THE A-Z OF
BUDDY HOLLY
AND
THE CRICKETS

THE A-Z OF BUDDY HOLLY AND THE CRICKETS

Alan Mann

MUSIC MENTOR BOOKS
York, England

© 1994, 1996 and 2009 Alan Mann. All rights reserved. Third edition. Previously published as *The A-Z of Buddy Holly* (Sound of Tex-Mex, 1994 and Aurum Press, 1996).

The right of Alan Mann to be identified as Author of this Work has been asserted in accordance with the UK *Copyright, Designs and Patents Act 1988.*

Every effort has been made to trace the copyright holders of material used in this volume. Should there be any omissions in this respect, we apologise and shall be pleased to make the appropriate acknowledgments in future printings.

A full list of illustrations and photo credits appears on page 316. The trademarks Brunswick, Coral, Decca, Rollercoaster and Vogue-Coral appear by kind permission of the owners.

Throughout this book, various references are made to unauthorised (bootleg) recordings and illegal reissues of copyright material. Details of these are included solely for the purpose of review and historical record, and should not be construed or interpreted as an endorsement of the practice of record piracy either by the author or the publisher.

All rights reserved. No part of this publication may be reproduced, stored in a retrieval system or transmitted in any form by any means, electronic, mechanical, reprographic, recording or otherwise without prior written permission from the publisher.

This book is sold subject to the conditions that it shall not, by way of trade or otherwise, be lent, resold, hired out or otherwise circulated without the publisher's prior consent in any form of binding or cover other than that in which it is published and without a similar condition including this condition being imposed on the subsequent purchaser.

Whilst every effort has been made to ensure the correctness of information included in this book, the publisher makes no representation – either express or implied – as to its accuracy and cannot accept any legal responsibility for any errors or omissions or consequences arising therefrom.

British Library Cataloguing-in-Publication Data
A catalogue record for this book is available from the British Library.

ISBN-13: 978-0-9547068-0-7

Published worldwide by Music Mentor Books *(Proprietor: G.R. Groom-White)*
69 Station Road, Upper Poppleton, York YO26 6PZ, North Yorkshire, England.
Telephone: +44 (0)1904 330308 *Email:* music.mentor@ntlworld.com

Cover by It's Great To Be Rich, York.

Printed and bound in Great Britain by Inc Dot Design & Print, York.

**This book is dedicated to Johnny Vallis
…who made it happen!**

Front cover photo

Left to right: Niki Sullivan, Joe B. Mauldin,
Buddy Holly and Jerry Allison
at WIBX, Utica, New York in 1957.

Foreword by John Beecher

In the fourteen years since I wrote the short foreword below to the first edition of Alan's book, nothing much has changed... we have been waiting and waiting for a complete Buddy Holly box set, and at last it looks as though something is on the way, as a set has been scheduled for around the time this book is published. Holly fans have continued to be fascinated by every aspect of Buddy's life, and a few previously unheard recordings have surfaced. Now, Alan's book has got even better with the addition of more entries and more detail in this new edition. So what are you waiting for? Skip the original *Foreword* below and get on with reading the book!

John Beecher
2008

It's been a long time since 1957 and 'That'll Be The Day', although to some of us it seems like only yesterday; especially if you've had all the mirrors removed from your house in case you catch a glimpse of someone over fifty. But the fascination for rock'n'roll and all things 1950s has remained strong even for those born long after that decade. In fact, there are probably more rock'n'roll records and books available now than there ever were when the Establishment was telling us this 'jungle music' would never last.

When Alan Mann told me he was putting together a book called *The A-Z of Buddy Holly* for his 'retirement thesis', I wasn't surprised, for if ever there was a labour of love this would have to be it. Alan was a founder member of the Buddy Holly Appreciation Society in the early 1960s, and his enthusiasm for the music and unearthing information about those artists has never diminished. This enthusiasm comes alive through the entries in this book, and Holly fans can be certain of a 'good read' all the way from ABBA to Zapata. In between, you're sure to discover all sorts of things you never knew, had almost forgotten, or didn't realise you ought to have known in the first place. In any event, Alan's book is going to be a useful addition to the Holly and the Crickets bookshelf, and I for one am happy he's got it together.

John Beecher
1994

Acknowledgements

The list has to start with my forgiving wife Pam (*'there have always been three people in our marriage'*) and our beloved children, Karen, Nicola and Richard, who have proffered their encouragement at every turn. Or maybe that was carefully disguised pity? Of our many grandchildren, the teenage James Buxton must be singled out as he, more than any other, has become infected by the music of the Buddy Holly era. However he sensibly holds his enthusiasm in check and finds time to follow more contemporary music. As an embryonic drummer, James still cherishes the very first lesson he had, which was in Las Vegas at the hands of Jerry Zapata – someone who was around Buddy during those Clovis days, as the final entry in this book attests. Meanwhile, my wonderful daughter-in-law Jane (Penrose) has also been incredibly helpful and given freely of her extensive knowledge of the publishing world in which she works.

The remaining list has deliberately been kept to a manageable level, so many will have to accept that they are contained within a heartfelt blanket of thanks. But some names must be singled out – none more so than John Beecher and John Ingman.

The former started up the British Buddy Holly Appreciation Society in the '60s and eventually collaborated with John Goldrosen in republishing his definitive Buddy Holly biography (retitled *Remembering Buddy*), which still remains the last word on the singer. Anything subsequently published is surely little more than a postscript. John Beecher willingly allowed me to reprint his original pithy *Foreword*, the tenor of which hopefully stands the test of time, and was also kind enough to contribute an update. He heads up his Rollercoaster Records empire from deepest Gloucestershire and continues to put out essential Holly-related releases at regular intervals. His love for Holly's music remains undiluted despite the toll of passing years.

The other John, namely Ingman, continues to be the most indefatigable of all British Holly researchers. John's eye for detail is incredible and he has a deep love for the music of Buddy Holly, the Crickets, and anything remotely musical that has come out of post-war West Texas. He came to stay with me for several vital days to ensure I never wavered in my resolve to complete the project. It would have been a poorer work without his considerable input. But, of course,

John and any others are not responsible for any errors that may have crept in: the author alone must take the rap.

Jim Carr, who wrote the definitive account of the Crickets' 1958 UK tour, and who's put out the *Holly International* magazine from his Doncaster home for close on fifteen years, is gratefully thanked. Miraculously, he continues to turn up fresh revelations – not to mention previously unseen pictures – on a regular basis. Also from Doncaster is *Crickets File* veteran John Firminger, who kindly provided me with a wealth of information about the group. For those who don't subscribe to either publication, details are given at the end of the book.

Geoff Barker of BBC Swindon (he has many other strings to his bow) has also been extremely encouraging right from the start: such support as his has helped when the author began to flag and doubted whether the project would ever be completed. Trevor Cajiao of *Now Dig This* and Stuart Colman in Nashville have likewise been ever-ready to help if called upon.

The other individuals who need mentioning are listed in the paragraphs below. All are friends who have helped in a myriad of ways over the years: they must know how grateful I am, although if your name isn't included and you helped please accept the oversight. Some of the above have an entry under their names, as has Bill Griggs, who started his *Reminiscing* magazine back in 1976, and who has gone on over the years to do so much pioneering investigative work which culminated in his series of *Buddy Holly Day By Day* booklets. We all owe him a deep debt of gratitude.

The residual list must include the members of the Norwich Thorpe St Andrew's Rotary Club, Ken Coombes of The Friends of Mike Berry, Lawrence Cross, John Davidson-White, Mike and Liz Delf, Steve Derby, Cicely Fancy, Peter Feast, Nick and Lavinia Ganley, Peter Gibson, Trevor Hardy, Ian and Denise Higham, Paul and Dot King, Derek James from the local press in Norwich, the late Trevor Manger, Goff Pattinson, Simon and Susie Pritchard, Chris Rees, Peter Rodger, John Sendall, Brian Shepherd, Wayne Smith, Bob Watson, Ian Westgate, Eric White of Out of Time Records in Norwich, and Barry Whiting, a new friend who recently made himself known to me by ringing my doorbell and introducing himself.

From the USA and Australia several friends deserve special thanks, and these include Bob and Sue Dees, Dennis and Patti Farland, Howard and Mary Olson, Jerry and Kathy Zapata, and Damian and Therese Johnstone. And I mustn't forget that ace Holly impressionist

Nicky Walker, who has relocated to Spain and is much missed by us all.

Otherwise, the author's ambit doesn't intersect with that of the musicians themselves, but there have been odd exceptions to prove the rule. The names follow in random order. Sherry Holley, Buddy's niece (and Larry Holley's daughter), who is an artist in many senses of the word and still lives and works around Lubbock, Texas. Albert Lee, guitarist extraordinaire, is another who has been supportive, while Tommy Allsup and Kevin Montgomery, whose names are known to any self-respecting Holly fan, can be bracketed together here too. From his home just outside Nashville, Tennessee, Sonny Curtis has been gracious enough to liaise via the wonders of email on behalf of Jerry and Joe B., while my good friend, musician (and nowadays German resident), Tony Sheridan – a huge fan of Buddy's music – is most warmly thanked, as is his wife Anna – even though she confessed to preferring Elvis!

Medium, psychic consultant, broadcaster and Billy Fury devotee Philip Solomon has also championed the new book from the start, and has already interviewed the author on air in advance of the publication. Legendary broadcaster Keith Skues, MBE, now ensconced in deepest Norfolk, has likewise been highly supportive. Penultimately – but most crucially – the Canadian entertainer Johnny Vallis, to whom this book is warmly dedicated, fortuitously put me back in touch with Music Mentor Books. He realised that my publisher was there all the while: Johnny's help and encouragement have been constant from that first long-distance telephone call to the present.

Last of all, but of course the last shall truly be first, is the redoubtable George Groom-White of Music Mentor Books, whose meticulous eye for detail has been of tremendous help throughout the project, and who made sure the author toed the line and met every deadline as the days got shorter and shorter. Thanks, George, and thanks also to your own long-suffering wife, Verena, and the girls.

Alan Mann
Little Melton
November 2008

Contents

Introduction 15

Technical Notes 17

The A–Z 19

Selected Bibliography 313

Useful Addresses 315

Photo Credits 316

Introduction

Welcome to the completely revised and expanded 50th Anniversary Edition of *The A-Z of Buddy Holly and the Crickets*, now much improved and more comprehensive than anything that has gone before. Not only that, but the eagle-eyed reader will have spotted that the Crickets are now incorporated into the title, and thus there is more about the group post-1959 than there was before. As with Holly himself, new nuggets of information continue to come to light and supplement the already substantial information base. It has occasionally meant that what we accepted as fact needs to be re-examined in the light of some fresh discovery. Sometimes this has led to an entry being amended, whilst new headings have been inserted and one or two quietly dropped. For example, it's been established beyond doubt that Buddy Holly didn't play on a session by the Nighthawks, and this obviously renders any entry for that obscure group redundant. As to the latter-day Crickets, they may have slowed down a tad, but their long-running career remains ongoing. Even as these words were being written, they were off to Nashville to collect another industry award.

As the anniversary date of 3 February 2009 reminds us, fifty years have now rolled by since that fateful day in 1959 when the news emerged that Buddy Holly, Ritchie Valens, the Big Bopper and pilot Roger Peterson had perished in the wreckage of a light aircraft somewhere in the wastes of Iowa. It's also worth reminding ourselves that times were completely different back then, and news of the disaster went largely unreported outside of the tabloid press, who gleefully had their headlines for the day, if little else. Younger readers might also be surprised to learn that in the '50s it was considered ghoulish to champion the music of someone no longer with us.

Fortunately, times have changed for the better, and there's surely no difference between listening to John Lennon, Freddie Mercury, Buddy Holly, or anyone else. Could it somehow be that the consciousness of the human race has expanded over the past half-century, and that outmoded attitudes and beliefs of the past have fallen away? Is there some element locked in Holly's music that's penetrated the outer layer of our collective consciousness? High-blown words perhaps, but we somehow knew that this man was a musical giant and that his music wouldn't die. Hadn't he written a song – 'Not Fade Away' – almost hinting at that very thing? But then, wasn't his whole musical career sandwiched between two strangely prophetic song titles: the stark 'That'll Be The Day' [when I die] and the more perceptive 'It Doesn't Matter Anymore'. Of course, I'm not suggesting the singer knew his life would end in an Iowa cornfield back in 1959, but equally his brother Larry insists that Buddy always needed to do everything in a hurry – as if, deep down, he realised that he didn't have much time to achieve what he wanted.

But, to end on a less fanciful note: it's been a joy over the years to see just how far the man and the music have reached out and connected up with the lives and music of others – and not only from the world of rock'n'roll. As we delved, we'd discover his country & western roots and, perhaps more unusually for a youngster growing up in Texas, his love of rhythm & blues too. Later, we found out that he also linked in with folk music, and many a folkie has since dipped into his songbook. And so it has gone on: the stories and the connections have kept on coming and coming. But perhaps we always knew they would. He may not have known it himself because he was just a good ole boy from Lubbock, Texas, but Buddy Holly was a genuine musical genius. His music still reaches out and enriches the lives of so many people even if he himself is long gone.

What follows are some 400 entries on artists from ABBA to Zapata, as well as every worthwhile Holly record title and recording session with as much background information as is considered practical in a work this size. The author hopes that the text collects together in one book most of the key information that is out there pertaining to Buddy Holly and the Crickets.

It's also poignant to note that a considerable number of individuals central to the story of Buddy Holly and his music – Waylon Jennings, Niki Sullivan, Norman and Vi Petty, George Atwood and many others – have since passed on to their final reward. The underlying hope is that the author has treated all the players as kindly as possible within these pages, given many are no longer able to exercise their right of reply. While there were undoubtedly some heroes and villains where the career of Buddy Holly was concerned, it's important to remember that ultimately it's all about the music – and nothing can take that away from us. *Rave on!*

Technical Notes

1   To save space, where luminaries such as Elvis, Paul McCartney, etc are concerned, only the briefest mention is made of their career achievements, as such information is readily available elsewhere.

2   Although Jerry Allison is usually addressed as 'J.I.', he is referred to as 'Jerry' throughout the text.

3   The majority of US chart listings are taken from *Billboard*, the music trade paper. Their rivals, *Cash Box*, are occasionally quoted as an alternative.

4   Session information is listed beneath each Buddy Holly song title in the following order:

- Month/year recorded and location.
- Personnel on the session.
- Personnel overdubbed.

Rather than try to pinpoint exact dates, which is often near-impossible, the author has preferred to give an approximate date.

5   All of Buddy Holly's recordings were made in mono, except for those made during his final studio session in October 1958. However, later overdubbing – most notably by the Fireballs – led to the creation of many stereo masters.

6   In 1984, the Picks overdubbed new backing vocals onto 35 Holly recordings in Houston, Texas. These overdubs should not be confused with their overdubs of the Crickets' recordings in 1957.

A

ABBA

As we did in the previous editions, we kick off with possibly the most tenuous of links with the music of Buddy Holly and the Crickets, in that Benny Andersson, one of the driving forces behind the legendary Swedish group ABBA, had earlier been a member of the Hep Stars, who recorded a version of Mike Berry's UK 1961 hit, 'Tribute To Buddy Holly'. Although the group didn't put out their version until 1965, it quickly went into the Swedish Top 10. Incidentally, the Hep Stars were no minor Scandinavian group – they were Sweden's top rock act in the '60s, outselling even the Beatles and the Rolling Stones.

ACETATE

A word on acetates is needed, as the word is not common currency these days, but it crops up at various points throughout this book.

In recording terms, an 'acetate' is a metal disc covered with a thin coating of lacquer, from which a test record is produced – not from a stamper, as is usual, but by a special machine that cuts a groove directly into the lacquer. Acetates were widely used throughout the music industry in pre-tape days to produce demo records, but the downside was that they were very easily damaged.

Buddy Holly cut his share of acetates in the early-to-mid 1950s, including the hillbilly recordings he made with Bob Montgomery ('My Two Timin' Woman', 'Footprints In the Snow', 'I'll Just Pretend', 'Take These Shackles From My Heart' and his solo demo of 'I Forgot To Remember To Forget'). The Holley family also have some acetates that are so badly damaged that some of the titles are unknown. It is known that these include part of a mandolin-based instrumental and a scrap of Jimmie Rodgers's 'Blue Yodel No.6'.

ADVERTISING

Although it took a while for Holly's music to fully penetrate our consciousness, it wasn't long before it began to be regurgitated in the form of advertising jingles promoting anything from jelly babies to new cars (remember *'That'll be the Daewoo'*?). Even older readers in the UK will no doubt recall the animated skeleton that was used to advertise Scotch cassette tapes with lyrics based on 'Not Fade Away' (the hook was *'re-record, not fade away'*), while Terry's Old Gold chocolate cleverly used 'True Love Ways' in 1988 and even helped Holly's recording get back into the British charts thirty years after it was first written. In the 1990s, a youth movement in the United States chose the slogan *True Love Waits* (get it?) as an effective counter against the rush towards pre-marital sex, although that was no more than a play on words. Coming up to date, the last time the author was in the USA, he recalls a pizza commercial on TV which used Holly's recording 'Take Your Time' to promote their product. Of course, an avalanche of tunes from the pens of other '50s composers have been used over the years, but probably none more than those lifted from the Buddy Holly songbook. And remember, his song catalogue was composed in little more than a short two-year time-span.

'AIN'T GOT NO HOME'
Recorded late 1956 at Buddy's home in Lubbock, Texas
Personnel: Buddy Holly (guitar, vocals), Jerry Allison (drums), unknown (double bass)

Originally written and recorded by R&B singer, pianist and native of New Orleans, Clarence 'Frogman' Henry, this novelty number became both a regional and national hit for Henry towards the end of 1956, spawning *(sic)* his 'Frogman' soubriquet. Prior to hitting the big time, Holly recorded his own rough demo of it – along with a batch of others – in Lubbock. In trying to emulate the Frogman's version, Buddy manages to sing unconvincingly in three different registers, although to be fair the Texan's run-through was never intended for release.

However, it did see the light of day in 1969, when former manager Norman Petty oversaw the release of the *Giant* album, a mix of such early tracks and several much later numbers. All were heavily overdubbed by the Fireballs, by virtue of which the mono originals were turned into stereo masters. It was to be many years before the raw, undubbed mono version of the song finally came out. We also eventually realised that 'I'm Just A Lonely Boy', long rumoured to exist, was simply an alternative name for this recording, being part of the lyrics.

Henry (who was born in 1937) went on to have a lengthy professional career, but his peak years were undoubtedly in the early 1960s, when he had several international chart hits including 'But I Do', which made the Top 5 in both the UK and the USA.

Surprisingly, the Band, led by Robbie Robertson, later had a minor US pop hit with their version of 'Ain't Got No Home' in 1973. Carl Mann, Bruce Channel and the New York Dolls are among the few others who have also recorded the song.

ALBUMS – *See* **EPs** *and* **LPs**

'ALL FOR YOU' *(Buddy Knox)*
In the past, it was mooted that Holly may have played guitar and sung background vocals on this recording made by Knox at Clovis in February 1958, but it has since been established that Holly was on tour in Florida at the time and the guitarist was actually Sonny Curtis.

STEVE ALLEN
Steve Allen (1921-2000) was a showbiz institution for years in the United States but remained largely unknown beyond North America. He was renowned as the host of the *Tonight Show*, as well as the primetime *Steve Allen Show*, on which Elvis Presley memorably sang 'Hound Dog' to a lugubrious real-life Basset Hound! Allen also brought a wild Jerry Lee Lewis to the nation's 1950s television screens, and for a time it was rumoured that the Crickets may also have appeared on the show. We eventually learnt that this wasn't so, though the Crickets did make several major television appearances, of which the most prestigious were the *Ed Sullivan Show*, *Arthur Murray's Party* and Dick Clark's *American Bandstand*. The band played live on almost every occasion, and lip-synching or miming (as on *Bandstand*) was the exception.

Despite showcasing several rock'n'roll acts on his shows, Allen was known to be an outspoken critic of the emerging music, which he insisted was nothing more than a cacophony of noise. A jazz buff and composer himself, he later received a Grammy award for one of his thousands of jazz/popular compositions. Sadly, he died unexpectedly from complications following a minor road traffic accident in 2000.

This entry faced deletion on the grounds of being tenuous until the author learnt that Crickets drummer Jerry Allison was of the firm opinion that Buddy had based his choice of heavy-framed spectacles on those worn on TV by Steve Allen! Quite an intriguing thought, although we know that Phil Everly also suggested to Buddy that, if you have to wear glasses on stage, you should wear ones that would get noticed. Perhaps Phil also gave the same advice to Elton John?

JERRY IVAN ('J.I.') ALLISON

Where to start? Well, perhaps to point out that any brevity here is because so much of the book refers to Jerry Allison as it does to Holly himself, given that they co-founded the Crickets.

Jerry's name was linked with Buddy's almost from the start, which is fairly remarkable given that there was some 2+ years' difference in ages (Buddy having been born in late 1936 and Jerry in 1939). Perhaps if they had linked up later, rather than sooner, the age gap would have been an irrelevance, but back in 1954-55 when they were both attending Lubbock High School, their respective ages were 17 and 15, which was quite a difference. However, as an emerging drummer, Jerry was already playing regularly with Cal Wayne & The Riverside Ranch Hands and was pretty precocious for his age, so that the gap was never much of a problem for them. Disappointingly, however, it meant that Jerry, who was still attending school, wasn't able to take part in Buddy's original Decca session in Nashville in January 1956). At the time, that must have been just a tad frustrating.

On a personal note, in 1958 Jerry and Buddy married Peggy Sue and Maria Elena respectively and shared a joint honeymoon in Acapulco.

Jerry Allison, Joe B. Mauldin, and Sonny Curtis are all names that have been synonymous with that of the Crickets ever since 1959 – albeit sometimes intermittently – and, of course, Jerry still owns the name. A minor wobble set in at the time of the 1962 Cuban Missile Crisis, when Jerry was called up as a reservist in the US Air Force. That was a particular downer, as a UK tour had already been lined up and a substitute drummer, Don Groom, had to be drafted in.

Although Jerry's been at the heart of the Crickets ever since, there was also a lengthy period (1978-83) when they hooked up and toured almost exclusively with Waylon Jennings. It's also fair to say he is an underrated songwriter: 'Cruise In It', 'Holly Would' and 'He's Old Enough To Know Better' are titles known to all Crickets fans. All told, he's either written or co-composed close to 100 songs, while as a session drummer he's backed Johnny Rivers, the Everly Brothers, Eddie Cochran, and even got pulled in to rehearse with Elvis Presley in Las Vegas before Ronnie Tutt recovered in time to go on stage. His Texas drumming style is unique, and he surely must be one of the greatest rock'n'roll drummers ever.

See also **SCOTTY TURNER**.

KEITH ALLISON

Briefly a member of the post-Holly Crickets and unrelated to his namesake Jerry Allison (although, as a multi-instrumentalist, he did deputise for Jerry when the latter was drafted). Keith Allison's main involvement with the Crickets occurred when he played guitar on their final 1964 UK chart hit, '(They Call Her) La Bamba' – the group having temporarily hitched a ride on the all-pervading surfing craze – and also appeared in a 60-minute US TV special, *Aloha A-Go-Go*. He was a long-time member of the US TV show, *Shindig!*, and was often termed 'the American Beatle'. Allison later had a lengthy involvement with Paul Revere & The Raiders, a prominent act of the late 1960s and early '70s. He has worked within the music industry ever since, but should not be confused with the Australian actor of the same name.

ALLISONS

In the months and years that followed Holly's tragic death in 1959, a handful of lookalike or soundalike artists surfaced, and a brief trawl through of some of their names appears under the blanket heading of **SOUNDALIKES**. Of these, the Allisons, a duo from the UK, achieved a great deal of early success with their decidedly Holly-ish 'Are You Sure'. The song was selected as Britain's entry for the 1961 *Eurovision Song Contest* and came second. Even so, it reached No.1 on most UK charts and stayed in the hit parade for months.

Amusingly, a storm in a teacup blew up in the British press when the story broke that the duo, Brian Alford ('John Allison') and Colin Day ('Bob Allison') weren't actually real brothers. What a shock! One can only assume that real news must have been a bit thin at the time.

Although their career at the top proved to be short-lived, the Allisons did release an album of some interest to Holly fans, in that it contained covers of three of his songs including his first and last major hits, 'That'll Be The Day' and 'It Doesn't Matter Anymore'. The duo eventually split up in the mid-'60s, but have reunited on numerous occasions over the years for oldies tours or other selected events.

TOMMY ALLSUP

One of the group that backed Buddy on the *Winter Dance Party* tour, Tommy (born 24 November 1931, the twelfth of thirteen Allsup children from Owassa, Oklahoma, a small town north of Tulsa) was Holly's senior by several years. Remarkably, even as these words are being written in mid-2008, Allsup, together with fellow countryman

Kevin Montgomery, are touring the UK and performing a set that concentrates on the music of Tommy's late friend, Buddy Holly.

Holly had originally met Allsup – a superb guitarist himself – when both were at Norman Petty's Clovis studio, Buddy quickly lining him up to play lead on some upcoming sessions. Although seldom listed as an official Cricket back then, Allsup went on to play on several major Holly/Crickets recordings ('Heartbeat', 'It's So Easy', 'Lonesome Tears', 'Love's Made A Fool Of You' and 'Wishing'), although at the time most fans were unaware of his involvement.

In July 1958, Tommy and his band, which included vocalist Earl Sinks, toured the Midwest with the Crickets as the *Summer Dance Party*, almost foreshadowing what was to come later. Having cemented a friendship with Buddy, Allsup joined the Crickets for the *Autumn Edition* of *The Biggest Show of Stars for 1958*, and it wasn't surprising that, following his split with Jerry and Joe B. in October 1958, Buddy asked him to play backup for him on the 1959 *Winter Dance Party* tour.

Also accompanying Holly on that tragic last tour were future country legend Waylon Jennings on electric bass and Carl Bunch on drums, although such was the ongoing battle with the elements during that winter, that by the time the tour package reached the Surf Ballroom in Clear Lake, Iowa in February, Bunch was already hospitalised with frostbite and Buddy had co-opted fellow headliner Ritchie Valens to accompany him on drums.

It's been well documented over the years that Allsup and Jennings were set to join Buddy on the final fatal plane flight, but that Ritchie Valens took Allsup's place at the eleventh hour, a toss of the coin having decided who would fly. However, because he had given his wallet containing his driving licence to Buddy, Allsup was briefly identified as one of those who had perished.

Having experienced the trauma of losing a fellow musician and friend, Tommy had to endure playing out the remaining tour dates. (In fact, they were barely halfway through the planned dates, so promoters GAC drafted in some fresh acts and the tour limped on until each date had been fulfilled.) Given the crash took out three of the main four headliners, one is forced to conclude that the maxim *'The show must go on'* was invoked with a vengeance. Decades later, Waylon Jennings recalled in his autobiography that the group completed the tour in a state of numbness.

In 1964, Tommy returned to Clovis and joined up with Jerry

Allison and others to complete an instrumental album of favourites entitled *The Buddy Holly Songbook*, which has recently been reissued on CD by Rollercoaster with extensive liner notes by John Ingman. But it wasn't until 1994, some thirty years later, and accompanied by super-fan Bob Dees, that Tommy finally managed to get back to the Surf Ballroom and join in the annual tribute show that had first been put together in the 1970s by deejay The Mad Hatter. In one form or another it's been running ever since.

Despite his rock'n'roll past, Allsup's first love has always been country music, and he went on to accumulate a lengthy CV that also included producing the likes of Asleep At The Wheel and even Bob Wills, when he made what would become his final studio album. His full list of studio credits is far too numerous to list here, for he has played on close to ten thousand sessions including many country Number Ones. Chances are that the reader could turn to his or her own record collection and find stacks of country albums to which Tommy has contributed (George Jones, Tammy Wynette, Charlie Rich, and Johnny Paycheck are just a few of many top artists he has backed). Widening his talents, he also owned his own recording studio (see **ZAGER & EVANS**), as well as a doomed club in Dallas which he rather bizarrely named Tommy's Heads Up! At one time, he even held a corporate post with a Nashville label, but eventually returned to his first love of country picking.

See also **WINTER DANCE PARTY**.

'ALMOST PARADISE' *(Norman Petty Trio)*

This little-known title refers to a Petty composition recorded at Clovis which entered the *Billboard* 'Top 100' in the last week of February 1957 and remained on the chart for three months, peaking at No.56. Versions by pianist Roger Williams and Lou Stein also charted.

All of which is fairly uninteresting until one realises that the February debut date was the same week that the Crickets recorded 'That'll Be The Day' in Petty's Clovis studio! In stumbling upon this bit of trivia, the author also noticed that the Petty Trio's final US chart hit, 'The First Kiss', entered the charts on 12 August 1957 – the *same day* that the Crickets debuted in the charts with their first hit! As coincidences go, this has to verge on the surreal. However, it also reminds us that, for a short period, Petty must have been torn between pursuing his own chart success and managing the career of the Crickets. An interesting thought.

Readers who saw the Crickets on their 1958 British tour might recall that 'Almost Paradise' was listed in the tour programme as part of the Holly/Crickets repertoire. But it was the odd title out, and there seemed no logical reason for its inclusion. Certainly, the Crickets never performed the instrumental during the tour.

AMERICAN BANDSTAND

Like the British pop series, *Top Of The Pops*, which limped on into the present century, *American Bandstand* also tarried awhile but eventually disappeared from view in 1989. It was originally screened in the Philadelphia area as far back as 1952 before its growing popularity saw it networked coast-to-coast via some 67 stations. Thereafter it continued to be aired nationally for over thirty years. Hosted by the smooth and personable deejay Dick Clark, it was hugely successful and even survived the payola crisis of late 1959 that seriously rocked the whole industry and unseated the unlucky Alan Freed.

The Crickets made three appearances on *American Bandstand*: firstly back in August 1957 after 'That'll Be The Day' hit the charts, and twice in October 1958 with 'It's So Easy' and 'Heartbeat'. Ironically, the group had effectively broken up by then, although Dick Clark was unaware of this fact when he interviewed them. This interview (and most others) is still available on the 2002 Rollercoaster CD EP, *That's What They Tell Me – That's What They Say*, and, given the circumstances surrounding the group, makes for slightly uncomfortable listening. Sadly, no footage survives of their *Bandstand* appearances.

It's also ironic that, at that time, neither Holly nor the Crickets had a record in the charts, apart from 'Real Wild Child' by Ivan (Jerry Allison), which reached No.68.

A brief postscript before we leave. Virtually all the acts who appeared on *American Bandstand* lip-synched to their latest records. A rare exception to this were the Big Beats, an instrumental group from Dallas, who Dick Clark allowed to perform live (see **BIG BEATS** and **JERRY ZAPATA** for more information).

AMERICAN GRAFFITI

A celebrated 1973 film set in the California of a decade earlier, and memorable for several things including its predominantly 1950s soundtrack which included a couple of the Crickets' biggest hits, 'That'll Be The Day' and 'Maybe Baby'. (Despite being Crickets recordings, the soundtrack lists them as being by Buddy Holly – but at least it differentiated them from recordings by the post-Holly group).

Set around 'cruising the strip' in small-town America, it won several awards and launched the career of a slew of big names including *Star Wars* director George Lucas, Ron Howard and a youthful Harrison Ford. Charles Martin Smith, bassist for Gary Busey in *The Buddy Holly Story* five years later, also made an appearance. Vocally, the star of the picture was probably the crazy deejay Wolfman Jack, who played himself. And it was also in this movie that one of the characters had the memorable line, *'Rock'n'roll has been going downhill ever since Buddy Holly died.'*

'AMERICAN PIE' *(Don McLean)*

A defining moment in the career of the hitless Don McLean, who, although he'd been around on the folk scene for some time, suddenly rocketed to the top of the US pop charts in 1971 with this extraordinary self-composed eight-minute paean of nostalgia telling the tale of Holly's passing through the eyes of a youngster delivering newspapers. Although the record never even mentioned the singer by name, it managed to give a cryptic nod along the way to the myriad of elements that made up American music.

A *tour de force* of musical nostalgia, which simultaneously resurrected the posthumous career of Buddy Holly in his homeland and became a huge hit all over the world. The album that accompanied the single was dedicated to Holly, and McLean was always quick to confirm his love of his music in subsequent interviews.

Because Don McLean has other links with Buddy Holly, a separate entry appears under his name. However, there is just one piece of fiction that requires correction: 'American Pie' was *not* the name of the plane which Holly and his party charted that fateful night. Quite how that extraordinary piece of nonsense gained any credence is not known, although doubtless the Internet was involved somewhere down the line.

AMPEX TAPE RECORDER

Norman Petty moved into tape technology with the purchase of a 1953 Ampex to record his own trio, but purchased further machines to allow him to do overdubs. It was originally thought that Petty's Ampex machine was one of the first on the market, but they had actually been around for quite some time.

In late 1958, one of the machines was acquired by Holly, and it was on this that he recorded his final demos in New York In his *Buddy* biography, Philip Norman notes that he paid $2,000 for the machine and a microphone.

'AN EMPTY CUP'
Recorded September 1957 at Tinker US Air Force Base, Oklahoma
Personnel: Buddy Holly (guitar, vocals), Niki Sullivan (guitar), Jerry Allison (drums), Joe B. Mauldin (double bass)
Overdubbed October 1957: The Picks (backing vocals)

This was one of four tracks recorded in the Officers' Club at Tinker US Air Force Base in Oklahoma when the Crickets were on the road (see **TINKER US AIR FORCE BASE** for details of how that unusual session came about). The song is one of a couple of Roy Orbison numbers that the Crickets recorded – coincidentally both at the same session. The distinctive backing vocals were added a couple of weeks later at Clovis, in line with a pattern that was developing, whereby Norman Petty called upon the Picks to embellish Holly's vocals. Buddy and the boys were seldom in the studio on those occasions, but were happy to let the producer dub the backing vocals before the record's eventual release.

'An Empty Cup' and 'You've Got Love' had been left with Petty by fellow Texan Orbison, who had recorded a version of the former song at Clovis some time earlier. Petty's name was added to the composer credits to give him a cut of the royalties, a common industry practice back then.

Fans first heard the song on the *Chirping Crickets* LP. It's certainly a great, plaintive vocal performance by Holly and, although the tune is excellent, it has rarely been covered over the years. It was included on the 1960 UK EP, *That'll Be The Day*, and also on the flip of the 1964 UK Top 40 hit, 'You've Got Love'. The four original cuts from this session without the Picks' overdubs have never surfaced, and it's uncertain whether the tape still survives.

CARROLL ANDERSON

Carroll Anderson (1921-2006) was manager of the Surf Ballroom in Clear Lake, Iowa, and it was he who liaised with the *Winter Dance Party* troupe when they arrived at the venue to perform on that fatal February night. After the show, he drove Holly, Ritchie Valens and the Big Bopper to the Mason City airport in his station wagon and helped them board the small chartered plane. The following day, he had the heartbreaking task of performing the initial identification of the victims' bodies. A well-liked individual, Anderson played host to Buddy's parents, Mr & Mrs L.O. Holley, who visited the crash site on more than one occasion. He stayed on at the Surf until 1967, and later in his life became a local councillor.

HARVEY ANDREWS

Years after the 1959 plane crash, British folk artist Harvey Andrews (born 1943) recorded one of the most genuine tribute records to Buddy Holly. While some of that genre (eg 'Three Stars', 'Gold Records in the Snow') were incredibly maudlin, his composition, 'Please Don't Get On That Plane', had been twenty years in germination and was lyrically all the better for it. Sadly, it never got much of an airing and didn't chart. The singer/songwriter was quoted as saying that Holly has been a great influence on him over the years, along with the likes of Fats Domino and Little Richard. He has also recorded 'Learning The Game'.

Interestingly, Andrews seems to have specialised in tribute discs, having also recorded eulogies to Harry Chapin and Phil Ochs. A sensitive individual, he has also looked beyond the field of music for his inspiration, composing a paean to the First World War poet, Wilfred Owen, and even a 'Song For Anne Frank', one of the most poignant victims of the Second World War. He is still active in the world of folk music, touring and performing all over the world.

ANGELIC GOSPEL SINGERS

This black gospel group was formed in 1944 by Margaret Allison from South Carolina, who often performed soprano lead whilst playing piano accompaniment. The driving force behind the group, she also helped to compose most of their repertoire, as well as arranging their versions of traditional gospel numbers. Over the years, the Angelics had a succession of releases on the Nashboro label and they were known favourites of Buddy Holly, who had some of their recordings in his personal record collection. It's said that the melody of the Holly composition 'True Love Ways' is based on their recording of 'I'll Be Alright', and aural evidence shows there's certainly some similarity. What is certain is that Buddy loved black music at a time when it wasn't very fashionable for a white Southerner to do so, and his appreciation of other black acts such as Ray Charles, Little Richard, Bo Diddley, Mickey & Sylvia and others is woven throughout the text.

The Angelic Gospel Singers are still in existence, although their longevity has brought about several enforced changes in personnel.

PAUL ANKA

A precocious 16 year old whose first hit, 'Diana', sold nine million copies worldwide, Paul Anka is included here as he not only toured Australia with Holly and the Crickets in early 1958, but also met up with him in New York that October and passed him a new song he had just finished writing, 'It Doesn't Matter Anymore'. Buddy was given the song while he was in New York, and the distinctive string arrangement was composed on the spot by Dick Jacobs. Prophetically, it was to be part of his final studio session and, of course, one of his biggest hits. Holly and Anka had formed quite a close relationship and may well have collaborated together, had Buddy lived. Certainly, Anka mentions Holly's name to this day in interviews.

Although he is now a naturalised American citizen, Paul Anka was born Ottawa, Canada in 1941 and is of Lebanese descent. The singer/songwriter has gone on to carve out a lengthy career with successes too numerous to list, although penning lyrics to 'My Way' for Frank Sinatra was a highlight, as was writing an international No.1 for Tom Jones ('She's A Lady'), and later being inducted into the Songwriters' Hall of Fame. Part of his varied CV has seen him headlining in Vegas and the Copacabana, New York. In earlier years he appeared as a teen-idol in a few rock'n'roll movies before graduating to a weightier acting role in the epic war film, *The Longest Day*. Strangely, he never had a UK chart album until 2005, when *Rock Swings* remedied that particular oversight.

APARTMENT TAPES

The more avid Holly fan will have come across the phrase 'the Apartment Tapes' many times. The reference is, of course, to a batch of songs discovered on Buddy's Ampex tape recorder in his New York apartment (Apartment 4H, The Brevoort, 11 Fifth Avenue), which he had recorded in December 1958 and January 1959, prior to embarking on that fateful final tour. There are about a dozen songs in all, but bootleg evidence indicates that there are also a few fragments, some chatter and one instrumental number.

The material dates from a period of intense creativity, especially the period just prior to Christmas 1958. The half a dozen numbers from December ('Crying, Waiting, Hoping', 'Learning The Game',

'Peggy Sue Got Married', 'That Makes It Tough', 'That's What They Say' and 'What To Do') were all brand-new compositions and intriguingly all dealt with lost love – a curious state of affairs for someone newly married. Buddy gave tapes of these songs to Dick Jacobs soon after and asked him to score Count Basie-styled arrangements for them, which would possibly have taken his career in a different direction.

One small mystery is that Tommy Allsup recalls helping Buddy out on 'That Makes It Tough' shortly before setting off on the *Winter Dance Party* tour in January 1959, as there was a minor chord that was giving Buddy problems. This recording is clearly not the same one that Holly gave to Dick Jacobs a month earlier, and remains untraced.

The second batch of titles, completed in January just prior to Buddy leaving on tour, was decidedly different in character and mostly by contemporary black artists that Holly loved and would have been highly familiar with (eg 'Love Is Strange' by Mickey & Sylvia). The author's pet theory about these latter recordings is discussed more under the entry for Ray Charles.

Although most of the material has long been available in overdubbed form, it's extraordinary that these undubbed recordings have remained unissued for so long. However, shortly before this book went to press it was announced that Universal would finally be releasing the songs in 2009.

APOLLO THEATER, NEW YORK

It was in August '57 that the Crickets, who had just entered the *Billboard* 'Top 100' for the first time with 'That'll Be The Day', famously found themselves on a bill at the Apollo Theater in Harlem, New York. They were the only white act amongst a host of black stars which included Clyde McPhatter, the Cadillacs and Lee Andrews & The Hearts.

The assumption is that the bookers had assumed the Crickets were the black rhythm & blues vocal group led by Dean Barlow, who had had a R&B hit in 1953 with 'You're Mine', but whose career had tailed off since. The scene that followed, of Buddy and the boys on stage in front of an initially silent, if not hostile, all-black audience was captured perfectly – if with a touch of Hollywood – in the '70s biopic of Holly's life. But it's a myth to assume that no white acts ever played the Apollo. They did do occasionally: for example, the Johnny Burnette Trio had played there in 1956, as well as Buddy Knox and

Jimmy Bowen in early 1957. White jazz bands would also sporadically appear at the venue.

Despite the onset of a multiracial rock'n'roll scene from the mid '50s onwards, there was still a residue of segregation hanging about in America, and it impacted both on the artists and their audiences. But it was music that helped to sweep away the long-lived and ingrained racial prejudice. In the '70s, several years before the *Buddy Holly Story* biopic appeared, Jerry Allison and Tom Drake wrote a film script around the group's appearance in such an all-black venue (see **NOT FADE AWAY** *(Film)*), although the project was aborted.

ARMED SERVICES

Back in the '50s, many a budding music career faced derailment through circumstances outside anyone's control when Uncle Sam beckoned and military service followed. Two contrasting examples can be briefly mentioned here, a negative one being Bobby Bare, who left a 1958 demo of 'All American Boy' behind when entering the Services: infuriatingly for him, it reached No.2 in the *Billboard* 'Hot 100' in his absence, and he had to wait years before his hit-parade career could be revived, long after his return to Civvy Street. However, for a more positive example we needn't look beyond the well-known tale of Private (later Sergeant) Elvis Presley. Despite being in the military from 1958 to 1960, he never stopped charting, thanks to the wiles of his manager, Colonel Tom Parker – a lesson in media manipulation that has seldom been surpassed.

As regards the three main Crickets, Buddy flunked his medical mainly because of eyesight problems that saw him classified 4F, and so remained a civilian. After his death, the younger Jerry and Joe B. had the dubious honour of passing medicals and both saw some involvement with the military, as did Sonny Curtis.

GEORGE ATWOOD

The late George Atwood (1920-2005) is an unsung hero of the Buddy Holly story. Indeed, there's little doubt that, had Holly lived, he would have gone on to play a major role in his life, for plans were well underway for Buddy to build a recording studio in Lubbock (see **PRISM RECORDS**). Atwood had already been lined up as PR manager, and this is confirmed by paperwork that the author has seen.

George Atwood played bass on many Clovis sessions from around 1955 onwards. He first met Buddy in 1956 whilst recording a

George Atwood in the studio, June 1957.

Clyde Hankins album session (*Swing Fever*), at which the latter, who had just returned from one of his Nashville sorties, was a bystander. In the spring and summer of 1957, Atwood (double bass) and Holly (guitar) played together on various sessions for Sherry Davis, the Norman Petty Trio, Jack Huddle, Jim Robinson and Charlie Phillips. As can be seen, Buddy was earning money as a session guitarist well before his own career took off.

Atwood had an interesting past as a circus clown (called Go-ee) – something he was immensely proud of – and he also hosted a children's TV show in Lubbock. However, his principal career was as a musician, and he worked with the likes of Gene Krupa, Tommy Dorsey, Ray Price, Eddy Arnold and, as mentioned elsewhere, Carolyn Hester. It didn't matter whether it was folk, country or big band jazz, he was an incredibly versatile musician and very much in demand. Asked by the author to define his musical talents as part of a Question and Answer session, he put it like this: *'I was known in the business as a 'utility bassman', that meant I played stand-up, electric bass, slap-bass, tuba and the sousaphone. The low instruments were my speciality, and I also wrote, arranged and copied scores, conducted and taught.'* Photos from those days confirm him to be a larger-than-life individual.

Atwood was never an official Cricket – he was a generation older than Holly and more of a father figure – but, because of his adaptability, he did get to play bass on 'Heartbeat' at Buddy's request, as well as demos of two songs that Buddy had written for the Everly Brothers, 'Wishing' and 'Love's Made a Fool of You'. Sadly, Don and Phil never recorded them. Buddy's own versions eventually came out as 'A' sides of separate Coral singles and both made the UK Top 40 during the '60s.

Born in Tuscaloosa, Alabama of an ancestry that included English and Native American, George Atwood spent most of his working life based in West Texas, where he worked with such luminaries as Roy Orbison, Waylon Jennings (via KLLL radio), Jimmy Dean, Tennessee Ernie Ford and even comedian Tom Ewell. In declining health throughout the '90s, he took delight in corresponding with friends, and one felt this helped to keep him going. Indeed, he managed to survive numerous health crises until his death in 2005.

AUSTRALIAN TOUR

In January 1958, just prior to their lengthy UK tour, the Crickets embarked on a short tour of Australia accompanied by Jerry Lee Lewis, Paul Anka and Jodie Sands, preceded by a show in Hawaii *en route*.

The Australian bill was an exceptionally strong line-up except for Sands, a little-known songstress from Philadelphia who had just one US Top 20 hit to her name ('With All My Heart' – covered by Petula Clark, who had much the bigger international hit with it). Bolstering the bill was Australia's leading rock'n'roll star Johnny O'Keefe. Yodelling balladeer Frank Ifield was added to the Sydney dates.

For years, there was a paucity of documented information about the Australian tour, apart from an occasional photo and an interview that Buddy had with local deejay, Pat Barton. (Nearly every known interview with Buddy Holly, including this one, is to be found on the 2002 Rollercoaster CD EP, *That's What They Tell Me – That's What They Say.*) Recently, however, a new book by Roderick Jordan, *Buddy Holly & The Crickets – Musical History In Australia*, has appeared, giving us far more detail. What was always certain was that the shows were well received, although the bedlam of the earlier Little Richard tour of Australia didn't happen. But Holly and the Crickets certainly gained a set of fans that have stayed loyal to them over the years.

AUTOMOBILES

An earlier edition of this book had a lengthy entry under this heading, but, while the interest in Holly's music continues, the curiosity as to just what cars Buddy drove back then is now of passing interest only. Tinker Carlen, a friend of his from Lubbock, recalls that Buddy first drove his father's Hudson Hornet as a juvenile, while Buddy's brother Larry remembers him also driving early model Chevrolets and Cadillacs. He received a 1955 Oldsmobile from his parents as a graduation present. Towards the end of his life, the singer had a 1958 Cadillac, and reputedly had a 1959 model on order at the time of his death. Sharing a keen interest in cars, the three Crickets managed to fit in a visit to the Austin motor works at Longbridge during their 1958 British tour. Buddy also owned a motorbike (see **MOTORCYCLES**) and had flying lessons – definitely a man in a hurry.

FRANKIE AVALON

An American star of the late '50s and '60s, Francis Avallone *aka* Frankie Avalon was born in 1939, but is seldom mentioned in reference books except when bracketed together with a group of singers (the 'Bobbys' Rydell, Darin, Goldsboro and Vee), who helped to usher in a softer era of ballads. Whatever the true reasons for the watershed, the death-knell of rock'n'roll in its original raw state had already been sounded by then.

Holly and Avalon had first met up on package shows after Frankie's twin Top 10 hits of 1958 ('Dede Dinah' and 'Gingerbread') earned him automatic bookings. Certainly, he played some dates on the *Summer Dance Party* tour, as his name appears on posters from those times. He also made frequent appearances on *American Bandstand*, which wasn't a surprise as he came from Philadelphia, where *Bandstand* was transmitted from. The fact that he was also ridiculously handsome may have helped too.

Frankie wasn't originally part of the 1959 *Winter Dance Party*, but sadly he and others were used to plug the gap when the three main headliners perished in the early hours of 3 February. By all accounts, it was a traumatised tour that continued throughout the Midwest, although times soon got better when his new release, 'Venus', charted that same week in the US and quickly went to No.1. Thereafter, he appeared in thirty or more 'beach party' movies, a popular feature of American culture in the '60s.

Years later, he recorded 'Roses Grow Beyond The Wall', a song that makes mention of Buddy Holly within its lachrymose lyrics. In 1978, he bridged the generation gap when appearing in the hit musical, *Grease*, and also toured in several stage versions of the same.

A remarkably well-preserved individual to this day (he turns 70 in 2009), he is still active in the entertainment business, and has also branched out in later years by marketing his own brand of health products.

B

'BABY I DON'T CARE'

Recorded December 1957 at Norman Petty Recording Studios, Clovis, New Mexico
Personnel: Buddy Holly (guitar, vocals), Jerry Allison (cardboard box percussion), Joe B. Mauldin (double bass), C.W. Kendall Jr (piano)

One of several recordings by Buddy and the boys which weren't self-composed, but were contemporary material that they liked. Most readers will remember Elvis singing this number at a poolside party in one of his best films, *Jailhouse Rock*, and the track was included on the million-selling EP of the same name.

It was one of two numbers from the prodigious Leiber & Stoller songbook that Buddy recorded, the other being 'Smokey Joe's Café', one of the Apartment Tape tracks. This songwriting team penned many of Elvis' best songs: 'Baby I Don't Care' was a particular favourite of their pal, Eddie Cochran, so it was natural enough for Buddy to include it when they were rooting around for stuff to complete the *Buddy Holly* album.

Initially mistitled 'You're So Square (Baby I Don't Care)', Buddy's version is superb, and all the more impressive when one remembers that Jerry Allison's drumming was performed on a stout cardboard box. (Interestingly, unlike Elvis, Holly makes no mention of *'hot rod races'* in his reading of the song. One can only speculate why it was omitted.) It became a surprise double-sided UK hit in 1961 when, coupled with 'Valley of Tears', it reached No.12.

In 1984, the Picks overdubbed backing vocals onto this

recording (see **OVERDUBS** and **PICKS** for more info).

Although it wasn't a hit for Elvis, popular US folk singer Joni Mitchell took a version into the US Top 50 in the early '80s – the only time that the song made the US singles chart.

'BABY IT'S LOVE' *(Buddy & Bob)*
Recorded 1954 or 1955 at KDAV, Lubbock, Texas
Personnel: Buddy Holly (guitar, vocals), Bob Montgomery (guitar, vocals), Sonny Curtis (fiddle), prob. Don Guess (double bass)

This is one of several songs that Buddy Holley (as he still was at this time) cut as a demo with his friend Bob Montgomery at a local radio station, KDAV. Styling themselves 'Buddy & Bob', as was the fashion for country duos at the time, they hadn't yet fallen under the spell of Elvis, although they very soon would. Around this time, the boys played locally wherever and whenever the opportunity arose, even if their earnings amounted to only a few dollars.

This recording was never meant to be released, but surfaced in the mid-'60s with heavy overdubs by the Fireballs on the *Holly In The Hills* album put together by Norman Petty. All the Buddy & Bob songs were credited as being written by either Buddy, Bob or Don Guess, although exactly who wrote what is mostly a matter of some conjecture. However, the main point is that the material they were trying out was their own stuff and not covers.

Holly In The Hills was the latest attempt to satisfy fans' insatiable appetite for anything with Buddy's name on it, and the decision was presumably justified when the LP reached No.13 on the UK charts. 'Baby It's Love' wasn't included on the US version of the album, which had a slightly different track listing (see **HOLLY IN THE HILLS** for details). To date, the original undubbed takes have not been released.

Although the song hasn't engendered many covers, back in 1958 Jimmy Lee Fautheree recorded a great rocking version in New Orleans under the pseudonym 'Johnny Angel', though it never got much airplay.

'BABY LET'S PLAY HOUSE' *(Buddy & Bob)*
Recorded June 1955, probably at Nesman Recording Studio, Wichita Falls, Texas
Personnel: Buddy Holly (guitar, vocals), Jerry Allison (drums), Larry Welborn (double bass)

This number, which Elvis had recorded in early 1955 at Sun, was high in the *Billboard* C&W chart by the time Buddy & Bob decided to try it. Whereas much of their material is closer to downhome country, this is an R&B number through and through. The original cut, in which Holly handles the vocals, is quite commercial and could probably have been released as it stood. However, as so often happened, Norman Petty had the Fireballs overdub it, thereby creating the version that fans are familiar with from the 1965 *Holly In The Hills* album. Years later, the undubbed track finally popped up on the 1995 4-CD Vigotone bootleg, *What You Been A-Missin'*.

The song was written by Arthur Gunter, a blues singer from Nashville, who had a string of releases on the Excello label including this one, but sadly didn't achieve much commercial success during his lifetime. He passed away in 1976 within one week of reaching fifty. In the early '70s, he was quoted as saying that his biggest payday *wasn't* in writing the Elvis number, but in winning $50,000 on the Michigan State Lottery!

His song has only rarely been covered, although Sleepy LaBeef cut a memorable version, while Johnny Burnette's 'Oh Baby Babe' is essentially the same song, even though it's not credited to Gunter. When the Holly version first came out, it was mistitled 'I Wanna Play House With You' – the title of an old Eddie Arnold composition, to which it bears no resemblance whatsoever. Interestingly, Mike Berry included 'Baby Let's Play House' when he teamed up with Jerry Allison and Sonny Curtis to put together *Buddy Holly – A Life in Music*, a superb alternative recording to the West End show, *Buddy – The Buddy Holly Story*, and (for the purist) much more faithful to the original storyline of Holly's life.

'BABY WON'T YOU COME OUT TONIGHT'
(1) Recorded late 1955 Nesman Recording Studio, Wichita Falls, Texas
Personnel: Buddy Holly (guitar, vocals), Sonny Curtis (guitar), Jerry Allison (drums), Don Guess (double bass)
(2) Recorded December 1955 Nesman Recording Studio, Wichita Falls, Texas
Personnel: Buddy Holly (guitar, vocals), Sonny Curtis (guitar), Jerry Allison (drums), Don Guess (double bass)
(3) Recorded early 1956 at Norman Petty Recording Studios, Clovis, New Mexico
Personnel: Buddy Holly (guitar, vocals), Sonny Curtis (guitar), Jerry Allison (drums), Don Guess (double bass)

The version of this song that fans are familiar with is the 1956 recording above (heavily overdubbed by the Fireballs to create a stereo master) featured on the 1963 *Reminiscing* album. It was another twenty years before the unadulterated mono original, complete with surface noise, got an official release, thus enabling listeners to hear how the song was originally laid down at Clovis at a time when Buddy's style was still developing. Although he'd already visited Nashville to record by then, he would still have a short time to wait before he could actually get to hold a copy of his first record, 'Blue Days, Black Nights' *b/w* 'Love Me', in his hands.

'Baby Won't You Come Out Tonight' (originally titled 'Moonlight Baby') is credited as a Holly composition, although the situation is clouded by the fact that, during his lifetime, bass player Don Guess received the composer royalties on it. As indicated above, the same group of musicians had attempted the song twice before at the Nesman Recording Studio in Wichita Falls, Texas, though the only recording that has surfaced from those sessions (Rev-Ola CD, *Gotta Roll! The Early Recordings 1949-1955*) includes extraneous noise.

Seldom covered, the song was recorded by singer Willie Alexander – a former member of the Velvet Underground – whose version appeared in 1989 on the *Everyday Is A Holly Day* tribute album issued by the French new wave label, New Rose.

HANK BALLARD & THE MIDNIGHTERS

Buddy's influences came as much from the black artists that he listened to on the radio, as the more prevalent, and predominantly white, country singers that he was surrounded by during his upbringing in the Lone Star State. Sonny Curtis recalls that Holly and his friends would often tune into a clear-channel R&B station they were able to pick up on the outskirts of Lubbock at the dead of night.

One firm favourite was Henry Bernard Ballard *aka* Hank Ballard – the 'nearly' man of rock'n'roll, who wrote and recorded 'The Twist' in 1958, only for Chubby Checker to take the plaudits and introduce the dance to the masses. As the Midnighters' lead singer and driving force, Ballard was truly ahead of his time. Their risqué songs 'Work With Me Annie' and 'Annie Had A Baby' – both R&B chart-toppers in the mid-'50s – must surely have been the influence behind 'Midnight Shift' (even if the composers, Earl Lee and Jimmie Ainsworth, claimed otherwise), and Holly's own composition, 'Rock-A-Bye Rock', owed not a little to the Midnighters' 'Sexy Ways'.

Ballard was belatedly inducted into the Rock and Roll Hall of Fame in 1990. He died in 2003 at the age of 76.

DEAN BARLOW – *See* **CRICKETS** *(Dean Barlow group)*

BENNIE BARNES

A minor figure in the world of country music, Bennie Barnes (1936-87) hailed from Beaumont, Texas and was a contemporary and friend of J.P. Richardson *aka* the Big Bopper, who was from the same locale. Barnes had one huge country hit back in 1956, when 'Poor Man's Riches' on Starday (a Richardson composition) went to No.2 in the *Billboard* C&W chart. His links with the Big Bopper were perpetuated after his death, when Barnes recorded the plaintive 'Gold Records In The Snow', a self-penned paean to the three victims of the 1959 plane crash. However, the record didn't break out nationally.

Barnes later joined Mercury, sharing both the same label and manager as the fallen singer/deejay, and recorded several other numbers from his prolific pen including 'Beggar To A King' and 'Fastest Gun Alive'. He enjoyed an active career as a country performer, but only had one more national country hit of any note, 'Yearning', in 1961. Bear Family recently issued his complete '50s recordings.

BEACH BOYS

Too famous to need a pen-picture here, this legendary Californian group weren't formed until 1961 and their first major appearance was at the inaugural *Ritchie Valens Memorial Dance* in Long Beach Civic Auditorium on New Year's Eve that same year. Although the group spearheaded surfing music, they were still heavily influenced by the waning rock'n'roll era. One of their biggest hits was a cover of the Regents' 'Barbara Ann', with lyrics that included a mention of *the* Peggy Sue.

In 1965, at the height of the surfing craze, the Beach Boys, Lesley Gore and the (post-Holly) Crickets, who were then based in Los Angeles, made an appearance in a quickie 'surfing' movie, *The Girls On The Beach*.

In 1978, and with the *Buddy Holly Story* biopic having received an Oscar nomination, the Beach Boys recorded and charted – albeit only at No.59 – with their very own version of Holly's classic, 'Peggy Sue'. They were inducted into the Rock and Roll Hall of Fame in 1988.

BEATLES

If it's possible to write a complete book about the sole meeting between Elvis and the Beatles, then perhaps a trilogy could be worked up to discuss the strands connecting the Beatles with Buddy Holly and the Crickets, both as individuals and in their group entities. But so many of these links are common currency (McCartney owning Holly's song catalogue, the Beatles recording Holly's 'Words of Love', etc), that mention of the Scousers here is purely confined to flagging up a few other random links.

So, what are the links that are worth mentioning? Well, it's known that the Beatles' 'insect' name (originally the 'Silver Beetles') was inspired by the Crickets, and the lads even wrote a fan letter to the group in the early 1960s, delighted to put on record their deep admiration for the group.

Of course, the Beatles featured Holly material live on stage from the very start of their career, particularly during those grinding Star-Club sessions in Hamburg in 1961-62. Certainly, Holly's 'Reminiscing' was included on the *Beatles Tapes* Polydor album from those days, while another Holly number, 'Crying, Waiting, Hoping', was one of the songs they performed at their famously unsuccessful Decca audition. Most significantly perhaps, the Beatles recorded the classic 'That'll Be The Day' before they even landed a recording contract, and the rare demo finally saw the light of day in the '90s on their *Anthology* project. It's also ironic to recall that, back in the '60s, in the wake of the Beatles' huge American successes, the latter-day Crickets recorded almost an entire album of Beatles covers! It certainly adds weight to the phrase 'what goes around comes around'.

The Beatles were inducted into the Rock and Roll Hall of Fame in 1988.

See also **JOHN LENNON** *and* **PAUL McCARTNEY**, *in particular McCartney's involvement with the Holly song catalogue)*. Although there are no separate entries for George and Ringo, they have also had plenty of involvement with Holly's contemporaries, as well as regularly supporting Paul McCartney at his annual *Buddy Holly Week* bash.

'BECAUSE I LOVE YOU'
Recorded early 1956 at Norman Petty Recording Studios, Clovis, New Mexico
Personnel: Buddy Holly (guitar, vocals), Sonny Curtis (guitar), Jerry Allison (drums), Don Guess (double bass)

A pretty ballad with sincere lyrics, this was one of a batch of numbers written by Buddy while he was still trying to hit the big time. Like many others, it wouldn't see the light of day during his lifetime. It first appeared on the 1963 *Reminiscing* album, as a stereo track with additional instrumental overdubs by the Fireballs. However, fans were always aware that an undubbed version existed, and this eventually surfaced in 1983 on the *For The First Time Anywhere* album. There are no backing vocals on either version, however some rather intrusive ones were added by the Picks in 1984 (see **OVERDUBS** and **PICKS** for more info).

Although Dutch fans voted it one of their favourite all-time rock'n'roll records in a 1998 poll, 'Because I Love You' has seldom been covered and deserves to be more popular than it is. (Coincidentally, in 1958 Buddy's pal, Bob Montgomery, wrote a song with the same title, which he also recorded at Clovis. However, they are entirely different compositions.)

BEECHCRAFT BONANZA

The type of aircraft that proved to be Buddy's undoing when he hired one to ferry him to the next gig on the *Winter Dance Party* tour back in February 1959. The small plane in question was a ten-year-old, standard 4-seater in red-and-white livery – the sort regularly chartered by anyone back then who could afford the going rate (receipts show that the fare charged on the night was $36 per passenger). The craft that young pilot Roger Peterson flew that night was numbered N3794N (contrary to some suggestions, it was not named *'American Pie'* or anything else). It was owned by Dwyer's Flying Service based in Mason City, Iowa, close to the Clear Lake venue where the artists had performed.

A Civil Aeronautics Board report later concluded that the crash was primarily the result of pilot error (for more info see **CRASH**). For the complete story of the *Winter Dance Party* tour and the accident, see Larry Lehmer's book, *The Day The Music Died*. Although highly detailed, it's tastefully written and is heartily recommended. Touchingly, it's dedicated to the family and friends of the pilot, Roger Peterson – the oft-overlooked fourth victim.

JOHN BEECHER

The owner of Rollercoaster Records, John remains totally unassuming and will only admit to being born sometime during the last century – though the author suspects that it was nearer the end of World War Two. But John is less secretive where Buddy Holly and the Crickets are concerned, and has led the thirst for knowledge to which many have subscribed over the years.

In 1960, he took over the running of the fledgling British Buddy

Holly Appreciation Society from Chris Griffin, who (masquerading as 'Tony Kent') had left to work for Joe Meek, a name mentioned elsewhere in these pages. But John's task wasn't always straightforward, as to champion a dead singer back then was considered one step short of necrophilia. Indeed, a national newspaper ran a leader about such fans in 1960 headlined *'We Give The Cult 5 Years'*, insisting that the ardent followers of the late singer were little more than ghouls – a ludicrous attitude that curiously didn't seem to extend to fans of the Glenn Miller orchestra! But that type of unenlightened thinking has long since faded away and sounds positively anachronistic in the more enlightened twenty-first century.

Starting at the bottom in the music business, John eventually formed Rollercoaster Records in the late '70s, enabling him to give full rein to his love of specialist music, for which he felt there was a niche in the market left by the majors. These days, Rollercoaster and John are based in Gloucestershire, from where he oversees a wide-ranging catalogue that includes a goodly share of Holly-related recordings.

John is deeply knowledgeable on the post-war music scene with a CV that's too long to list here. But briefly, he helped to compile the MCA *Complete Buddy Holly* box set in 1979, and later collaborated with John Goldrosen to update and publish *Remembering Buddy*, the definitive biography of the singer. Apart from masterminding several seminal Holly releases (among them the 1986 LP, *Something Special From Buddy Holly* and a 2002 CD EP containing all available Buddy Holly interviews called *That's What They Tell Me – That's What They Say*), Rollercoaster have also put out several (post-Holly) Crickets and Sonny Curtis releases for good measure. John's most recent coup was assembling a whole host of early Holly material – with far superior sound – on the 2007 CD, *Ohh! Annie!*, including a previously unheard alternate take of 'Midnight Shift'. Why isn't this man in the Honours List for heaven's sake?

BELL SOUND STUDIOS

Buddy Holly cut material in quite a few studios during his brief career, although the main one was obviously Norman Petty's installation at Clovis, where the vast bulk of his demos and commercially-released recordings were laid down. Prior to this, he'd used a couple of small studios in Texas (Nesman and Venture), and in 1956 had on three occasions ventured further afield to record at Bradley's Barn in Nashville, but none of these early recording attempts had resulted in any real breakthrough.

Of the other studios used by Holly, the most interesting ones were probably the ones in New York. The first of these was Bell Sound, based at 237 West 54th Street, which he visited in January 1958 to record 'Rave On' and 'That's My Desire'. Later that same year, he twice visited Decca's legendary Pythian Temple.

Incidentally, the post-Holly Crickets also recorded some of their Coral material at Bell Sound too. However, given they have been recording for some fifty years, they've probably recorded in almost as many studios over that time. Nowadays, however, they mostly record at their own studio in Jerry Allison's home in Lyles, near Nashville, Tennessee.

According to his autobiography, Bob Thiele, who was A&R Director at Coral at the time, supervised the 'Rave On' session. He describes Bell Sound as having a state-of-the-art set-up, the most distinctive feature of which was the ability to isolate each instrument, so that the sound could be picked up clearly. Specifically, this enabled the rhythm to be clearly heard, rather than end up getting 'submerged' in the mix. He'd put these facilities to the test when he recorded the McGuire Sisters at Bell Sound and produced a gold record and a US No.1 with 'Sugartime'. 'Rave On' didn't quite match that, but it did make the US Top 40 and No.5 in the UK, and has been perennially popular ever since.

CHUCK BERRY

It would be remiss not to include the name of Charles Edward Anderson 'Chuck' Berry in an *A to Z* such as this, even though the only number that Buddy recorded from his impressive songbook was 'Brown-Eyed Handsome Man'. He attempted the number twice as a demo, although the recordings didn't surface during his lifetime.

The Crickets and Berry first met up immediately after 'That'll Be The Day' charted in 1957. They often appeared together on those mammoth American package shows, like the Alan Freed *Big Beat Show* they headlined the following year. In interviews, Joe B. has frequently harked back to the happy memories when they and Chuck would shoot craps together in the gangways of the tour bus. He also recalls riding in Berry's Cadillac.

Of course, Holly and his group frequently performed Berry's material on stage (as the Crickets still do), and a staple of their 1958 UK tour was their version of 'Sweet Little Sixteen'. Justice was done when both Chuck Berry and Buddy Holly were inducted into the Rock and Roll Hall of Fame at the inaugural ceremony in 1986.

MIKE BERRY

If there is a British Buddy Holly, then it is surely Mike Berry. Born Michael Bourne in 1942, he first came to record buyers' notice as a protégé of record producer Joe Meek, morphing from Kenny Lord & The Statesmen into Mike Berry & The Outlaws thanks to Joe's foresight. (His demos for Meek included 'Peggy Sue Got Married', which later appeared on a Rollercoaster compilation album.) Over the years, the group contained some notable musicians including Chas Hodges (later of Chas & Dave), Heinz (of 'Just Like Eddie' fame) and guitarist Ritchie Blackmore (Deep Purple). Mike actually became the group's singer after vocalist/bass player Heinz Burt left to pursue a solo career, and immediately exhibited an uncanny ability to sound like the late Buddy Holly. Although a shoal of singers circa 1960-61 were also busy mimicking Holly's vocal mannerisms, nobody seemed to have the natural style and sound that Mike exuded, which reached a peak in 1961, when he charted with the classic 'Tribute To Buddy Holly'.

As his music career tailed off somewhat during the late '60s, he began to turn more and more to acting, appearing in the *Are You Being Served?* comedy sitcom, *Worzel Gummidge* and countless TV commercials. Nevertheless, he also had a string of chart hits in Europe in the '70s including a re-recording of 'Tribute to Buddy Holly' that went to No.1 in the Netherlands (the 1976 re-cut for Polydor avoided the irritating *'snow was snowing'* alliteration), while in Britain he reinvented himself as a balladeer and enjoyed a second chart career in the early '80s with 'The Sunshine Of Your Smile', which reached the Top 10, earning him a silver disc and triggering a hit album.

In 1998, Berry fulfilled a lifetime ambition to appear on stage with the Crickets when they were scheduled to headline the *Eddie Cochran Tribute* show in Chippenham, and Sonny Curtis had to pull out for family reasons. Here a link was forged that would never be relinquished.

Six years later, he went on to record a complete album with the Crickets entitled, appropriately enough, *About Time Too!* (Incidentally, this wasn't a collection of Holly covers – though there were a couple – but rather material reflecting the artists' mutual favourites ranging from Dylan to Hank Williams.) In fact, Mike and the Crickets had been trying to get together for years, but something had always turned up to

Mike Berry, UK, mid-'60s.

scupper plans. The album, produced by Chas Hodges at the Crickets' own studio in Lyles, just outside Nashville, Tennessee, is excellent and is still available from Rollercoaster.

After a lifetime in music, Mike Berry must have sung just about every Buddy Holly song there is, but he still manages to delight fans with his ability to interpret some of the less well-known Holly numbers – an ability that received international recognition when he was invited to headline the 2006 *Clovis Music Festival*. It's only a prediction, but having performed for Paul McCartney at nearly every *Buddy Holly Week* tribute over the years, chances are he'll be appearing soon at a Holly tribute near you. One thing is for sure: he's come a long way since he first hesitantly covered the Shirelles' 'Will You Love Me Tomorrow'.

BIG BEATS

A superb instrumental outfit, the Big Beats – Donny McCord (rhythm guitar), Earl Slocomb (bass guitar), Chester Ware Kendall Jr (piano), Larry Randall (saxophone) and Jerry Zapata (drums) – first got together in Dallas, initially with Trini Lopez on vocals. After Lopez's departure they turned more to instrumentals, but despite some good exposure including an appearance on Dick Clark's *American Bandstand* on 16 July 1958, they somehow missed out on having a national hit,

The Big Beats at East Texas State University, 1 May 1958. *Left to right:* Donny McCord, Larry Randall, Jery Zapata, Earl Slocomb and C.W. Kendall Jr.

though 'Clark's Expedition' did see some regional chart action.

They first went to Clovis in 1957 at the instigation of Buddy's dad, Lawrence, and regularly undertook session work there. Amongst the artists they backed were Sonny West (on 'Rave On') and Terry Noland (on 'Don't Do Me This Way' b/w 'Patty Baby'). They also had a couple of instrumentals released on Columbia, as well as several on smaller labels, but never made the big breakthrough. Later on, Norman Petty would often express his surprise in interviews that the group never made it bigger.

Sonny Curtis remembers the group well, and photos of the Crickets and the Big Beats together exist from those days. Not only that, C.W. Kendall Jr, the Big Beats' pianist, both wrote and played on Holly's 'Little Baby'. There is undoubtedly unissued material by the group still lying in the Clovis vaults.

See also **TRINI LOPEZ** and **JERRY ZAPATA**.

BIG BOPPER

All rock'n'roll fans know the basics: that the Big Bopper was born Jiles Perry (*aka* 'J.P.', 'Jape' or 'Jay') Richardson Jr in Sabine Pass, Texas in 1930, and that he perished along with Buddy, Ritchie Valens and pilot Roger Peterson in an Iowa cornfield on 3 February 1959. However, it is salutary to reflect that, although he earned a posthumous gold record with his composition, 'Chantilly Lace', he was, as far as the bulk of the record buying public were concerned, a one-hit wonder. He certainly was in the UK, where his record barely scraped into the Top 30. Even in the US he would only have two other hits, both sides of his follow-up single ('Big Bopper's Wedding' *b/w* 'Little Red Riding Hood') charting separately.

This, of course, only relates to his career as a recording artist, but there was a lot more to J.P. Richardson. Prior to his recording career, the Big Bopper had been a well-known deejay for years in Beaumont, Texas, and had set a record of sorts in the '50s when he spun platters (the word of the day!) on KTRM radio non-stop for 122 hours and 8 minutes in a sponsored 'disc-a-thon'.

He was also a blossoming country songwriter, and even before such exploits had found time to compose dozens of songs, of which the biggest was 'Poor Man's Riches', a No.2 C&W hit for Benny Barnes in 1956. Ironically, it wasn't until after his death that a string of his compositions followed that into the charts, mostly thanks to George Jones (a friend of his), who took 'White Lightning' to the top of the *Billboard* C&W listing in March 1959, where it stayed for five weeks. Hank Snow's 'Beggar To A King', another Richardson song, reached No.5 C&W in 1961, while 'Running Bear' by Johnny Preston shot to the top of the 'Hot 100' in 1960, earning a gold disc into the bargain. (Release of Preston's records was actually postponed following Richardson's death. Intriguingly, the background grunts and chants on the track were by George Jones and Richardson himself. Jones had also written an answer disc to 'Chantilly Lace' called 'Bopper 486609', but that too was held up because of his passing.) The Big Bopper's posthumously-released album was also entirely self-composed, bringing the tally to twenty or more compositions without a dud amongst them.

There is a sad postscript to this entry which, in some ways reflects the times we're all living in now. Briefly, because of ongoing innuendo and rumour regarding the crash, and the fact that the Bopper's body was found some distance away from the others, suggestions had arisen that somehow foul play – even guns – may have contributed to

The Big Bopper poses at the Riverside Ballroom, Green Bay, Wisconsin on 1 February 1959.

the accident. With Richardson's son, Jay Perry, carving out a performing career for himself as the 'Big Bopper Jr', the whole thing had begun to prey on his mind to the extent that he became determined to find out exactly what had happened.

And so, in 2007, a fresh autopsy was ordered at the family's request, which proved conclusively that there were *no* gunshot wounds, and nothing inconsistent with the singer having died instantly of a broken neck, crushed skull and other injuries resulting from a devastating impact. Death had been instantaneous. Yet another case (the Diana inquest springs to mind) where there seems to have been a reluctance to accept the blindingly obvious, but some prefer to look for any alternative conclusion, however preposterous that might seem.

On a happier note, a few years ago the Crickets backed the Big Bopper Jr on 'Teenage Moon' and 'The Monkey Song' on his 1997 album, *The Legacy Of The Big Bopper*.

BIG D JAMBOREE

The *Big D Jamboree* in Dallas, Texas was one of several centres scattered throughout the South (the *Louisiana Hayride* in Shreveport was another), where country & western music was regularly performed and broadcast over the airwaves to enthusiastic audiences. The roll-call of artists who played the *Jamboree* is a veritable Who's Who of Southern country, rockabilly and rock'n'roll and includes Johnny

Horton, Carl Perkins, Sherry Davis, Ferlin Husky and Johnny Carroll.

Sid King (of Sid King & The 5 Strings, who were from Dallas but performed regularly at Lubbock's Cotton Club during the '50s) recalls Buddy Holly and Sonny Curtis travelling down to Dallas and making a brief appearance on the show, playing either two or three numbers. This would have been around '55 or '56 – well before he'd made the big time. In recent times, Rollercoaster Records have put out several albums of live recordings from the *Big D Jamboree*, although, sadly, no recordings of Holly's appearance exist.

BIOGRAPHIES – *See* **LITERATURE (BIOGRAPHIES)**

BLIND FAITH

Short-lived supergroup which included Rick (sometimes 'Ric') Grech, a fine bass player with a quality pedigree who later joined the Crickets after being introduced to them by Glen D. Hardin. Although Blind Faith barely lasted a year, their one and only album (which included a fine version of Holly's 'Well... All Right') topped the British charts in 1969. Since the group also included Stevie Winwood and Eric Clapton – both renowned Holly fans – perhaps it wasn't surprising that they would cover at least one of his songs.

'BLUE DAYS, BLACK NIGHTS'
Recorded January 1956 at Bradley's Barn Studio, Nashville, Tennessee
Personnel: Buddy Holly (vocals), Sonny Curtis (guitar), Grady Martin (guitar), Don Guess (double bass), Doug Kirkham (percussion)

This was one of a quartet of tracks that Buddy, Sonny Curtis and Don Guess cut on their first visit to Nashville, aided and abetted by some of the future country capital's finest sessionmen including the legendary Grady Martin on rhythm guitar. (Jerry Allison and Joe B. Mauldin were not there because the former was still attending school in Lubbock, while the latter was playing with the Four Teens and hadn't yet linked up with the others.)

Buddy often listened to local country artist Ben Hall on Lubbock radio station KDAV and had approached him for material for the session. Hall gave him 'Blue Days, Black Nights' and also 'It's Not My Fault', which Holly later cut a demo of in the spring of 1956. Hall also cut a demo of 'Blue Days, Black Nights' around the same time in a more relaxed country style, but in 1960 reworked it as a more uptempo number.

Coupled with 'Love Me', another cut from the session, 'Blue Days, Black Nights' became Buddy Holly's first single. Released by Decca in April 1956, it went nowhere. Released in the UK that July on the Decca subsidiary, Brunswick, it likewise sank without trace. Needless to say, the few pressings of the single that survive are extremely hard to find, making it a very collectable record. In 1984, the Picks overdubbed backing vocals onto this recording (see **OVERDUBS** and **PICKS** for more info). On a recent Rollercoaster reissue, the engineer can be heard announcing *'Take 6'*, which is the only surviving take of the song.

'Blue Days, Black Nights' has inspired surprisingly few cover versions, although Bob Luman cut an excellent version on Imperial in the '50s, while Bobby Vee included this as one of his very eclectic choices on his 1999 Holly tribute album, *Down The Line*, and also sang it accompanied by Nanci Griffith and the Crickets on the 2004 *Crickets And Their Buddies* album.

And, while there is no copyright on the phrase *'blue days, black nights'* and Ben Hall may not have been the first to use it, it is also interesting to note that it later cropped up in the lyrics of the 1977 ELO hit, 'Telephone Line'.

'BLUE MONDAY'
Recorded late 1956 at Buddy's home in Lubbock, Texas
Personnel: Buddy Holly (guitar, vocals), Jerry Allison (drums)

This Dave Bartholomew song was first recorded by Smiley Lewis in December 1953 for Imperial, but, of course, it is Fats Domino's classic version from *The Girl Can't Help It* – a Top 5 hit in the US in 1957 – that is remembered nowadays.

Buddy tried the number out during 1956, when he was endlessly rehearsing new material, and it is that rehearsal performance – heavily overdubbed by the Fireballs and transformed from mono into a stereo master – that fans first heard a decade or so later on the 1969 *Giant* album. The undubbed version surfaced in the UK in 1986 thanks to the pioneering release on Rollercoaster of *Something Special From Buddy Holly*.

Holly also recorded Fats's 'Valley of Tears' but, thankfully, it was at a later full Clovis session rather than the rough demo we have for 'Blue Monday'. Of course, there have been many covers of 'Blue Monday' over the years. Even the Crickets, when they were based in California in the early '60s, did a version for Liberty.

'BLUE SUEDE SHOES'
Recorded late 1956 at Buddy's home in Lubbock, Texas
Personnel: Buddy Holly (guitar, vocals), Jerry Allison (drums)

This number was laid down at the same session as 'Blue Monday' and much of the above information applies here too. Briefly, it was initially released in overdubbed form on the 1964 *Showcase* album, and the undubbed original first appeared in the UK on the 1986 Rollercoaster LP, *Something Special From Buddy Holly*.

Carl Perkins first wrote and recorded this rockabilly classic for Sun back in December 1955, and it catapulted him to No.2 in the US charts in 1956 before a near-fatal car accident seriously derailed his career for a time. We know this was a song from Buddy's 'To Learn' list – this and well over 50 others! Nearly every major rock'n'roll singer got around to recording their own version, but only Perkins, Presley and Boyd Bennett made the charts (all in 1956). Then, in the '70s, Johnny Rivers reached the Top 40 with his interpretation. (Coincidentally Buddy's pal, Eddie Cochran, also recorded the song, which, like Buddy's recording, was released after his death.)

'BO DIDDLEY'
(1) Recorded late 1956 at Buddy's home in Lubbock, Texas
Personnel: Buddy Holly (guitar, vocals), Jerry Allison (drums), unknown (double bass)
(2) Recorded prob. late 1956 at Norman Petty Recording Studios, Clovis, New Mexico
Personnel: Buddy Holly (guitar, vocals), unknown (guitar), Jerry Allison (drums), Larry Welborn (double bass)

This is a number that Buddy and the boys loved to do live on stage, but for the Holly collector things can get puzzling, as there are four different versions out there, but only two different lead vocals. The familiar hit version (*(2)* above) was the one that Buddy and Jerry had polished up at Clovis while hoping to hit the big time. Released with instrumental embellishments by the Fireballs, it became a huge posthumous hit in the UK in 1963, reaching No.4 in the charts. (It's also indicative of the difference in popularity of Holly in the US and UK at that point, as in his homeland it only struggled to No.116!)

In 1983, the undubbed version was issued on the *For The First Time Anywhere* album. This lacks the strong lead guitar line of the hit version (supplied by George Tomsco) and is all the poorer for it. Later still, a much looser demo in which Buddy shouts *'Break time!'* to Jerry on the drums surfaced in 1995 on the 4-CD Vigotone bootleg, *What You Been A-Missin'*, and in the UK on 1986's *Something Special From Buddy Holly* on Rollercoaster. Fascinating stuff.

Finally, there is the strange 1984 overdub by the Picks (see **OVERDUBS** and **PICKS** for more info) during which they occasionally chant *'Papa-oom-mow-mow'* in the background, courtesy of the Rivingtons 1962 hit record of the same name! Strange days indeed, mama.

With hindsight, it seems ironic that Bo Diddley didn't make the *Billboard* 'Top 100' with his own superb recording, although it did top the R&B lists of 1955 and certainly helped him launch a long and successful career that only came to an end with his passing in 2008. Numerous singers have covered this original number over the years – even Little Richard – while Diddley himself went back into the studio and recorded a new version in 1969.

It's known that Holly based his 'Not Fade Away' on the 'Bo Diddley' riff, so it was entirely fitting that Bo recorded a version of 'Not Fade Away' for his 1976 album, *The 20th Anniversary of Rock'n'Roll* album.

BO DIDDLEY *(artist)* – See under DIDDLEY

MARK BOLAN

A legendary and much-missed performer (1947-77) who sadly died in a road accident just weeks before his 30th birthday and exactly one month to the day after Elvis Presley's sudden passing. In fact, like 1959, the year 1977 was an incredibly sad one, as a whole handful of musical legends passed away over a twelve-month period including Billie Holiday, Mario Lanza and Bing Crosby. Marc, along with other show business celebrities, had attended the annual *Buddy Holly Week* party in London that year and it was reported that a badge inscribed *'Every Day is a Holly Day'* was found in the car's wreckage.

BOOKS – *See* LITERATURE (BIOGRAPHIES), LITERATURE (FICTION)

PAT BOONE

Born Charles Eugene Boone in Nashville in 1934, Pat was a contemporary of Buddy Holly and the Crickets. However, their careers intersected little, as the deeply religious singer declined to get involved in the big rock'n'roll packages of the day. In the '60s, however, he recorded 'That'll Be The Day' for his *Great! Great! Great!* album, which contained covers of many rock'n'roll hits of the day.

Throughout his career, Boone has attracted flak for his sanitised versions of rock'n'roll hits, although he has always strenuously defended his motives. In later years, he moved into country and gospel music, and several members of his family (notably daughter Debby) have gone on to success in the music field. His late father-in-law was Red Foley, the legendary country artist from the '40s.

Jimmy Bowen backstage at
at unknown venue, late '50s.

JIMMY BOWEN

James Albert Bowen was born in Santa Rita, New Mexico in November 1937 and attended West Texas State University in Canyon (near Amarillo), where he took up bass and met guitarist Donnie 'Dirt' Lanier and drummer Donnie Mills. Lanier introduced Bowen to guitarist Buddy Knox, and it wasn't long before they formed a group. They called themselves 'The Orchids', after the orchid-coloured shirts they wore on stage.

At Roy Orbison's suggestion, they approached Norman Petty in Clovis about making a record. Knox had written a song called 'Party Doll' as far back as the late '40s(!) and this, coupled with Bowen's 'I'm Stickin' With You', came out on the local Triple-D label in 1956. Picked up for national distribution by New York's Roulette label, both sides were reissued as separate singles. 'Party Doll', credited to Buddy Knox & The Rhythm Orchids, shot to No.1 in the US charts, while 'I'm Sticking With You', credited to Jimmy Bowen & The Rhythm Orchids, reached a respectable No.14.

During their time at Clovis, Bowen and Knox got to know Holly and various Crickets. Bowen collaborated with Jerry Allison on a composition called 'I'm Keepin' You', which he subsequently recorded for Roulette in 1958.

Like many other aspiring musicians, Bowen's life had been transformed after seeing Elvis on stage in Amarillo, and he had decided there and then to pursue a career in music – primarily, it seems, to meet members of the opposite sex! He also admits in his memoirs, *Rough Mix*, that he really wasn't much of a bass player and he feared that, if the girls ever stopped screaming, he'd be found out. He did go on to have a series of singles on Roulette and, although several were minor hits, he realised that a career change was on the cards. He was far more suited to being a backroom boy than standing in front of a microphone.

After a period with KYSN, Colorado Springs, he got the chance to make records and quickly graduated from being an engineer to producing entire sessions for the likes of Sammy Davis Jr, Dean Martin and Frank Sinatra (notably 'Strangers In The Night', where the singer memorably ad-libbed *'dooby-dooby-doo'* at the song's end).

He eventually became a record company executive, holding senior positions at Capitol, MGM, Elektra/Asylum (where he signed Sonny Curtis to Elektra in 1969) and latterly MCA, concentrating mostly on country music. These days he's enjoying a well-deserved retirement in Hawaii.

BOWMAN BROTHERS

The original Bowman Brothers comprising Dee, Lowell and Jay (brother Monte would join later) were from a small community near Clovis, but located just over the border inside Texas. They were a fine vocal group and, as with the Picks and the Roses, were one of many contemporaries associated with Norman Petty's studio in the '50s. In 1958, they even had a record out on the Columbia label ('Hey Punkin'), on which Tommy Allsup played guitar. However they were mostly used by Petty as session artists, and feature on many recordings including the Petty Trio's chart debut, 'Almost Paradise'. The brothers also cut a version of 'Mailman Bring Me No More Blues' at Clovis, but it wasn't released. They were undoubtedly contemporaries of Holly's and one of several candidates (Don Guess and Terry Noland being the others) for being responsible for introducing Buddy to Norman Petty and Clovis in the first place.

The greatly missed David Box.

DAVID BOX

Fans of the Crickets will be familiar with the sad story of Harold David Box (1943-64) and the tragically familiar tale of a young man who was inspired to follow in the footsteps of Buddy Holly and the Crickets. He achieved his ambition of recording a 1960 single with the group, but only a few years later lost his life in a plane crash at the age of 21, just when it seemed his career was about to take off.

A native Texan from Sulphur Springs, Box came from a musical background, his father Harold 'Boxey' Box being an outstanding Western swing musician of many years' standing. From a young age his son also relentlessly pursued a career in music, first by heading a local group called the Ravens, and then miraculously, on his seventeenth birthday, got to record with the Crickets in Los Angeles. The resulting single, 'Peggy Sue Got Married' *b/w* 'Don't Cha Know', with Box on lead vocals, was their final Coral release. Sadly, it didn't chart.

Box returned to school for a while, but shortly after made a series of superb singles which came out on the Joed and the Candix labels. Although popular locally, none were hits. In 1964, having been offered a recording contract with RCA, he lost his life the day before he was due to travel to Nashville in circumstances a bit too similar to that of his hero.

It would be close to forty years before most of the late singer's released and unissued material was gathered together by lifetime British fan John Davidson-White and released as *The David Box Story* by Rollercoaster – a long-overdue tribute to a unique young talent. Seek out his music if you have not yet done so.

David Box was posthumously inducted into the West Texas Walk of Fame in Lubbock in 2006. His sister, Rita, accepted the award on his behalf.

HAROLD BRADLEY

A lifetime session guitarist (though he was also adept at banjo and most other stringed instruments) and brother of the legendary country producer Owen Bradley (see below), Harold backed Buddy Holly on his third and final Nashville session in November 1956.

OWEN BRADLEY

Legendary country producer who fans may recall was portrayed in *The Buddy Holly Story* movie as someone with whom Holly would clash in the studio. Anyone who has read the true story of Holly's rise to fame will know that this was pure Hollywood fantasy.

Bradley (1915-98) had an impressive musical pedigree, and amongst other things enjoyed a US Top 20 hit in 1957 with the instrumental 'White Silver Sands', as well as heading Decca's A&R division and eventually rising to become Vice-President of MCA (previously Decca). He was inducted into the Country Music Hall of Fame in 1974.

It's often said that Owen Bradley and Nashville weren't ready for Buddy Holly's rocking sounds in 1956, yet we can counter this by reflecting that both the Johnny Burnette Trio and Gene Vincent recorded some of the wildest, most potent rock'n'roll sessions ever in that very studio during that same period.

See also **NASHVILLE SESSIONS**.

'BROWN-EYED HANDSOME MAN'
(1) Recorded late 1956 at Buddy's home in Lubbock, Texas
Personnel: Buddy Holly (guitar, vocals), Jerry Allison (drums), unknown (double bass)
(2) Recorded prob. late 1956 at Norman Petty Recording Studios, Clovis, New Mexico
Personnel: Buddy Holly (guitar, vocals), unknown (guitar), Jerry Allison (drums), Larry Welborn (double bass)

Chuck Berry was a particular favourite of all the Crickets and it's not surprising that, whilst cutting demos, they would tackle at least one of his songs. As with 'Bo Diddley', Holly recorded two different versions of 'Brown-Eyed Handsome Man', but it is the Clovis one with which we are all familiar. Overdubbed by the Fireballs, it produced his biggest posthumous hit since 'It Doesn't Matter Anymore', reaching No.3 in the UK and staying on the charts for an unlikely four months – well above the average life expectancy for a hit record. It was also a Top 10 hit in Australia where, despite Holly's demise, his popularity continued unabated. In contrast, his reputation back home appeared to be at a low ebb, and the record only managed to get to No.113, barely scraping into *Billboard*'s 'Bubbling Under' chart.

Unlike 'Bo Diddley', where the searing guitar line was overdubbed by George Tomsco of the Fireballs, this time it was Buddy's own lead that we heard on the hit.

The undubbed version eventually surfaced in 1983 on the *For The First Time Anywhere* album, while a second, noticeably looser version where Buddy momentarily forgets the words was first heard on the 1986 Rollercoaster album, *Something Special From Buddy Holly*.

Curiously, although both Buddy Holly and Paul McCartney have charted with 'Brown-Eyed Handsome Man' in Britain (the latter as late as 1999), it wasn't a pop hit for Chuck Berry, either back home or in the UK (it was actually the flip of the No.7 R&B hit, 'Too Much Monkey Business'). Various artists have recorded the song over the years, but given that it was conceived in 1956 as an R&B number it is ironic that probably the most successful version Stateside was by Waylon Jennings: a No.3 country hit in 1969. However, the one that is definitely the most fun to listen to are the repeated attempts by Elvis, Carl Perkins and Jerry Lee Lewis to remember the words during their impromptu 'Million Dollar Quartet' session.

DAVE BRUBECK

The innovative jazzman is now an octogenarian. An earlier edition of this book suggested that Brubeck may have met up with Holly backstage at the London Palladium when the Crickets were touring the UK, but research has since revealed that Brubeck was not in England at that time. Mistaken identity it seems, although the snippet did appear in the musical press of the day. Brubeck was contacted a few years ago and couldn't recall having met his compatriot, so it would appear they never locked horn-rims.

BUDDY – THE BUDDY HOLLY STORY

If we reflect deeply, there must have been something quite unique about the man and his music for his death in 1959 not to have been the end, but to have triggered off a chain reaction whose ripples are still felt today. Out of sight and deceptively slow, the seed had been planted and shoots would soon be seen in a myriad of ways, as articles led to books, brief film clips of the singer metamorphosed into a full-length Hollywood biopic, and occasional impersonations of the singer blossomed into a full-length stage musical. In the end it took some thirty years, but the legend was now so visible you could almost touch it, and eventually commemorative stamps and statues would even enable you to do just that.

But enough of the rhetoric. This entry must bring us down to earth and concentrate briefly on the stage show, *Buddy – The Buddy Holly Story* (aka *Buddy – The Musical*)*,* which burst forth close to twenty years ago. In fact, it opened in London's West End on 12 October 1989 and it's for certain that, somewhere in the world, a version is playing as you read these words. And, if a stage musical about the man himself doesn't appeal, there are other productions – *Rockin' On Heaven's Door* and *That'll Be The Day* are just two current examples – that feature Holly's music as part of their programme. There have been many others.

Buddy itself was written by Alan Janes and, with a dose of poetic licence as an ingredient, was a barnstorming success: a celebration of the man and the music which we could all enjoy and relate to, and all somehow encapsulated on one stage in the course of a two-hour show. With Bruce Welch of the Shadows acting as musical consultant, a high level of musicianship was in evidence from the very start. Indeed, it paved the way for other such musicals in a new genre – but it's worth remembering that it wasn't a foregone conclusion it would be a hit, and one or two early reviews were decidedly lukewarm. Now in its twentieth year, and having been seen by a worldwide audience of over twenty million, it seems likely to run and run, proving – as if we didn't know – that the appeal of Buddy Holly's music is both durable and timeless.

BUDDY & BOB

Before he went to Nashville in January 1956 for his first shot at stardom, Buddy was part of a country duo known as Buddy & Bob, their business card proclaiming their repertoire as *'Western and Bop'*. The 'Bob' part of the act was singer/guitarist Bob Montgomery, who went on to enjoy a long career as a producer and publisher in Nashville. Bob would typically play rhythm guitar and sing the lead vocals on ballads, while Buddy played lead guitar or banjo and sang on uptempo material. The duo were supported by Larry Welborn on bass and managed by Hi-Pockets Duncan.

Most of the group's performances were in and around Lubbock – promotional events at car dealerships, supermarket openings and the like – and appearing on local KDAV radio at weekends. A particular highlight among a wealth of minor gigs came in 1955 when they were drafted onto the bill on the night Bill Haley came to town (see **BILL HALEY**). Also at the show was Nashville talent scout Eddie Crandall, through whose good offices Holley (as he still was then) ended up being offered a recording contract by Decca.

Although Buddy & Bob cut various demo discs between 1952 and 1955, none of this material was issued at the time. Indeed, what we have today, as exemplified by the 1965 *Holly In The Hills* album, would have stayed well hidden if Holly hadn't eventually attained such legendary status.

BUDDY & JACK

Buddy's first real musical pairing took place in 1953, when he had just turned seventeen. His partner was Jack Neal, originally from

Fort Worth and a couple of years Buddy's senior. The duo had first met when Neal was working with Buddy's dad. Although both could sing and play guitar, the only known performances that exist from then, 'I Heard The Lord Calling For Me' and 'I Saw The Moon Cry Last Night', feature vocals by Neal with instrumental backing by Holly. They've cropped up on several recent releases after having been unavailable for years.

Buddy & Jack had a weekly slot on KDAV radio and built up a bit of local popularity, with listeners being encouraged to send in their requests for them to play live on air. Their repertoire, unlike the later Buddy & Bob material, usually featured a *de rigeur* gospel number in addition to the usual country stuff made popular by acts like the Louvin Brothers or Flatt & Scruggs. It's known that Buddy & Jack also occasionally appeared on local TV, including a talent show hosted by Jack Huddle called *About Lubbock*.

See also **JACK NEAL**.

BUDDY HOLLY *(LP)*
I'm Gonna Love You Too / Peggy Sue / Listen To Me / Look At Me / Valley Of Tears / Ready Teddy / Everyday / Mailman, Bring Me No More Blues / Words Of Love / Baby I Don't Care / Rave On / Little Baby

Released in March 1958 in the USA and July 1958 in Britain, a few months after the Crickets toured here, the *Buddy Holly* album was undoubtedly well received, but only made the little-known *Record Mirror* chart (the fact that five of the twelve tracks were already available on singles wouldn't have helped sales). Although it never charted in America, it has remained popular and has rarely been out of catalogue since.

Most of the tracks on it were the group's own compositions, while the remaining three were covers of Elvis ('You're So Square'), Fats Domino ('Valley Of Tears') and Little Richard ('Ready Teddy'). This LP was one of only two issued during Holly's lifetime: only the absence of backing vocals differentiated it soundwise from the earlier *Chirping Crickets* album. Incidentally, Niki Sullivan, who had left the group in 1957 and didn't make the UK tour, appeared on some of the above tracks.

BUDDY HOLLY LIVES – 20 GOLDEN GREATS *(LP)*
That'll Be The Day* / Peggy Sue / Words Of Love / Everyday / Not Fade Away / Oh Boy!* / Maybe Baby* / Listen To Me / Heartbeat / Think It Over* / It Doesn't Matter Anymore / It's So Easy* / Well... All Right / Rave On / Raining In My Heart / True Love Ways / Peggy Sue Got Married / Bo Diddley / Brown Eyed Handsome Man / Wishing
[Tracks marked * were Crickets recordings]

This album was compiled by Malcolm Jones and John Beecher. and was released in early 1978 to tie in with the new Holly biopic, *The Buddy Holly Story*. The publicity surrounding the film, plus TV-promotion of the album certainly had an effect, for, although various 'greatest hits' packages had been in existence for years, this one shot to the top of the charts in Britain and hung around for twenty weeks in total, earning a platinum disc for sales in excess of 300,000 units.

In the USA, it reached a more modest No.55 and spent twelve weeks in the charts, but still earned a gold disc. It was particularly gratifying for Crickets Jerry Allison and Joe B. Mauldin, who found themselves being presented with the award by none other than the head of MCA in Nashville, Jimmy Bowen – the same Jimmy Bowen they'd known back in Clovis two decades earlier.

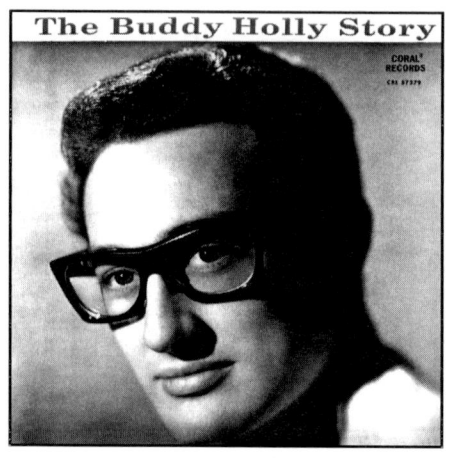 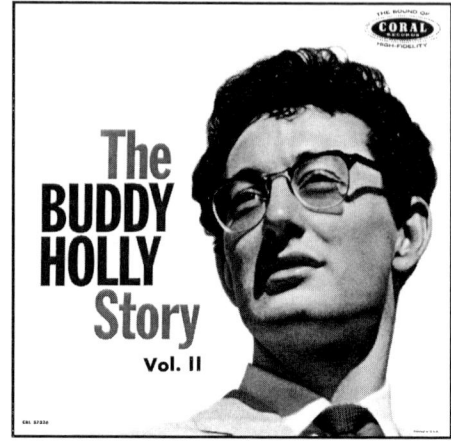

THE BUDDY HOLLY STORY *(LP)*
Raining In My Heart / Early In The Morning / Peggy Sue / Maybe Baby / Everyday / Rave On / That'll Be The Day / Heartbeat / Think It Over / Oh Boy! / It's So Easy / It Doesn't Matter Anymore

THE BUDDY HOLLY STORY: VOLUME II *(LP)*
Peggy Sue Got Married / Well... All Right / What To Do / That Makes It Tough / Now We're One / Take Your Time / Crying, Waiting, Hoping / True Love Ways / Learning The Game / Little Baby / Moondreams / That's What They Say

Looking back, it has to be said that the first *Buddy Holly Story* album was rush-released, as it came out in the USA in the month following the singer's death and was in the UK shops the month after that. Although for years it seemed as if Buddy Holly was largely forgotten in the USA, it's worth reflecting that the memorial album stayed on the *Billboard* 'Top LPs' chart for almost four years – an incredible period of time. In the UK, it was one of the biggest-selling albums to date and only the phenomenal *South Pacific* soundtrack prevented it from reaching the No.1 spot. With a sombre black & white cover photo from a recent shoot by Bruno of New York, matched only by the mawkish sleeve notes from *Billboard* journalist Ren Grevatt (who four years later would pen a similar eulogy to Patsy Cline), the album nevertheless soon found its way into nearly every fan's collection, even though there was nothing new on it.

By August 1970 it had gone on to sell a million, which led to

Mr & Mrs Holley being presented with a gold record in their home town of Lubbock – a tangible, if slender consolation for Buddy's elderly parents. It was later outsold by 1978's TV-advertised *Buddy Holly Lives (20 Golden Greats)* LP, which became the singer's (and the Crickets') biggest-selling album ever.

Whilst the original *Buddy Holly Story* album was a wonderful collection of Holly/Crickets hits, *Volume II* – released in 1960 – consisted mainly of unissued solo material. Although eagerly welcomed by the more avid fans, the waxings were of less interest to the more casual fan, and the chart action that followed reflected this: it briefly dented the 1960 UK Top 10, but never made the American charts at all. However, the packaging was more uplifting, with a striking colour cover and sleevenotes credited to the singer's widow.

It shouldn't be overlooked either that Holly (under both solo and group names) had a huge number of UK EP releases during the 1960s, resulting in the majority of these tracks being available on singles, EPs and LPs. The career of the late, great singer was showing little sign of slowing down.

THE BUDDY HOLLY STORY *(film)*

This film biography didn't emerge from a major studio, but was a joint Innovisions-ECA production that got underway in 1977 and went on general release after its Dallas premiere in 1978. There will be few reading this entry who won't have seen the movie at least once, and the way in which it portrays Buddy's rise to fame from the days he played a Lubbock roller rink circa 1954/55 through to his final appearance on stage at the Surf Ballroom in Clear Lake, Iowa on the night of 2 February 1959, where it ends with a freeze-frame.

Anyone wishing to be pedantic can certainly pick endless holes in the storyline, such as the way in which it portrays Buddy's family as not supporting his music, the omission of the Crickets as an entity (the hit-making Crickets originally comprised four individuals, rather than the strangely named 'Jesse' and 'Ray Bob' who back-up Holly in the film) and the airbrushing-out of Buddy's producer/manager, Norman Petty... and that's just for starters.

If the film gives a Hollywood gloss to Buddy's life, few could doubt Gary Busey's sincerity in playing the leading role – even if at 33 he was possibly a little too advanced in years to be playing a 22 year old. Perhaps, like the *Buddy* musical that turned up in the late '80s, it should simply be approached as a celebration of the singer's life and unique achievements.

Despite these shortcomings, it is compulsively watchable and was certainly a big box office success, easily recouping its $2 million dollar outlay. Oscar-wise, pickings were thin, with just one awarded for Original Score Adaptation, but Busey did at least got nominated for the Best Actor award. In Britain, the soundtrack album was to have been promoted on TV, but a strike hampered sales. Fortunately, the best-selling Holly/Crickets *Buddy Holly Lives (20 Golden Greats)* album was still in the shops.

Perhaps Sonny Curtis got it right after all. Having been to the premiere, and bemused by what he had seen up on the screen, he went home and immediately wrote 'The Real Buddy Holly Story'. For many fans that song tells Buddy's story far more accurately than the celluloid representation. Timewise too, he only needed around 3 minutes compared with the luxury of the film's 114 minutes.

Finally, a postscript: an earlier attempt to film Holly's life story had gone into pre-production a few years earlier, and the entry **NOT FADE AWAY** *(Film)* explains more. It is also part of the reason that, awkwardly, the Crickets were not referred to by name in the Busey film.

BUDDY HOLLY WEEK

It is well known that Paul McCartney acquired Buddy Holly's music publishing catalogue in 1972. This was a match made in heaven, as the ex-Beatle is a huge Holly fan and immediately decided to do something special to celebrate the singer's life on an annual basis.

And so it came to pass that a special week of Holly-related events was launched in September 1976, a date that handily coincided with what would have been the late singer's 40th birthday. The highlight of that very first *Buddy Holly Week* was a special luncheon for the great and the good of the music business, with the guest of honour, Norman Petty, flown in from New Mexico. Every year thereafter, a programme of events marked the anniversary in a special and eye-catching way. Far too many years have rolled by to do anything other than touch on a few of the highlights below.

The '70s were a thrilling time in *Buddy Holly Week* terms, and after the launch, the following year (1977) saw the Crickets returning to Britain to headline a concert at the Gaumont State, Kilburn – the same venue they'd played back in 1958. 1978 was special too, as this coincided with the London premiere of the *Buddy Holly Story* film at the Odeon, Leicester Square. In 1979, it was back to the concert format with a show at the Hammersmith Odeon headlined by the Crickets, at the end of which they were joined on stage by Paul and Linda McCartney, Denny Laine, Bob Montgomery, Don Everly, Rick Grech and others for a big musical finale.

During the '80s, there were jive competitions, Holly lookalike contests and a memorable *Rock'n'Roll Movie Week*, while in 1995 a couple of concerts in Shepherd's Bush featured the Crickets, Carl Perkins and Bobby Vee. A markedly different event was conceived for 1997: fans could compose *A Poem For Buddy*, the best of which would be published by the Poetry Society. Some excellent poems were submitted, but the award for the most inventive title must surely go to the one entitled *Rock In Peace*.

'BUDDY'S GUITAR'
Recorded December 1959 in Apartment 4H, The Brevoort, 11 Fifth Ave, New York
Personnel: Buddy Holly (acoustic guitar, vocals)

There's not too much to say about this snippet, which was discovered among Holly's famous Apartment Tapes, recorded weeks before his death. A rare Holly instrumental (the only other two being 'Holly Hop' and 'Honky Tonk'), the melody is similar to the Ray Charles song, 'Leave My Woman Alone', but is taken at a much slower pace akin to the Everly Brothers' version. Although it still awaits a legal release, this cut did appear some years ago on the 1995 4-CD Vigotone bootleg, *What You Been A-Missin'*.

See also **INSTRUMENTALS**.

CARL BUNCH

Born 1939 in Big Spring, Texas, Carl Bunch had originally wanted to become a dancer, but early health issues put paid to that and he turned to drumming instead. At the age of sixteen, he joined Ronnie Smith & The Poor Boys, a small but popular Texan group who ended up making some records of their own at Clovis. (Smith later committed suicide in October 1962.)

Towards the end of 1958, Bunch was approached by Tommy Allsup to join Buddy Holly and Waylon Jennings for a major tour of the Midwest called the *Winter Dance Party*. From Carl's viewpoint this was his big break, it paid well, and was one that he couldn't afford to turn down. And so he ended up playing drums for Buddy (who nicknamed him 'Goose') on that disastrous final tour until he was

Carl Bunch, late '50s.

hospitalised with frostbite several days before they reached Clear Lake. The extreme winter weather that year, compounded by inadequate bus heaters, saw the musicians literally setting fire to papers in the bus aisles in a desperate attempt to keep from freezing to death.

Incredibly, Bunch was discharged from hospital and rejoined the tour in Sioux City, Iowa just one day after the plane crash that claimed Holly's life. Of course, the accident and its aftermath affected him deeply, although he was initially unaware of what had happened until his mother phoned him in hospital!

Bunch's life has been full of twists and turns ever since. After a spell in the US army, he returned to music and briefly played with Roy Orbison, and for a while with Hank Williams Jr. Always spiritually inclined, he and his wife became missionaries before he returned to higher education and obtained a Doctorate in Clinical Psychotheology. He later worked in commerce, but has never turned his back on music and has played tribute events in Lubbock, Clovis and Clear Lake. A hugely likeable individual and a great humanitarian, he has been in poor health for some time.

JOHNNY BURNETTE

On the surface there's little to link Buddy Holly and Johnny Burnette (1934-64), but there are so many 'near misses' that it's worth recording a few while juxtaposing their parallel careers. They both fronted rock'n'roll trios, both were signed to Coral and both apparently recorded under the auspices of heavyweight producer Bob Thiele. Both groups had previously tried their luck down the talent show route, but while the Crickets had drawn a blank with Arthur Godfrey, Johnny's group had more luck and won three times in a row on the *Ted Mack Amateur Hour*. And, believe it or not, they both made their recording debuts in the same Nashville studio in July 1956, only a couple of weeks apart. Famed guitarist Grady Martin, who played rhythm on some of Burnette's recordings also played rhythm for Holly on two of his three Nashville sessions. Most spookily of all, both men's deaths were accidental and had associations with Clear Lake: Holly perished after performing at Clear Lake, Iowa, while Burnette sadly drowned in Clear Lake, *California* in a tragic fishing accident.

JAMES BURTON

Legendary lead guitarist of the rock'n'roll era born 1939 in Minden, Louisiana, James Burton usually plays the Fender Telecaster and needs little introduction. It's often claimed that he single-handedly introduced the Telecaster into the world of rockabilly in the '50s (indeed, he's a member of the Rockabilly Hall of Fame as well as the more high-profile Rock and Roll Hall of Fame). In his time, he's played with Ricky Nelson, John Denver and also Elvis – firstly as a member of his backing group, and since his death as part the *TCB* tour band who still back the King via the giant video screen.

Burton didn't have any connections with Buddy Holly, but he did appear on a few of the recordings the post-Holly Crickets made in the '60s for Liberty, including several Beatles and surfing covers. Unfortunately, he didn't tour with them.

GARY BUSEY

Born in Goose Creek, Texas and raised in Oklahoma, Gary Busey was a professional drummer with several bands in the '60s and '70s, including those of Leon Russell, Kris Kristofferson and Willie Nelson. He later styled himself 'Teddy Jack Eddy' and amongst other gigs got to play with the upcoming Leonard Cohen before turning his hand to acting.

A potential breakthrough arose in 1975, when he landed the role of drummer Jerry Allison in the film, *Not Fade Away*, the first attempt to base a film on the life and music of Buddy Holly, but the project was never completed. In 1978, however, he got a second bite of the cherry when he was offered the leading part in *The Buddy Holly Story*.

Whatever the merits of the film may have been, the fact is that he played his own forceful lead guitar and also did the vocals 'live'. By any yardstick his performance has to be a *tour de force*, even if it's quite unlike Buddy Holly. Undoubtedly sincere, Busey has turned up in documentaries down the years expressing his undying admiration for Holly and reputedly purchased Buddy's Gibson guitar at auction for around $250,000 in 1990.

Gary Busey made a string of movies in the wake of the Holly biopic, but his career was put on hold in 1988 when he received life-threatening injuries in a motorcycle accident. But he's since recovered and has made more than thirty films, even if he's developed something of a reputation for eccentricity.

C

LLOYD CALL

Another obscure name from the annals of West Texas music. In 1958, Call dubbed vocals onto 'Little Cowboy' and 'If I Had Known' using a backing track laid down by Buddy Holly (acoustic guitar), Jerry Allison (drums), Vi Petty (piano) and George Atwood (bass). Neither of these has been issued, although Lloyd lip-synched to 'Little Cowboy' at the 1987 *Norman & Vi Petty Music Festival* (see **CLOVIS**). In June 1958 Homer Tankersley added his vocals to 'If I Had Known' and this was duly issued on Petty's Nor-Va-Jak label. Never a full-time musician, Call spent much of his working life as a school administrator in Portales, New Mexico.

GLEN CAMPBELL

Born in Arkansas in 1936, Glen Campbell is one of those artists whose achievements are never-ending. He was a member of the Champs ('Tequila'), the emergent Beach Boys, and even backed Gene Vincent on a Challenge album in the mid-'60s. (David Gates, Dash Crofts and Jimmy Seals were also in the band at that last Vincent session – quite a stellar line-up.) And, if a surfing record was being cut (eg the Hondells), chances are he was involved there too.

Even so, it's still a surprise to discover that, for a short while, he was also a Cricket, albeit only in the recording studio. Most famously, he played on their 1962 British Top 10 hit, 'Don't Ever Change'. He also did frequent session work with Jerry Naylor.

Glen has gone on to enjoy an incredible career peppered with gold records and other prestigious industry awards, but the abiding image these days is of a kilted Campbell playing the bagpipes as the finale to his stage act.

RAY CAMPI

A legendary bass-slapping rockabilly star from the '50s, Ray Campi was born in New York City in 1934, but moved to the Deep South as a child. Although not a name you'll find in the standard book of hit singles, he's nevertheless spent a lifetime in and around the music business while moonlighting in well over thirty outside jobs. An occasional visitor to Britain from the rockabilly revival days of the '70s onwards, he has also recorded for a variety of minor record labels including Ronny Weiser's Rollin' Rock imprint and is deservedly in the Rockabilly Hall of Fame.

Campi was one of the first artists to pitch in with a tribute disc in the wake of the '59 plane crash. Within days of 3 February, he recorded the self-penned 'The Man I Met (A Tribute To The Big Bopper)', while the flip, 'Ballad of Donna and Peggy Sue', was dedicated to the other two stars. The single came out on Pappy Daily's D label, which also released 'Gold Records In The Snow' by Bennie Barnes. Unlike Tommy Dee's maudlin 'Three Stars' (see **DEATH DISCS**), neither of these releases made the national charts. Ironically, Campi had corresponded with Holly and spoken to him on the phone, but they never got the chance to meet. He later recorded at Clovis, although nothing from these sessions was issued.

TINKER CARLEN

A figure on the edge of the Buddy Holly story, Tinker Carlen is the epitome of a good ole Texas boy. He was a contemporary of Holly's at school and ran around Lubbock with him and others during the early '50s. He's also known to have briefly jammed with him (Bill Griggs has published a picture of Buddy and Tinker together), but was never in any of Holly's groups.

In 1983, Carlen got together with Larry Holley and put out a single on the latter's Cloud 9 label: the evocatively titled 'Looking For The Hi-D-Ho' *b/w* a duet with Sherry Holly of 'Raining In My Heart'.

Still living in Lubbock, Tinker recently published a memoir of his life in 1950s Lubbock with the rather fanciful title of *Tinker Carlen: An Original Cricket*. He's mentioned here with much affection, but the consensus must surely be that he wasn't ever officially a Cricket, although no-one would wish to deny him his time in the sun.

CARLSBAD

A small town in New Mexico, about 150 miles from Clovis, Carlsbad is mostly famous for its huge bat caves. It was also the place where, on 2 March 1957, the Crickets made their very first stage appearance under their new name. For several years rumours persisted that Bobby Peeples had taped the show, but like so many others it came to nothing.

See also **RUMOURS**.

BUZZ CASON

James Elmore Cason was born in Nashville, Tennessee in 1939 and has spent a lifetime in music – sometimes as the front man, although increasingly as a songwriter and music publisher.

He started his career in 1956 with the Casuals (Nashville's first rock'n'roll group, probably best known as Brenda Lee's backing band), while he also later made the US Top 20 for Liberty during 1960 as 'Garry Miles' with 'Look For a Star'. Shortly after, he charted with 'Blue Velvet' as a member of the Statues vocal trio. As a composer, probably his biggest earner was 'Everlasting Love' a 1968 British No.1 for Love Affair.

Cason first met the Crickets in the early '60s, when the group relocated to California and he was helping Snuff Garrett with A&R for Liberty. (His other claim to fame back then was as the speeded-up voice of Alvin on the Chipmunks' US hits, although his role was uncredited.)

When the Crickets' lead singer, Jerry Naylor, fell ill in 1964, the opportunity arose for Buzz to join the group as vocalist, and British fans got the chance to meet him when the group toured here that same year. In 1993, he was again involved with the Crickets when helping on their *Double Exposure* album.

In 2004, Cason published his autobiography, *Living The Rock'n'Roll Dream*, which can be obtained from www.buzzcason.com.

'CHANGIN' ALL THOSE CHANGES' – *See* **'I'M CHANGIN'...'**

RAY CHARLES

It's well documented that Buddy Holly was a huge Ray Charles fan, and that he cherished the dream of collaborating with Charles musically if the opportunity ever arose. In fact, Maria Elena is on record as saying that she and Buddy called at his house shortly before Buddy left for that last tour, but Ray wasn't at home.

Ray, like Buddy, was ahead of his time, although as a commercial act he had yet to sell a million, and back then was still mainly known for his R&B offerings such as 'I Got A Woman'. Nevertheless, the fact that Charles willingly collaborated with all manner of other musicians throughout his career and liked nothing better than crossing musical boundaries makes the likelihood of him getting together with Holly both possible and intriguing.

Indeed, their paths had briefly crossed in the spring of 1957, just after 'That'll Be The Day' came out, when the Crickets played a date on a Southern bill which Ray was headlining. Even so, it's still a great pity that Holly never got the chance to attempt more of the Ray Charles songbook, and all we have are a few frustratingly short snippets. These include a fragment of Buddy jamming with Jerry Lee Lewis on 'Hallelujah I Love Her So' (a Charles composition) and singing part of 'Drown In My Own Tears' (No.1 R&B hit for Charles in 1956, composed by Henry Glover). A short clip of the latter song was also discovered on the Apartment Tapes.

In some ways, it was perhaps fitting that Charles and Holly were both included amongst the inaugural group of inductees into the Rock and Roll Hall of Fame in 1986

RAY CHARLES SINGERS

This was a white ensemble who had absolutely no connection with Brother Ray. They frequently appeared on TV and had a string of chart hits themselves in the '60s. They were used in 1959 and 1960 by Jack Hansen to overdub Holly's December 1958 Apartment Tape recordings in New York.

CHIPMUNKS

These animated characters (Alvin, Simon and Theodore) with their speeded-up-tape voices were a Stateside sensation over the Christmas 1958 season, and the novelty 'Chipmunk Song' held the top spot in the US pop charts for weeks on end. But why mention this here? Well, the really strange, slow version of 'Slippin' and Slidin'' recorded by Holly in his apartment in January 1959 was made at the same time that the Chipmunks record was monopolising the airwaves. Not only that, Holly recorded it at half the normal speed: play it back at normal speed, and you could be listening to the Chipmunks! It may sound crazy, but Ross Bagdasarian's TV characters really were flavour of the month and maybe Buddy was fooling with the tape recorder to amuse himself or his wife. Interestingly, the Big Bopper also utilised the 'Chipmunk' technique on 'Purple People Eater Meets The Witch Doctor'.

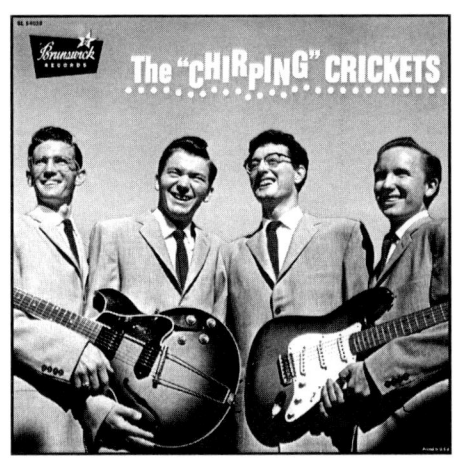

THE CHIRPING CRICKETS *(LP)*
Oh Boy! / Not Fade Away / You've Got Love / Maybe Baby / It's Too Late / Tell Me How / That'll Be The Day / I'm Looking For Someone To Love / An Empty Cup / Send Me Some Lovin' / Last Night / Rock Me My Baby

This was the first-ever Buddy Holly/Crickets LP and was released in the USA in November 1957. It was natural to follow up the monster hit, 'That'll Be The Day', with an album full of the group's best material, but it is salutary to reflect that many of the songs on it had already been recorded prior to the hit single entering the charts. The group – still a quartet at this point – were at their most creative during the opening months of 1957, and three of the tracks ended up being US Top 20 hits, and even higher (Top 5) in the UK.

The album itself was a big seller. Released in Britain in March 1958 to coincide with the Crickets' UK tour, it peaked at No.5 in the *Record Mirror* chart, and has remained in catalogue indefinitely.

Certainly for teenagers living in monochrome '50s Britain, the LP was worth the price for the cover picture alone – four grinning Crickets holding their Fender guitars against a clear blue sky – said to have been taken on the roof of the Brooklyn Paramount Theater in New York. Little did we know that, despite the cover image looking perfect, it concealed the fact that Jerry and Niki had recently had a fight, leaving the former with a badly bruised eye!

But it remains an iconic image and one that excited every would-be musician at the time. And the fact that two of the group wore spectacles was highly significant to those with eyesight problems including John Lennon, Hank Marvin, Brian Poole, John Ingman(!) and yours truly, who was forever impressionable back then. We later learnt that Hank Marvin had immediately arranged to import a Stratocaster as soon as he could afford it – the first, but certainly not the last British musician to do so.

CHRISTMAS RECORDS

Buddy never recorded any Christmas material in his own right, though he apparently had plans to team up in 1959 with bandleader/arranger Neal Hefti for a Christmas album, the title of which was *Deck The Halls With Hefti Holly*! Sadly, these came to nothing. He did, however, play guitar on both 'Christmas in Killarney' and 'Hurry Santa, Hurry' on a still-unissued Carolyn Hester session at Clovis in June 1958. That same session also generated 'A Little While Ago', written by Hester, as well as an update of Buddy's 'Take Your Time'.

In 1990, the Crickets (Gordon Payne on guitar and vocals, Jerry Allison on keyboards (!) and Joe B. Mauldin on bass) specially recorded 'Deck The Halls' for a various artists album called *Rock and Roll Christmas*. With its allusion to holly/Holly, the song was an obvious choice, and has since surfaced on numerous other seasonal compilations.

JIMMY CLANTON

Born in Baton Rouge, Louisiana in 1940, Jimmy Clanton was one of the trio of singers drafted in on 4 February 1959 to replace the three stars who had perished the previous night, tour management GAC insisting that 'the show must go on' – a daunting prospect one suspects. The singer was no doubt picked on the back of his double-sided million-seller from late 1958, 'Just A Dream' b/w 'Letter To An Angel', presaging a career that would continue with two other huge hits in 'Go, Jimmy, Go' and the Neil Sedaka composition, 'Venus In Blue Jeans'.

Ironically, Valens and Clanton knew each other particularly well, as both had appeared in the 1958 film, *Go, Johnny, Go!*, although Clanton had the starring role while Valens's appearance was limited to a rather tame lip-sync to 'Ooh, My Head'. Clanton had also met Holly when they headlined the lengthy *Biggest Show of Stars* tour in 1958.

In 1961, Clanton also starred in another quickie film, *Teenage Millionaire*, co-incidentally appearing alongside Dion, the most prominent survivor of the *Winter Dance Party* tour. He's continued to perform as a singer down the years, although during much of the '70s he was a disc jockey on WHEX in Columbia, Pennsylvania.

ERIC CLAPTON

Yet another superstar (see **GLEN CAMPBELL**, **SIR PAUL McCARTNEY**, etc) whose name can be legitimately linked with either Buddy Holly or the Crickets. Although their guitar styles bear little resemblance to each other, Clapton admits to being a long-time fan of Holly and his Fender Stratocaster, and has revealed that the first LP he ever purchased was *The Chirping Crickets* when he was just thirteen.

But an even more tangible relationship exists between Clapton and the latter-day Crickets, and evidently started when Eric asked Sonny and Jerry to help out with backing vocals for his first solo album, *Eric Clapton*. One of the tracks, 'After Midnight', even became a US Top 20 hit. The favour was later returned when Eric (and Delaney Bramlett) played on the Crickets' 1971 Barnaby album, *Rockin' Fifties Rock'n'Roll*, and on 'Someone, Someone' on 2004's *The Crickets And Their Buddies*. One senses the link is a permanent one.

Clapton was inducted into the Rock and Roll Hall of Fame in 2000.

DICK CLARK

By the time you read this, Dick Clark will have reached his 80th birthday – a sobering thought for someone seen as perennially young (indeed, he was still billed as *'The World's Oldest Teenager'* until relatively recently). He even managed to look younger than most of the audience on his programme, *American Bandstand*, if TV footage is to be believed. An astute businessman who rode out the payola scandal he enjoyed a high-profile career in the music business before becoming the host to long-running US TV quiz show, *The Pyramid Game*. He's always come across as friendly and approachable. Indeed, only a few years ago he penned some affectionate reminiscences of the Big Bopper for the late singer's son's CD tribute to his father. Clark's later years have been notable for the profusion of industry awards he's received including, in 1993, his induction into the Rock and Roll Hall of Fame.

Fans of Holly will mostly be familiar with Clark's name via the recorded interview with Buddy, Jerry and Joe B. during the Crickets' *Bandstand* appearance on 28 October 1958 (still available together with most of Holly's other interviews via the good offices of Rollercoaster Records). Sadly, film of that appearance wasn't preserved.

See also **AMERICAN BANDSTAND**.

JUNE CLARK

June Clark was the sister of Buddy Knox's guitarist, Donnie Lanier, and as such was someone who Holly and his friends knew well from the Lubbock music scene circa 1956-57. In fact, a biography of Holly from a few years ago claims she and Buddy carried on a clandestine affair for a short while.

A famous set of publicity photos was taken in June's house in a break between rehearsals showing Buddy, Jerry and Joe B. in a variety of rock'n'roll poses, instruments to the fore. It's evident that, although they'd recently become a quartet, Niki Sullivan wasn't present when the pictures were taken. Although she was usually around when the boys rehearsed 'That'll Be The Day', June didn't travel to Clovis for the actual recording session.

She was also a cousin of Gary Tollett, who, with his wife Ramona, famously sang backing vocals on 'That'll Be The Day' and 'I'm Looking For Someone To Love'. In an act of reciprocity, which was by no means unusual, Buddy later played on several of the Tolletts' own sessions.

See also **GARY & RAMONA TOLLETT**.

BO CLARKE

Drummer Bo Clarke is seldom mentioned in the Buddy Holly story, but it's a name that shouldn't be overlooked as he played a small but important role at the Clovis studio, even if it was often on other artists' sessions. He first came to Norman Petty's studio with the Roses, who sang backup for Jerry Allison on his 1958 Ivan single, 'Real Wild Child' *b/w* 'Oh You Beautiful Doll', on which he played drums.

The only actual Holly recordings that Bo played on were demos of 'Love's Made A Fool Of You' and 'Wishing'. However, his close friend, bassist George Atwood, remembers Buddy, Bo and himself playing together on a couple of Jerry Engler cuts ('What A You Gonna Do' and 'I Sent You Roses') in September 1958, though they weren't issued at the time. He also played on the two tracks Waylon Jennings cut that same month, 'Jole Blon' and 'When Sin Stops'.

Bo Clarke sadly passed away in 1993. According to Atwood, he was a consummate drummer and among the finest he ever worked with.

STANLEY CLAYTON

Song-writing pseudonym for Bob Thiele.

See also **DON CORNELL**, **'MAILMAN, BRING ME NO MORE BLUES'**.

CLOVIS

A small settlement in New Mexico some seven miles from the Texas border which originally went under the name of Riley's Switch, but was later renamed Clovis, after a Frankish monarch of the fifth century. It was here, in a small, unprepossessing building that Buddy Holly and the Crickets created their greatest recordings.

The group had to travel around 100 miles from their homes in Lubbock to reach Norman Petty's studio at 1313 West Seventh Street (see also **NORMAN PETTY RECORDING STUDIO / NOR-VA-JAK**). The usual pattern was to hang around practising or dozing most of the day, as Petty, who engineered the sessions, insisted that recording at night was the best time for the studio acoustics (plus any external noises were also at a minimum during the wee hours). In the early '60's, Petty purchased the Mesa Theater and later converted it into a multi-track recording studio and radio station, whilst the original studio has now been restored and is periodically opened for tours.

In 1986, Jerry MacNeish and John Ingman persuaded Petty's widow, Vi, to inaugurate a music festival to honour Buddy Holly and all those others who had associations with the town from the early days of rock'n'roll. Organised by Robert Linville (see **ROSES**), the *Norman & Vi Petty Music Festival* ran annually into the '90s, although the last few years were very low-key. Sadly, Linville passed away in 2001. In 2005, the Clovis Chamber of Commerce revived the *Clovis Music Festival*, which takes place every September, around the time of Buddy Holly's birthday.

Of course, to link the studio's name solely with that of Buddy Holly would be rather a distortion, as Roy Orbison, Buddy Knox, the Fireballs, the String-A-Longs and a select band of others cut some classic recordings there during the '50s and '60s. In 2008, Rollercoaster Records put out *Clovis Rocks: Stars of the Clovis Music Festival*, a compilation CD which includes the likes of Bobby Vee, the Crickets, the Roses and many other artists listed in these pages.

EDDIE COCHRAN

The Rock and Roll Hall of Fame was opened in 1986, but incredibly, two of America's foremost exponents of that home-grown art form were not be included in the first group of inductees. Carl Perkins and Eddie Cochran (1938-60) share the dubious honour of having to wait until the following year, 1987, before that accolade was bestowed upon them. It's also surprising to know that they had such a paucity of hits in their homeland: just three US Top 20 entries and two gold records between them – meagre reward for such outstanding artists. Fortunately, Perkins was alive and well at the time of his induction and able to attend in person, whereas Cochran belatedly achieved some posthumous fame for his contribution to rock'n'roll. (Coincidentally, Eddie Cochran and Buddy Holly both entered the Hall of Fame 27 years after their deaths.)

Buddy, Jerry and Joe B. had struck up a warm friendship with Cochran when they first met on the *Biggest Show of Stars for 1957* tour, but they would only get to see each other a handful more times before Holly's tragic accident. Jerry and Sonny Curtis both backed Eddie on the final famous Goldstar recording session which produced the classic 'Three Steps To Heaven'. As we know, he left immediately after to join Gene Vincent on what became a triumphal tour of Britain, only to lose his life in the 1960 Easter weekend car crash that also left Vincent and Sharon Sheeley seriously injured.

There is nothing too tangible to tie Holly and Cochran except their known close friendship. Buddy, Jerry and Eddie were all interviewed by Denver deejay Freeman 'Freddy' Hover in October 1957 while they were on tour together. The only photo of that meeting – taken by Holly – shows Hover with Cochran, Jerry Allison and Jimmy Bowen. In the interview with Buddy and Jerry, Buddy talks about the possibility of appearing with Eddie in one of his upcoming motion pictures – he would appear in several – but that was something that never happened. Many years after Eddie's demise, we learned that he'd recorded an emotional version of the tribute ballad, 'Three Stars' (see **DEATH DISCS**), but perhaps unsurprisingly this wasn't released at the time.

Cochran's place in rock'n'roll history is now assured and several books including a full-length biography have come out in the past few years. To this day, the Crickets routinely perform Cochran's 'Summertime Blues' on stage, with Jerry taking the lead vocals.

ED COHEN

Executive Producer of *The Buddy Holly Story* film from the '70s, he's mentioned here mainly to differentiate him from his namesake Paul Cohen below. They are not thought to be related.

PAUL COHEN

Paul Cohen was A&R Director for Decca in Nashville back in the mid-'50s. A recording of a lengthy telephone call made from Jerry Allison's home exists, in which Buddy tries to persuade Cohen to release some of his 1956 recordings. It's particularly interesting to listen to his pleading, knowing that he'd re-recorded 'That'll Be The Day' just a few days earlier, while saying he hadn't! (The boys presumably decided to record the call in the hope that Cohen would give them permission over the phone to record it elsewhere, and they, in turn, would have the proof on tape.) Recently released as part of the El Toro 3-CD set called *Not Fade Away: Buddy Holly – The Complete 1957 Recordings*, it makes for enthralling listening.

Also ironic is the fact that Cohen was promoted to head of Coral Records in 1958 and discovered that his No.1 artist was the same Buddy Holly of whom he allegedly said: *'Buddy Holly is the biggest no-talent I've ever worked with'*. Given that this phone call took place over fifty years ago, it really makes one wonder what else might one day turn up.

Cohen, whose reputation had been gained in earlier years from overseeing Decca's roster of country artists, died in 1970 in his early sixties.

'COME BACK BABY'
Recorded September 1958 at Norman Petty Recording Studios, Clovis, New Mexico
Personnel: Buddy Holly (guitar, vocals), Jerry Allison (drums), Joe B. Mauldin (double bass), King Curtis (tenor sax)

This classic, if little-known recording (composed by Fred Neil, although Norman Petty also copped for a co-writer credit) remained in the can and didn't surface until it and other posthumous Holly material appeared on the *Showcase* album in 1964. We later learnt that it was one of four tracks recorded at a session which Holly had produced, the others being 'Reminiscing', 'Jole Blon' and 'When Sin Stops' (the last two featuring Waylon Jennings on vocals and Holly on guitar). George Atwood has confirmed that he was the bass player, while the sublime saxophone work was supplied by ace horn-blower King Curtis, specially flown in from New York (see also **KING CURTIS**).

It's said that the released version is Take 2 and that Take 1 remains unissued, although this is unconfirmed. In 1984, the Picks overdubbed backing vocals onto this recording (see **OVERDUBS** and **PICKS** for more info).

Much has been written about the late Fred Neil (1936-2001), an iconic singer/songwriter with some wonderful song credits to his name including the Nilsson classic, 'Everybody's Talkin' '. A live version of 'Come Back Baby' appears on his 1971 Capitol album, *Other Side Of This Life*.

It's also interesting to note that Myron Lee & The Caddies, a well-known group in the Midwest, cut a version of the song for Norman Petty at Clovis in 1959. Although it was recorded after Holly's, it was actually released first.

COMMERCIALS – *See* ADVERTISING

DENIS COMPTON

The leading candidate for the most unlikely entry in the book surely has to be the late English cricket legend, Denis Compton, who with teammate Godfrey Evans was briefly introduced to Buddy, Jerry and Joe B. in March 1958 during the group's UK tour.

With the word 'cricket' as the flimsiest of links between the five men, they were nevertheless brought together at the Whiskey A Go Go in London (the upstairs room of the famous Flamingo Club), along with a posse of ladies from the staff of *Valentine* magazine (a weekly for girls of a suitably impressionable age) for a photo shoot. Falling some way short of an actual publicity stunt, several photos duly appeared in the music trade papers, as well as the fragrant *Valentine*.

Over the years, all the output from that 1958 photo session has surfaced. It would appear that several reels of film were shot and the photos themselves are delightful, if a trifle samey.

Several years ago, long-time cricket – and Crickets – fan, Sir Tim Rice managed to collar both Compton and Evans to ask them for their recollections of that occasion, and was even able to put together a lively article for the *Daily Telegraph* about it. Fairly predictably, both men were very polite, but memories had dimmed and not too many revelations appeared.

COLIN COOK

A name that is virtually unknown outside of his native Australia, Cook is a singer/songwriter with a huge pedigree who enjoyed considerable hit parade success in his homeland in the '60s at a time when the charts were dominated by British and American acts. He's listed here, as, with the help of some Australian contacts, he was chosen to record a couple of the songs that Buddy and Scotty Turner collaborated on shortly before Holly died. The tracks ('Am I Ever Gonna Find It' and 'September Hearts'), together with his own composition, 'Don't Let the Music Die', a heartfelt tribute to Buddy Holly and the music he did so much to influence, were issued in the '90s on the album *Colin Cook Sings The Lost Songs Of Buddy Holly*.

SAM COOKE

The paths of soul singer supreme Sam Cooke (1931-64) and Buddy Holly barely intersected. However, they both appeared on the same *Ed Sullivan Show* in December 1957 (Cooke's 'You Send Me' was top of the charts at the time), so they must have met at least on that occasion. Certainly, Buddy would have been attracted to Sam's music, as it is known that he liked both black gospel and R&B.

These days, Cooke is such an iconic figure that he was cast – fictitiously, but to great effect – as a major player both in the 1978 *Buddy Holly Story* biopic, and 1989's *Buddy* musical. He was also included in the first group of artists to be inducted into the Rock and Roll Hall of Fame in 1986.

COOL FOR CATS

One of a handful of early pop shows on TV in Britain, this one was hosted by Kent Walton, who became well-known nationally for popularising wrestling on TV. Holly was rushed to the ATV studios on 28 February 1958 to lip-synch on his own to 'I'm Gonna Love You Too', which was being released that very day.

CORAL RECORDS

The Coral logo will already be imprinted on the minds of Holly/Crickets fans from the '50s, but a few words of clarification are needed, as their label history is somewhat convoluted.

Buddy was originally signed as a solo act by Coral's parent company, Decca, back in 1956. When his one-year contract expired at the end of that year, he and the Crickets signed with Coral. However, because the group were producing so much good material, a decision was made to release records under Holly's name on Coral, and others, credited to the Crickets, on Decca's R&B subsidiary, Brunswick.

In Britain, almost everything that was released during Buddy's lifetime came out on Coral. The only exception was the 1956 Brunswick single, 'Blue Days, Black Nights' *b/w* 'Love Me' – both US

Decca recordings.

Decca was originally a British company which had started up around the time of the First World War, mainly to sell gramophones, and later acquired Brunswick so that it would have access to Bing Crosby's recordings! They didn't actually move into record production in Britain until 1929, and American Decca wasn't established until 1934. Thereafter, Coral was established in America in 1949 as a subsidiary of Decca, specialising in popular singers of the day.

Decca and its subsidiaries were eventually absorbed by MCA in 1971, and the musical family tree has become quite complicated since. As this book goes to press, Holly's record company, MCA, remains part of the Universal Music Group, who themselves are a subsidiary of General Electric. The entertainment conglomerate is one of the largest in the whole world. But, regardless of all these later changes, the Coral emblem is one that will always have a fond place in the hearts of all Holly and Crickets fans.

CORBIN BROTHERS

Glenn ('Sky'), Ray ('Slim') and Larry Corbin were brothers from the Lubbock area, and contemporaries of Buddy Holly and his friends at the time they were all beginning to flex their musical wings. With the help of their father, the brothers launched KLLL radio in 1958, in direct competition to the more established KDAV. Since both stations heavily featured country music, the situation which arose was, according to erstwhile KLLL presenter Waylon Jennings, *'all-out war'*!

It is Slim Corbin's name we need to spotlight here, as he got together with Jennings at the KLLL studio in late '58 and composed a tune with him for a bet. The result was 'You're The One', which they recorded with Buddy Holly on vocals, and Slim and Waylon clapping in the background. This intriguing tune first surfaced (untouched!) as part of the 1964 *Showcase* album, while later a heavily overdubbed version appeared on the 1969 *Giant* album.

See also **'YOU'RE THE ONE'**.

DON CORNELL

Balladeer and big band singer Don Cornell (1919-2004) is an unlikely entry here, but both he and Buddy Holly were on the US Coral label, and both had versions of 'Mailman Bring Me No More Blues' out at the same point (albeit both were 'B' sides of their respective singles and neither was a hit). 'Mailman' was co-written by Coral executive

Bob Thiele under the alias 'Stanley Clayton', to avoid his management knowing that he was moonlighting as a composer.

By this time, Cornell was coming to the end of a lengthy chart career which had started back in 1942, when he was vocalist with Sammy Kaye & His Orchestra. In the early '50s, he earned three gold discs for 'It Isn't Fair', 'I'm Yours' and 'Hold My Hand', but despite scoring several quasi-rock'n'roll hits in 1956 with 'Teenage Meeting (Gonna Rock It Up)', 'Rock Island Line' and 'See Saw', quickly faded from view thereafter.

COTTON CLUB

The Lubbock version of the Cotton Club bore scant similarity to its more famous New York prototype: a niterie that was for years the Mecca of the jazz world. There were many such 'Cotton Clubs' spread throughout the post-war South (the Land of Cotton), and no doubt the Lubbock one, owned by Tommy Hancock, was typical of many. What we can glean is that the Lubbock version was a converted Quonset hut on the outskirts of town, and more of a 'spit and sawdust' venue than anything else. Certainly, it played host to all manner of musical acts throughout those years – including Elvis Presley, who continually toured the South before he became a worldwide phenomenon. Indeed, it was on that very stage where Elvis and Buddy Holly met, and the author's lengthy treatise on this and later meetings may be found in *Elvis & Buddy – Linked Lives* (see *Selected Bibliography*).

The Cotton Club building of Buddy's day burned down in 1962 and was replaced by another one further out of town.

See also **FAIR PARK COLISEUM**.

COVERS

Strictly speaking, a 'cover version' is a record issued to compete with an original release of a song in an effort to grab some of the sales action. It was a common industry practice in the '50s, and many hits were made on the back of others. Indeed, some covers became bigger hits than the originals they had copied. Fortunately, Holly and the Crickets largely managed to avoid such unwelcome attention, possibly because much of their material was self-composed and pretty individual in nature. In Britain, however, Woolworth's cut-price Embassy label could be relied upon to cover virtually every chart hit there was, and so we had the Tunettes covering 'That'll Be The Day' and Paul Rich attempting 'Oh Boy!' and 'Maybe Baby', albeit somewhat painfully.

Interestingly, in 1958 Holly was prevailed upon by Coral Records to cut a cover of Bobby Darin's 'Early In The Morning' (see **'EARLY IN THE MORNING'**).

A looser definition of a 'cover' is simply a remake of a particular song by another artist, typically some time after the original appeared. In that respect, Holly and the Crickets have inspired hundreds, and it would require a weighty tome to list them all.

Within a short time of Holly's passing, solo singers and groups started tackling his songbook, either via the occasional single release or the occasional Holly/Crickets medley to, over the years, entire tribute albums full of such material (by the likes of Jimmy Gilmer, Skeeter Davis, Bobby Vee and Connie Francis, to the lesser-known Matlock, Runaway Express and Willie Logan... there really are too many to list).

Of course, the best-remembered of all are those many artists who have charted with Holly/Crickets titles. There have been some splendid efforts, as well as some real turkeys, but perhaps it depends on the listener's perspective as to which are which. At the peak of the '70s rock'n'roll revival era, Mud took 'Oh Boy!' to No.1 in Britain in 1975, while in the USA Linda Ronstadt mined a real streak of Holly gold with a trio of covers ('It Doesn't Matter Anymore', 'That'll Be The Day' and 'It's So Easy') that all went Top 50 there between 1975 and 1977.

Among some of the more unusual or unexpected covers that the author has come across are Dick & Dee Dee's 'Not Fade Away', recorded for Warner Bros. in 1964; Bo Diddley's 1976 version, which is much better; the Troggs' reggae-styled version of 'Peggy Sue', which is certainly interesting and highly listenable; and Ted & The Tall Tops' great version of 'Take Your Time' on the 1989 tribute album, *Everyday Is A Holly Day,* issued by the French new wave label, New Rose. Wreckless Eric's punk-styled interpretation of 'Crying, Waiting, Hoping' also deserves a mention.

Many other covers are listed throughout this book and, needless to say, anytime that Sonny Curtis, Waylon, Tommy Allsup, Bobby Vee or the latter-day Crickets covered the Holly songbook, it was always done well and straight from the heart.

EDDIE CRANDALL

A Nashville talent scout and Marty Robbins's manager, now long deceased, who was persuaded to watch Buddy & Bob perform in 1955 on a bill headlined by Bill Haley, and was enthused enough to send a telegram to Pappy Dave Stone at KDAV in Lubbock saying,

'Have Buddy Holly cut 4 original songs on acetate. Don't change his style at all. Get these to me soon as possible.' Within days, Buddy, Jerry Allison, Sonny Curtis and Don Guess were on their way to the Nesman studio in nearby Wichita Falls, Texas, where they cut a quartet of songs: 'Moonlight Baby' (later renamed 'Baby Won't You Come Out Tonight'), 'Don't Come Back Knockin' ', 'I Guess I Was Just A Fool' and 'Love Me'.

Upon receiving the demos, Crandall approached Colonel Tom Parker, but Parker had just taken over as Elvis's official manager and had his hands full. He then approached C&W talent agent Jim Denny, who, suitably impressed, undertook to get Buddy a contract.

Decca took the bait, and 1956 saw Buddy yo-yoing back and forth to Nashville for recording sessions, with little to show for his efforts except for a dozen titles taking up space in the company's vaults. Neither of the singles released by Decca that year saw any sales action.

CRASH

There cannot be many Buddy Holly fans who are unaware of the basic details surrounding the tragedy of 3 February 1959, but for the sake of completeness the essential details are given below as starkly as possible so as to avoid sensationalising the events.

The *Winter Dance Party* had played the Surf Ballroom in Clear Lake, Iowa on the evening of Monday, 2 February, and were due back on stage the following night at the Armory in Moorhead, Minnesota. At this point, they were almost halfway through a gruelling GAC-promoted tour of the Midwest, and weather conditions were far from good and getting worse.

Anxious to get to the next venue quickly to launder some clothes, and fed up with the dilapidated buses that were forever breaking down, Holly arranged to charter a small plane from Dwyer's Flying Services based at a nearby Mason City airstrip. The original plan was for Buddy and Tommy Allsup and Waylon Jennings from his backing band to fly, but Waylon volunteered to give his seat up to the Big Bopper, who was suffering from flu, while Ritchie Valens pestered Tommy for the opportunity to fly in a small plane. A coin was flipped, Ritchie won the toss and paid over his fare. Surf Ballroom manager Carroll Anderson drove the artists to the airport and saw them fly off. The plane was piloted by 21-year-old Roger Peterson.

The plane crashed in a cornfield on farmland owned by the Juhl family. Various sources give the time of the accident as anything

Grim scene the morning after.

between 12:44 and 1:07 a.m. on Tuesday. All those aboard the aircraft are thought to have died on impact.

The pilot's body was found pinned in the wreckage. Buddy's and Ritchie's bodies were about fifteen feet away, while the Bopper's body had been thrown over the demolished fence into the next field. All had severe injuries, and certainly in Buddy's case it involved a closed-casket funeral.

A mandatory Civil Aviation Authority enquiry followed and found that pilot error was to blame for the accident, though others insist that a weather front containing driving snow was the major contributing factor.

In a macabre postscript, a cache of personal effects that had been locked away in police files in the aftermath of the crash was uncovered over twenty years later and returned to the respective families.

Those are the barest of details. Many Holly biographies carry greater particulars of the sad events, but particularly well-researched is *The Day The Music Died* by Larry Lehmer (see *Selected Bibliography*), an exhaustive, in-depth study of the whole of the *Winter Dance Party* tour and its aftermath.

FRED CRAWFORD

Country singer and long-time deejay who had a variety of record releases on minor West Texas labels throughout the '50s, though his name is seldom stumbled upon in the musical annals of the period. Mention is made of Fred here, as he had 'By The Mission Wall' out on the Starday label during 1957, and Buddy Holly, Jerry Allison and (probably) George Atwood acted as session musicians. An unissued take also exists. In the '70s, he re-recorded the song for Tommy Allsup's AOK label, but again without commercial success.

MARSHALL CRENSHAW

A bespectacled and talented American singer-songwriter born in 1954 who emerged on the home-grown music scene in the early '80s, inviting comparisons with Buddy Holly, although in retrospect the similarities between the two were very slender. His career involved quite a bit of well-intentioned imitation and included playing the part of John Lennon in the US musical, *Beatlemania*. Comparisons with other stars continued when he landed a minor part in the '50s throwback movie, *Peggy Sue Got Married*, and then capped this by playing Holly himself in the Ritchie Valens 1987 biopic, *La Bamba* (he can be seen performing 'Crying, Waiting, Hoping' in the movie). He has also performed at the annual Surf Ballroom tribute concerts in Clear Lake, Iowa.

CRICKETS *(Dean Barlow group)*

The lead singer of the Crickets was Grover 'Dean' Barlow. Confused? Well, you should be, as the outfit that Barlow fronted were not our Crickets, but an R&B vocal group from the Bronx who had a spate of releases on the MGM and Jay-Dee labels in the early '50s, and enjoyed a Top 10 R&B hit in 1953 with 'You're Mine'.

However, by the time Buddy and the boys appeared on the scene, the Crickets had split up and Barlow was working as a solo act – though that didn't stop their manager Joe Davis from extracting a cash settlement from Holly's group for infringing his rights to the Crickets name. (That information, incidentally, came from the sleeve of a Dean Barlow/Crickets album, although the author doesn't recall reading it elsewhere.)

As for Dean Barlow, who had a great tenor voice, he died back in 1982. Search out his music!

CRICKETS *(post-Holly group)*

Most readers will know that Buddy Holly and the Crickets parted company in October 1958, just a few months before Holly's tragic demise, although there seems little doubt that they would have got together again. Indeed, Jerry Allison had apparently tried to get in touch with Buddy during the first few days of February 1959, when fate so cruelly intervened. What follows below is a (very) potted history of the Crickets' long and convoluted career from that point onwards, with advance apologies for any oversights.

The Crickets line-up that never was. *Back row:* Joe B. Mauldin, Tommy Allsup. *Front row:* Jerry Allison, Earl Sinks.

The Coral Years: 1958 to 1960

When Holly went solo in 1958, it left the group on the lookout for a new lead vocalist. As luck would have it, one was already waiting in the wings: Henry Earl Sinks had already recorded at Clovis earlier that year (as 'Earl Henry') and had also shared a tour bill with Holly and the Crickets that July as a member of Tommy Allsup's band.

The new Crickets line-up (Allison, Mauldin, Curtis and Sinks) quickly clicked into place and, with Norman Petty's involvement, it seemed that little had changed – outwardly at least – with a brand new single, 'Love's Made A Fool Of You' *b/w* 'Someone, Someone', lined up for release in February 1959.

Holly may no longer have been part of the group, but there's little doubt that his death had a seismic impact on them for all manner of reasons. Sure, they would continue to record, switching to Coral's Bell Sound studios in New York for a few sessions, and turning out some first-class recordings, as anybody who has heard the *In Style With The Crickets* album will testify. But something deep down had changed. The group had suffered a body-blow if only by association, and, although they still had a fan base in Britain and overseas, they needed to reorganise and contemplate a fresh start away from Clovis and the heavy memories it carried if they were to rise again.

On tour in Canada, 1961. *Left to right:* Glen D. Hardin, Jerry Allison, Sonny Curtis and Jerry Naylor.

The Liberty Years: 1960 to 1965

With their fortunes on the wane, Jerry, Sonny and Earl decided to relocate to the West Coast, while Joe Mauldin opted to stay in Lubbock. Jerry and Sonny soon found themselves involved in session work and were still pretty busy, even if the group were no longer chart-toppers.

It was about now that fate once again stepped in, with Sonny being conscripted into the US Army in May 1960 for a two-year stint. The change also coincided with the Crickets signing with the Los Angeles-based label Liberty, thanks to Snuff Garrett, their erstwhile associate from Texas, who was the label's A&R manager.

However, musical tastes were beginning to change and times were getting tougher. Disillusioned with the lack of work coming their way, Earl Sinks had left the group in 1959 and the Crickets once again found themselves searching for a lead vocalist so that they could mount an assault on the hit parade.

New boy Jerry Naylor certainly had the stage presence they were looking for, but would success ever return? It did as far as Britain was concerned, and 1962 found the Crickets riding high with a Top 5 hit ('Don't Ever Change') and an equally big hit album, *Bobby Vee Meets The Crickets*. They also backed up their old friends, the Everly Brothers, on a couple of lengthy overseas tours in 1960.

For a time they were back, but eventually the sales graph tailed off again and the Crickets found themselves embracing the surfing sound and – ironically – even covering Beatles material.

Out of favour and out of hits: The late '60s

It's tempting to term this period 'The Wilderness Years', as for a time any resemblance to the Crickets of yore ebbed away – accelerated somewhat by the loss of Jerry Naylor, who suffered a heart attack in early 1964, while only in his twenties. He returned to the group for a short time at the start of 1965, but, with their Liberty contract coming to an end and the hits having well and truly dried up, the future looked decidedly bleak.

In early 1965, Allison decided to officially mothball the Crickets and enrolled in Roger Miller's road band, though he would still occasionally slip in the odd 'Crickets' gig with the help of various back-up musicians such as Larry Trider.

But what about the rest of the group at this point? Well, the US Army had also caught up with Joe B., who found himself on a lengthy posting to Germany 1963-65, so he was out of circulation. Sonny Curtis had been signed up by Snuff Garrett for his new Viva label upon his discharge from the army, and the late '60s saw him enjoying a string of country hits as a solo singer and burgeoning success as a songwriter.

Overall, however, the picture was very fragmented, and as a group the Crickets were close to being down and out. If they were to keep going, things needed to change – but how?

The Country Rock Years: The '70s

During the early '70s, America rediscovered the sounds of the '50s, and it wasn't long before the Crickets were back in the studio revisiting the Holly songbook for their new album, *Rockin' Fifties Rock'n'Roll*, with the help of Glen D. Hardin's arrangements. It sold reasonably well, even if it didn't revive their chart fortunes. But they were back and got to play high-profile rock'n'roll revival shows in New York, amongst other dates, before embarking on yet another British tour.

Not only did they tour Britain in 1973, but, with the help of Bob Montgomery, they even cut a new album called *Bubblegum, Bop, Ballads & Boogie* while they were there.

But the days of gazing backwards at their '50s heritage were coming to an abrupt end, and in 1973 fans buying the group's new album, *Remnants*, were shocked to find that the Crickets had grown their hair, morphed into a sextet and were recording material that was decidedly different from what had come before. The title of their 1974 UK album, *A Long Way From Lubbock*, hit the nail on the head. Physically, they'd been away from West Texas for a long while and were based in Hollywood, but musically they were now even further from their roots.

However, life is all about change, and another chapter in the Crickets' history was around the corner in the formidable shape of their old friend – and now renegade country superstar – Waylon Jennings, who invited Jerry, Sonny and Joe B. to join his stage show in 1978.

Left to right: Gordon Payne, Jerry Allison and Joe B. Mauldin.

New Dimensions: The '80s and beyond

For five years, the Crickets had their own spot on Waylon's show, and they even got to back him in the studio on a fine Holly medley produced by Duane Eddy which appeared on his 1978 album, *I've Always Been Crazy*.

However, the long honeymoon came to an abrupt end in 1983, resulting in yet another bout of regrouping. But every cloud has a silver lining, and this one did too, for, while they had been touring, they had formed a rapport with Gordon Payne, a fine vocalist and guitarist in Jennings' backing band, the Waylors.

With Sonny Curtis electing to return to Nashville to pursue various solo projects, the opportunity presented itself for the Crickets to revert to being a three-piece once again. The ensuing nine-year period with Gordon Payne on lead vocals, Jerry on drums and Joe B. on bass was a long and fruitful one: it re-energised the group and brought about a new round of touring and recordings, as well as some recognition. In 1986, Jerry Allison, Joe B. Mauldin, Sonny Curtis and Niki Sullivan were all inducted into the West Texas Walk of Fame in Lubbock – a most singular honour bestowed by their hometown.

The passage of time also highlighted the importance of certain anniversaries, and MCA sponsored a tribute album called *Not Fade Away (Remembering Buddy Holly)* marking the fact that forty years had elapsed since Buddy Holly had first recorded in Nashville for Decca. It brought together a host of great artists to honour Holly's memory – needless to say including Crickets Jerry Allison, Joe B. Mauldin and Sonny Curtis.

The Crickets have remained active ever since and are still involved in various projects. However they are all now in their seventies (or nearly), and no longer tour as such, although they do still make occasional live appearances. Nowadays, they do most of their recording at their studio in Lyles, Tennessee. From time to time, they drive the few miles into Nashville to collect the latest music industry award that's come their way. It's been a long road, but the fans know it's been worth it, and hopefully when Jerry, Joe B. and Sonny look back, they think so too.

'CRYING, WAITING, HOPING'
Recorded December 1958 in Apartment 4H, The Brevoort, 11 Fifth Ave, New York
Personnel: Buddy Holly (acoustic guitar, vocals)

One of a batch of self-compositions that Buddy left on his tape recorder in his New York apartment. This consists of just one performance of around two minutes in length, although four different versions have appeared on record. In random order, these are the undubbed track (which came out on the 1995 4-CD Vigotone bootleg, *What You Been A-Missin'*), the June 1959 overdub by Jack Hansen in

New York, and the later overdub by Norman Petty at Clovis. The Hansen overdub is an instrumental/vocal overdub (the latter by the Ray Charles Singers), while the Petty one is a straight instrumental overdub by the Fireballs. Unusually for an overdub, the Hansen version was mixed down and only exists in mono. In 1984, the Picks overdubbed backing vocals onto the Fireballs version of this recording (see **OVERDUBS** and **PICKS** for more info).

Although the song has only rarely been covered, on the occasions when it has, the results have been wonderfully eclectic. For example, the Beatles did a version during their Decca audition on which George Harrison handled vocals, while a reggae cover by Dave Mason came out in the 1970s. As mentioned elsewhere, Marshall Crenshaw sang the song in the Ritchie Valens biopic, *La Bamba*, while – believe it or not – a punk version was put out by Wreckless Eric. There was even a country version (Marty Stuart & Steve Earle) which featured a slide guitar intro.

KING CURTIS – *See under* **KING**

SONNY CURTIS

The life and music of Sonny Curtis, born in Meadow, Texas (a small community close to Lubbock) in 1937, and Buddy Holly have been inextricably linked from an early age. They first came together as teenagers as a result of a shared interest in the guitar, and before long were hanging out and 'a-pickin' and a-grinnin' ' as the stereotype has it. However, early photos of Buddy, Sonny and others playing together are as likely to feature Sonny on country fiddle as on guitar.

There was also a one-off session in Wichita Falls during 1955, where Buddy played back-up on several of Sonny's demos including 'Queen Of The Ballroom'. (Holly had cut the same song at an earlier session in Lubbock with Sonny backing him.) All four recordings from Sonny's session have been in circulation among collectors for years, although they have never been officially released.

With Sonny beginning to develop his songwriting skills, it's perhaps surprising that the only Curtis composition Buddy tackled at his three 1956 Nashville sessions was the frantic 'Rock Around With Ollie Vee'. Curtis played on the January and July Nashville sessions, but was absent for the November one (which, incidentally, is when the alternative 'Rock Around With Ollie Vee' was recorded). Sonny wonders whether the sax was added in an attempt to give the later version a Bill Haley sound. An intriguing thought.

Sonny Curtis's musical CV is long and varied, and it's impossible to do it justice in these few lines. Of the hundreds of his song copyrights, probably the best-known to American audiences is 'Love Is All Around', the theme song to TV's long-running *Mary Tyler Moore Show*, which he also sang. On the worldwide stage, 'Walk Right Back' (Everly Brothers) or 'I Fought The Law' (Bobby Fuller Four, the Clash, Sam Neely, Iggy Pop) are probably the most recognisable titles. He was inducted into the Nashville Songwriters' Hall of Fame in 1991, having been the very first inductee into Tommy Hancock's select Club For Unappreciated Musicians (see **TOMMY HANCOCK**).

Although he's released a shedload of singles over the years (on Dot, Coral, Viva, A&M, Ovation, Mercury, Songworks, Liberty, Elektra, Capitol, Colt, Rollercoaster and others), he's seldom crossed over into the pop charts, though he did have a string of country hits, with 'Good Ol' Girls' reaching the Top 20 of the *Billboard* Country chart. His composition, 'I'm No Stranger To The Rain' (recorded by Keith Whitley) was the 'CMA Song Of The Year' in 1989, a tune Sonny has also recorded. But for the author the most pleasing creation was his Elektra single, 'The Real Buddy Holly Story', which was inspired (if that's not a complete contradiction) by the biopic of Buddy's life. Frankly, Sonny really didn't see much connection at all between the tale being told on the screen and the reality that he recalled. The single is a veritable *tour de force* and should be compulsory listening for any true Buddy Holly fan.

So far, this entry hasn't even touched on Sonny's long-term association with the Crickets, but of course he's been with them in one capacity or another since 1959, with the odd break or two when he went off to pursue personal projects – including one with Uncle Sam.

On a personal level, the man himself is the kindliest of individuals and a delight to know. At one concert, Sonny was presented with a Zimmer frame as a birthday gift: it was lowered onto the stage from above to cheers from the audience. Let's hope it won't be needed for some time to come.

D

HAROLD 'PAPPY' DAILY

Readers will find the name of Pappy Daily (1902-87) mentioned within these pages, and the principal connection without fail is with the Big Bopper. A legendary name in Texas, Pappy was a music entrepreneur who had his finger in many pies down the years, although he's perhaps best known for giving his name to the country label, Starday (Jack Starnes and Daily were the partners) and handling George Jones's first hits. He also founded the D label, and it was here that J.P. Richardson's career was launched with 'Chantilly Lace', before the record was picked up by Mercury. It's said that, when the Bopper brought the song to Daily, it was entitled 'That's What I Like', and he also suggested that the flip side, 'The Purple Eater Meets The Witch Doctor', was the potential hit! But, thanks to Pappy's intervention, a career was launched and the rest is history. Daily later handled Mercury's country music division, and also branched out into artist management, with the likes of Melba Montgomery, Gene Pitney and George Jones on his books.

BOBBY DARIN

If the author were desperate to link the names of Bobby Darin (1936-73) with that of Buddy Holly, it could truthfully be said that the former wrote 'I Want Elvis For Christmas', and the novelty number was recorded by the Holly Twins, a female duo featuring Holly's friend, Eddie Cochran, on guitar. But that smacks too much of quiet desperation and there is a much closer connection which came about when Buddy was rushed into a New York studio to cover 'Early In The Morning' and 'Now We're One', both Darin compositions (see **'EARLY IN THE MORNING'** for the full story).

Bobby and Buddy knew one another, and had certainly been on the same bill together, but it isn't known quite how close they were. However, it seems that, from the start, while others were looking to record rock'n'roll, Bobby was more likely to be eyeing up the songbooks of Cole Porter or Kurt Weill.

Darin was a complex and multi-talented artist who later also became a movie actor, though it is as a recording artist that he is most fondly remembered, scoring forty US 'Hot 100' hits ranging from outright rock'n'roll to folk music to show tunes.

Sadly, he lived most of his life with faulty heart valves after an early bout of rheumatic fever and died on the operating table at the age of 37. Like Holly, he remained popular after his death and was elected into the Rock and Roll Hall of Fame in 1990. Several books on the singer have been put out over the years, while perhaps the ultimate accolade was *Beyond the Sea*, the quality biopic made of his life in 2004 with Kevin Spacey in the lead role.

MAC DAVIS

Born in Lubbock, Texas in 1942, country singer Mac Davis was greatly inspired by the way Buddy Holly had achieved fame, despite coming from such an unfashionable area of West Texas. He went on to have a US pop No.1 with 'Baby Don't Get Hooked On Me' in the '70s, whilst some of his other material gave a direct nod to Holly (check out 'Texas In My Rear View Mirror' and 'Hooked On Music'). Thereafter, he branched out in a variety of directions. As a songwriter, he composed 'In The Ghetto' and 'Don't Cry Daddy' for Elvis, and 'Watching Scotty Grow' for Bobby Goldsboro. He also made a series of movies and had his own TV series for a while.

Davis later battled a drink problem but bounced back and is still in the entertainment business today. He was inducted into the Lubbock Walk of Fame in the '80s, when his plaque deservedly joined others set around the base of the Buddy Holly Statue.

SHERRY DAVIS

A female vocalist from Texas, born Gwendolyn Wilkinson, Sherry Davis was encouraged in her singing career by the legendary cowboy singing star, Gene Autry. She began recording around 1950 on minor labels and, after a period on the West Coast, returned to Texas to become a regular on the *Big D Jamboree* in Dallas. In October 1956, she achieved the unique honour of touring with Elvis shortly after he signed for RCA. In an active career, she had a gospel single ('God Speaks' *b/w* 'Did You Stop To Pray This Morning') out on the Crest label in 1955, and hosted the prestigious *Good Morning America* TV show during the '60s.

She's in these pages as, in 1957, she went to Clovis and recorded 'Broken Promises' and 'Humble Heart', which were released as a single on the small Fashion label. Backing her up with some powerful lead guitar-work was Buddy Holly, assisted by Jerry Allison on drums. Obviously, the single is long unobtainable, and any copies are probably in a bank vault somewhere as an investment, but it should be possible to track the music down on CD via the Rollercoaster or El Toro releases.

Davis retired from singing in the '70s.

SKEETER DAVIS

Born Mary Frances Penick in Dry Ridge, Kentucky, Skeeter Davis (1931-2004) had her first brush with fame as one half of the country duo, the Davis Sisters, scoring a No.1 C&W hit in 1953 with 'I Forgot More Than You'll Ever Know', said to be one of Elvis's favourites. Sadly, her partner, Betty Jack Davis (no relation), was killed in a car crash the month the record charted. Skeeter then embarked upon a hugely successful solo career which eventually led to her becoming a member of the *Grand Ole Opry*.

In the '60s, at the height of her popularity, she went to Nashville and, with the help of Waylon Jennings and Buzz Cason, recorded a tribute album to Buddy Holly. Photos on the album sleeve show Buddy's parents present during the recording session. The album was different from Skeeter's usual material and wasn't particularly successful saleswise. Perhaps this is why she didn't make any mention of it in her bittersweet 1993 autobiography, *Bus Fare To Kentucky*. She continued performing until shortly before her death from cancer.

'DEAREST'
Recorded December 1958 in Apartment 4H, The Brevoort, 11 Fifth Ave, New York
Personnel: Buddy Holly (acoustic guitar, vocals)

The first time Holly fans heard this recording was when it was released as the flip side of 'What To Do' on a 1963 UK single. Here was yet another 'new' track from the Apartment Tapes, albeit with a pizzicato-style overdub courtesy of the Fireballs. The title was peculiar too: 'Ummm, Oh Yeah', with composer credits specified as 'unknown'. Clearly not too much research had been done by either Norman Petty or Coral because, under its correct title, 'Dearest', the song had been a Top 100 US hit for Mickey & Sylvia in 1957. No doubt Coral were quickly appraised of that fact by the copyright holders, for later releases were correctly labelled.

A more heavily overdubbed version complete with backing vocals was released on the 1969 *Giant* album, while the undoctored cut was included on the 1979 *Complete Buddy Holly* box set. To complicate life for completists, an incomplete alternate take was also discovered amongst the Apartment Tapes.

The song's composers, incidentally, were Ellas McDaniel (Bo Diddley) and Mickey Baker, one half of the Mickey & Sylvia duo, whose 'Love Is Strange' Buddy also recorded.

Seldom covered by others, Holly's Texan contemporary Ray Ruff cut it as 'Ummm, Oh Yeah' on the Storme label in the early '60s.

DEATH DISCS

Although tragedy has brought us a long roll-call of artists who have left us prematurely, the decade that spanned the mid-'50s to the mid-'60s must surely have exceeded any other period for accidental deaths. From a series of car crash victims (Jesse Belvin, Eddie Cochran and Johnny Horton) and plane crash fatalities (Patsy Cline, Cowboy Copas and Jim Reeves) to stars who died in more unlikely circumstances (Sam Cooke, Bobby Fuller and Johnny Burnette) – the list is almost endless and we haven't even mentioned the three stars of the *Winter Dance Party*. In the decades since, the losses have continued unabated, but sadly seem to have been self-inflicted in the majority of cases.

But something that has thankfully gone away – perhaps itself a victim of changing times – is the 'death disc', which the '50s and '60s so typified. It seemed back then that, every time a new tragedy unfolded, another artist would be in the recording studio overnight to wax some paean of praise to the newly deceased. Some of these misfired badly, and were so maudlin that they verged on the downright embarrassing.

The loss of Buddy Holly, Ritchie Valens and the Big Bopper brought forth a real mixture of genuine tributes mixed with others that were obviously an attempt to cash-in. The big British chart hit following the February crash was by Indiana-born songstress Ruby Wright, whose 'Three Stars' – with its spoken monologue courtesy of US deejay Dick Pike – made the Top 20. The song had been penned by another deejay, Tommy Dee. Dee didn't know any of the artists, but his version was such a huge US hit that he notched up a gold disc for his efforts. But the saddest, and most unlikely version of all was surely that of Eddie Cochran which didn't surface until some seven years after his own passing in 1960. Unable to attend his friend's funeral, he instead went into the studio to pay his respects. He's so choked up on the recording (reputed to have been edited together from eight different takes) that it makes for uncomfortable listening. Listening to it one feels positively voyeuristic.

There was a flurry of other tribute records over the months that followed including 'The Great Tragedy' by Herschel Almond, 'Gold Records In The Snow' by Bennie Barnes, 'The Man I Met (A Tribute To The Big Bopper)' *b/w* 'Ballad of Donna and Peggy Sue' by Ray Campi, and 'The Stage' by Waylon Jennings. But the best of the bunch was probably Geoff Goddard's composition, 'Tribute To Buddy Holly', a 1961 UK hit for Mike Berry.

Since those days, the tributes have continued, but have usually been far more subtle and, with the passage of time, far less emotive. Don McLean's 'American Pie' from 1971 was by far the biggest in terms of record sales, but there have been some other very poignant records that have harked back to the events of February, 1959. Waylon Jennings penned a powerful tribute called 'Old Friend', while Lee Jackson's 'I Named My Little Girl Holly' was also recorded by Mike Berry and Buddy Knox.

Other, more overt tributes include two songs recorded by the Picks in 1982, 'Buddy Holly Not Fade Away' and 'Forever 22', two years before their Holly overdubbing sessions in Houston (see **OVERDUBS** and **PICKS**). Buddy's brothers, Travis and Larry Holley, also wrote and recorded 'Buddy Holly And The Crickets' for their 1980 Cloud 9 release, *Holly's House – A Family Album*. The list is endless, but it would be an oversight not to include Sonny Curtis's 'The Real Buddy Holly Story'. It may have taken a film to trigger it off, but by gosh it's one of those tributes that's straight from the heart and was worth waiting for.

JIM DENNY

Jim Denny (1911-63) was a well-known individual in the 1950s, and was at one time talent coordinator for the *Grand Ole Opry*. It's famously suggested that he said that Elvis should give up singing and return to driving trucks. Sadly, his name doesn't give off much better vibes where Holly is concerned.

Denny owned Cedarwood Publishing, which handled Holly's early Decca recordings, but complications arose when Holly re-recorded 'That'll Be The Day' with the Crickets and it became a colossal hit on Brunswick. As a result, the group ended up passing over 50% of 'Think It Over' to Cedarwood as a *quid pro quo* arrangement.

Despite the negatives highlighted here, Denny was well thought of in the industry and was elected into the Country Music Hall of Fame in 1966.

MURRAY DEUTCH

A small but important bit-part player who was largely responsible for the Crickets getting their first big break in 1957. Deutch was General Professional Manager of Southern Music in New York (where Holly also met his future wife, Maria Elena) and took the demo of 'That'll Be The Day' to Bob Thiele at Coral after it had been turned down by several others, most notably Mitch Miller of Columbia. (Deutch had been sent the disc by Norman Petty, who was trying to get a major label interested. And yes, the hit we remember was just that: a demo that was so good it didn't need to be re-recorded!)

Thiele is very complimentary about Deutch in his 1995 autobiography, *What A Wonderful World*, and it's also said that Deutch was approached to become Holly's manager in late 1958 after his split with Norman Petty, but had too many other commitments.

A must for any Holly fan's collection are the jingles where the Crickets sing couplets from 'That'll Be The Day' addressed to Deutch, Thiele and Bob Randall, all of whom had helped them get their big break (see **JINGLES** for more info).

DIAMONDS

It's often overlooked that the first chart action Buddy Holly enjoyed pre-dated the Crickets' 'That'll Be The Day' hit by a couple of months. It came about when Canadian vocal group the Diamonds took his composition, 'Words Of Love', into the US Top 20, thereby ensuring that Buddy became a best-selling composer well before he hit the jackpot as a singer. The Diamonds' record bears little resemblance to Holly's version, being set to a Latin beat similar to their big hit, 'Little Darlin' '. The group, and in particular their lead singer, Dave Sommerville, became friendly with the Crickets when they toured together with *Alan Freed's Big Beat Show* in 1958. The Diamonds' hit parade days ended in 1961, but they continued on the oldies circuit for years thereafter.

'DID YOU EVER GO SAILING'

This is rumoured to be the first song that Holly sang before a live audience as a juvenile. It's an old bluegrass favourite written by country gospel composer Albert E. Brumley ('I'll Fly Away', 'Turn Your Radio On', 'He Set Me Free', etc) that Buddy's mother had taught him.

BO DIDDLEY

Bo was born Ellas Bates to a teenage mother in rural McComb, Mississippi back in 1928 and was raised by her cousin. He went on to carve out a unique place in the history of R&B and enjoyed a long career before he succumbed to heart-related problems in his 80th year. A true pioneer, he was a musician's musician and was described by Phil Everly as *'the most under-rated rock'n'roller of the century'*. Certainly, he came up the hard way and had to overcome all manner of setbacks before becoming widely recognised as a singer – a talent he combined with a distinctive style in guitar playing, as well as excelling in composing and arranging. Considering his prowess, his actual successes on the pop charts were modest, but part of his legacy was in forging the 'Bo Diddley' beat.

As we know, Buddy Holly went on to record his own demo of 'Bo Diddley' which ended up becoming a massive posthumous hit in 1963. Years later, Diddley returned the compliment by recording his own version of 'Not Fade Away', the Buddy Holly song that owes everything to the 'Bo Diddley' rhythm.

In more recent years, a tape of Buddy and Jerry Allison rehearsing Diddley's 'Mona' has surfaced, although the vocals are off-mike. This recording has never been officially released, although it was included on the 1995 4-CD Vigotone bootleg, *What You Been A-Missin'*.

Bo was inducted into the Rock and Roll Hall of Fame in 1987.

DION & THE BELMONTS

Dion DiMucci from the Bronx, New York, and his group, the Belmonts, were the fourth headliners on the doomed *Winter Dance Party* tour, and the only ones to make it through to the final performance in Springfield, Illinois on 15 February 1959. The group had actually racked up their third Top 40 hit shortly before the tour commenced, and even the tragedy couldn't derail their career. Their next hit, 'Teenager In Love', went on to become their greatest ever. Often asked about his recollections of the tour, Dion remembers getting on well with Holly and his group, and that Buddy even sat in on drums for them when Carl Bunch was hospitalised with frostbite.

After splitting from the Belmonts in 1960, Dion enjoyed further hits throughout the '60s and has had a lifetime in the business. He's still in demand, though his style has undergone a metamorphosis since his doo-wop days of 1958. 1988 saw the publication of his candid autobiography, *The Wanderer*.

Dion was inducted into the Rock and Roll Hall of Fame in 1989.

DIXIE CHICKS

It's great to include a modern-day country act who obviously tip their Stetsons towards Buddy Holly and the music of that era as a distinct influence. The Dixie Chicks have recorded some wonderful cutting-edge material that simultaneously celebrates their American heritage. Not only that, they also include a country fiddle at the forefront of their act. They've picked up a string of country awards since 1999, although their career hit a temporary obstacle back in 2003 when they publicly attacked the American stance over the Iraq war.

Their most notable link with Buddy Holly is their 2006 pop and country chart-topping album, *Taking The Long Way*, which contains the track 'Lubbock Or Leave It' – a paean to the era and the music which mentions Holly and name-checks several of his hits.

The trio presently comprises lead singer Natalie Maines from Lubbock (her grandfather gave Buddy Holly a few guitar lessons!), and Martie Maguire and Emily Robinson from the East Coast. At this point in time their career shows little sign of slowing down.

FATS DOMINO

Antoine 'Fats' Domino was born in New Orleans in 1928 and turned 80 while these notes were being written. He first began recording R&B during the 1940s, but in the hands of Fats and his piano it became more of a fusion of Cajun, blues and jazz with its own unique sound. Some people argue that his 1950 R&B hit, 'The Fat Man', was the first-ever rock'n'roll record. But it's mostly his sequence of mid-'50s rock'n'roll hits that he is remembered for, and, while some acts didn't transfer to celluloid very successfully, Fats certainly did – as his appearances in *The Girl Can't Help It* (1956), *Shake, Rattle and Roll* (1956) and *Disc Jockey Jamboree* (1957) attest.

It is known that Buddy Holly loved black music, and artists such as Fats Domino, Ray Charles and Mickey & Sylvia were all big heroes of his. The Crickets toured together with Domino, and in Buddy's interview with Red Robinson at the Georgia Auditorium, Vancouver on 23 October 1957 he mentions that *'we go on right after Fats'*. It therefore comes as no surprise to discover that Holly also recorded some R&B numbers. Certainly, there would have been many more to come had he lived.

The Crickets meet Lonnie Donegan, March 1958.

As it stands, the only proper studio recording we have of Buddy performing a Domino song is 'Valley Of Tears', which was released in 1957 as a track on his first solo album, though it also charted in the UK when released as a single in 1961 (as did the other side, 'Baby I Don't Care'). After Holly's death, a demo version of Buddy and Jerry rocking their way through 'Blue Monday' came to light, but bears little resemblance to the legendary Domino version with his full band behind him.

Domino and Holly were simultaneously inducted into the Rock and Roll Hall of Fame in 1986. At the ceremony, Fats commented: *'I wish that Buddy, Elvis and Sam Cooke could be here to enjoy what's happening.'*

LONNIE DONEGAN

One of the most influential of all artists to come up in the 1950s, Anthony James 'Lonnie' Donegan (1931-2002) almost single-handedly spearheaded the skiffle revolution of mid-'50s Britain and then, by dint of his personality, remained a star of the musical firmament for the rest of his life. He inspired an entire generation of British musicians and, although always linked with skiffle, he had a touch of folk, jazz, gospel and blues all mixed in there somewhere.

The Crickets and Lonnie met up in 1958 when they were touring the UK, and there are several photos of them together. It's said that Buddy loved Lonnie's 'Rock Island Line', which had amazingly been a Top 10 hit in the US. Lonnie went to see the Crickets perform, and also took them to the midnight matinee at London's Dominion Theatre in aid of blues legend Big Bill Broonzy.

Donegan carried on entertaining to the end, dying in Peterborough while on tour at the age of 71 (not a bad innings for someone who had been diagnosed with heart problems as a young child). Shortly before his death he was awarded the MBE.

'DON'T COME BACK KNOCKIN''
(1) Recorded December 1955 at Nesman Recording Studio, Wichita Falls, Texas
Personnel: Buddy Holly (guitar, vocals), Sonny Curtis (guitar), Jerry Allison (drums), Don Guess (double bass)
(2) Recorded January 1956 at Bradley's Barn Studio, Nashville, Tennessee
Personnel: Buddy Holly (vocals), Sonny Curtis (guitar), Grady Martin (guitar), Don Guess (double bass), Doug Kirkham (percussion)

At the time of these recordings, lyricist Sue Parrish, who was then living in Lubbock, had pushed a couple of songs to Buddy (see also **'LOVE ME'**) prior to his first Nashville session in January 1956. The first time fans in Britain heard it was on one of a couple of Brunswick EPs of Nashville material released in July 1959 to help meet the insatiable demand for Holly's recordings.

Exactly how many versions of this particular song exist is unclear, but in 2007 the original release, together with portions of two incomplete takes were spliced together and issued on the superlative *Ohh! Annie!* CD on Rollercoaster. In 1984, the Picks overdubbed backing vocals onto the Nashville recording (see **OVERDUBS** and **PICKS** for more info).

A totally different, less polished version cut in December 1955 (easily identifiable by Buddy calling out *'Let's play it again boys, let's go!'*) was released by Buddy's brother, Larry, on his Holly House label in 1986 and has since cropped up on other releases. There is also believed to be another unissued demo of the song cut at the Nesman session.

'DOOR TO MY HEART' *(Buddy & Bob)*
Recorded prob. 1954 or 1955 at Nesman Recording Studio, Wichita Falls, Texas
Personnel: Buddy Holly (guitar, vocals), Bob Montgomery (guitar, vocals), Sonny Curtis (fiddle), Larry Welborn (double bass), Don Guess (steel guitar)

A Bob Montgomery composition, this is a Buddy & Bob recording from the earliest days. However, the only version that has ever seen the light is the one overdubbed by the Fireballs at Clovis in 1963, so it's impossible to be absolutely certain what the recording sounded like in its original raw state (though it is known that part of the additional instrumentation included drums). It was one of the many Buddy & Bob tracks that first surfaced on the 1965 *Holly In The Hills* album, and is also the title track of a rare Australian EP. Predictably, this little-known song hasn't inspired any covers.

'DOWN THE LINE' *(Buddy & Bob)*
(1) Recorded early 1955 at Nesman Recording Studio, Wichita Falls, Texas
Personnel: Buddy Holly (guitar, vocals), Bob Montgomery (guitar, vocals), Jerry Allison (drums), Larry Welborn (double bass)
(2) Recorded June 1955 at Nesman Recording Studio, Wichita Falls, Texas
Personnel: Buddy Holly (guitar, vocals), Bob Montgomery (guitar, vocals), Jerry Allison (drums), unknown (double bass)

This is a Buddy & Bob composition and, like the one above, first appeared in heavily overdubbed form on the 1965 *Holly In The Hills* album. Bob Montgomery recalls getting the idea for this song while hitch-hiking to see his future wife in the pouring rain and being miles from anywhere. The track was in effect a demo, but a pretty effective one and well worthy of release, if only posthumously. The undubbed version did surface eventually, as well as an earlier attempt also cut at Nesman. Montgomery also cut a solo version of the song (without Holly's involvement) at Clovis in June 1958, but it remains unissued.

Of all the Buddy & Bob recordings, this and 'Baby Let's Play House' are probably the closest to outright rock'n'roll. (NB. Around the same time, Roy Orbison & The Teen Kings recorded a song by the same title. This was actually a completely different composition by Roy and band member Billy Pat Ellis called 'Go, Go, Go' which had been renamed.)

This song hasn't been covered very often, but with impeccable taste Bobby Vee picked it for one of the tracks on his 1999 Holly tribute album, *Down The Line*. In 1989, the Slickee Boys recorded a manic version for the New Rose tribute album, *Everyday Is A Holly Day*.

'DROWN IN MY OWN TEARS'

(1) Recorded Feb. 1958 prob. backstage at Fort Hesterley Armory, Tampa, Florida
Personnel: Buddy Holly (guitar, vocals), Jerry Lee Lewis (piano)
(2) Recorded December 1958 in Apartment 4H, The Brevoort, 11 Fifth Ave, New York
Personnel: Buddy Holly (acoustic guitar, vocals)

We know that Buddy Holly was a big Ray Charles fan (this was confirmed by the Crickets, and also by Ella Holley, who said so in an interview following her son's death) and he loved Charles's recording of 'Drown In My Own Tears', a R&B No.1 in 1956. The song was written by Henry Glover, who had made quite a name for himself as a trumpeter with Tiny Bradshaw and Lucky Millinder, and also found success as a composer (eg the Midnighters' 'Work With Me Annie').

It's exasperating that less than the final twenty seconds remains of the version that Buddy recorded in his New York flat, the rest having apparently been taped over. A backstage recording made in Florida the year before exists, with Holly singing and Jerry Lee Lewis on piano, albeit this is very poor quality. There's also the briefest snippet of them jamming on 'Hallelujah I Love Her So' with Lewis on vocals.

Incidentally Holly's pal Eddie Cochran, who like Buddy did lots of session work, played guitar on Troyce Key's 1958 version of 'Drown In My Own Tears', though it never charted. The only time the song dented the US pop charts – and then only for one week – was via the Don Shirley Trio in 1961.

WILLIAM 'HI-POCKETS' DUNCAN

At one time a deejay at KDAV, Duncan got to know Buddy Holly well when the singer was on the way up and briefly managed Buddy & Bob in the mid-'50s.

A friendly individual, he accidentally coined his own nickname when on air and it stuck ever after. As a deejay, he had connections with many of the post-war Lubbock radio stations and is fondly remembered by all those he came in contact with.

When Holly's career began to take off, Duncan was happy to step down and release him without making any sort of claims on him. Anyone else in his position might easily have become litigious.

He was interviewed by John Goldrosen for his Buddy Holly biography, and is one of the main characters portrayed in the *Buddy* musical, where he's used at times to narrate Buddy's story. Hi-Pockets passed away in 1981, sadly too soon to see himself immortalised in musical theatre folklore.

JERRY DWYER

Owner of Dwyer's Flying Service from whom Buddy chartered the doomed Beechcraft plane. As of this date, he still owns the charter business and continues to reside in the Mason City area.

BOB DYLAN

Robert Zimmerman, better known as Bob Dylan, is one legend who is quick to acknowledge the debt that he and others owe to the pioneer work of Holly, Elvis Presley and other early rockers. The two men never met, and their careers barely overlapped, but Dylan remembers the powerful effect of seeing Holly on stage in Duluth, Minnesota on the very last day of January 1959.

Then, in mid-1959, just months after the crash that simultaneously killed Buddy and kick-started Bobby Vee's career, the latter hired a guy named Elston Gunnn *(sic)* as keyboard player for his band. It turns out that this was none other than Mr Zimmerman under an assumed name! Surely a case of fact being that much stranger than fiction. Interestingly, his studio debut was playing harmonica on a Carolyn Hester album on Columbia, which indirectly led to him being signed to the label.

Dylan would later be quoted as saying that Buddy Holly and Johnny Ace are as valid to him today as they were back in the '50s. One of his better biographers, Robert Shelton, also suggests that Dylan occasionally emulated Holly's naïve sweet vocal style, and that the feel of albums such as *John Wesley Harding* definitely owed something to the Texan. His award-winning career, on which all superlatives have been exhausted, is ongoing and includes his induction into the Rock and Roll Hall of Fame in 1988.

E

'EARLY IN THE MORNING'

Recorded June 1958 at Pythian Temple Studio, New York
Personnel: Buddy Holly (vocals), George Barnes (guitar), Al Chernet (guitar), Sanford Bloch (bass), Ernest Hayes (piano), Panama Francis and Philip Kraus (drums), Sam 'The Man' Taylor (alto sax), Helen Way Singers (backing vocals)

In the summer of 1958, Buddy Holly was summoned to the studio by Coral Records to record cover versions of both sides of Bobby Darin's latest single, 'Early In The Morning' *b/w* 'Now We're One'.

The story behind this request is somewhat convoluted, but basically Darin was signed to Atlantic's Atco subsidiary, hadn't had any hits with them and was going nowhere fast. Anticipating that he would be released from his contract when it expired later in 1958, he lined up a deal with Decca's Brunswick label and cut a single for them.

However, things did not work out quite as Darin had anticipated. Against all expectations, 'Splish Splash', a novelty number he had recently cut for Atco, entered the *Billboard* 'Top 100' in June 1958 and shot to No.3. Meanwhile, Brunswick released 'Early In The Morning', pseudonymously credited to the 'Ding Dongs'. When Atlantic discovered that the Ding Dongs were actually Darin, they compelled Brunswick to hand over the master and promptly re-released it on Atco as by the 'Rinky-Dinks'.

Not to be outdone, Brunswick quickly roped in Buddy Holly (who happened to be in New York at the time) to cut a cover with the same musicians that Darin had used. The session included gospel-styled vocal backings from the Helen Way Singers, a black quartet, and a great band which included Panama Francis on drums and Sam 'The Man' Taylor on sax.

And so, the world got to hear our favourite Texan on a gospel-flavoured number, with a performance probably as good as any other of his career. (Listening to his rendition, it comes as no surprise to learn that Buddy was trying to link up with Ray Charles at the time in the hope of collaborating on some blues or gospel recordings.)

The result was two sizeable hits. The Rinky-Dinks' single entered the *Billboard* 'Top 100' on 28 July and climbed to No. 24. Holly's, close behind, entered the 'Top 100' on 4 August and made No.32.

In Britain, the Rinky-Dinks never got a look-in and Holly's version went to No.17 in the hit parade, a couple of weeks after Darin debuted with 'Splish Splash'.

Although Holly's session was reputedly recorded in stereo, only mono masters survive. And, since the two songs were made to order, there are no alternate takes, overdubs, or any of the usual variations that are of interest to collectors. No matter, 'Early In The Morning' ranks as one of his greatest recordings, and Jerry Allison and Joe Mauldin have often said they wish they could have been on it.

Skeeter Davis, Bobby Vee and Connie Francis have all covered the song on albums they have made of Buddy's music.

DUANE EDDY

Twangy guitarist Duane Eddy was a permanent fixture in most of the world's hit parades from his debut in 1958 until the mid-'60s. His path crossed Holly's when they toured together in 1958.

After Buddy's death, he continued his association with the reformed Crickets – most notably in 1973, when he produced a Waylon Jennings session of (predominantly) Holly songs including 'That'll Be The Day' and 'It Doesn't Matter Anymore', with Jerry Allison and Sonny Curtis playing backup. 'Buddy Holly Medley' from the same session surfaced in 1978 on Jennings's *I've Always Been Crazy* album, and also on the flip of his 1980 British single, 'Nadine'.

Eddy enjoyed a mini-revival of sorts in the '80s when, with Art of Noise, a highly successful British group of the day, he charted with 'Peter Gunn'. In 1990, he completed a successful tour of Britain with the Crickets and Tommy Roe. In 1994, he was belatedly inducted into the Rock and Roll Hall of Fame.

DAVE EDMUNDS

Born in 1944, British singer/guitarist Dave Edmunds has always been a confirmed fan of Holly's and some of his own recordings (noticeably 'Queen Of Hearts') have a distinct touch of the Crickets about them. Although too young to have been directly involved with the Texan, he did have the honour of being included in a major 1996 Holly tribute album recorded in Nashville, *Not Fade Away (Remembering Buddy Holly)*, producing and playing on Suzy Bogguss's rendition of 'It Doesn't Matter Anymore'.

JOE ELY

Surely one of the greatest singer/songwriters ever to emerge from West Texas, Joe Ely was born in Amarillo in 1947, but was brought up 100 miles further south in Lubbock after his parents relocated when he was just twelve years old. In some ways, he remains underrated, and his undoubted ability hasn't been reflected in his meagre chart success. Like one of his heroes, Buddy Holly, he's always been loyal to the area in which he was raised, although Lubbock itself is often described as 'the city in the middle of nowhere' – with all the problems that can bring a musician seeking a break.

In his early years, he linked up with Jimmie Dale Gilmore (who was managed by Buddy's father for a time) and Butch Hancock to form the Flatlanders. Although they didn't hit the heights immediately, the cult group cut a wealth of material which has stood the test of time.

Ely has appeared in several Holly tributes over the years and also participated in the 1996 Nashville tribute album, *Not Fade Away (Remembering Buddy Holly)*, performing 'Oh Boy!' with the help of Todd Snyder. He was also inducted into the West Texas Walk of Fame several years back, and has his plaque in Lubbock alongside the Buddy Holly Statue.

JERRY ENGLER

Jerry Engler was the opening act on the 19 January 1958 show at Rochester Auditorium, New York on which the Crickets and the Everly Brothers were headliners, and it was agreed that Buddy would produce an Engler session at Clovis. It appears that Jerry took along three numbers he had written ('What A You Gonna Do?', 'I Sent You Roses' and 'Bayou Baby') to the session and asked Buddy to pick out the best two – it wasn't financially viable to record all three. Holly selected the first two.

The session started late in the day on 6 September 1958 and carried on past midnight into 7 September – Buddy's 22nd birthday! Engler recalls Holly playing guitar and bells(!) on the first number, while 'Roses' is really lounge music with Norman Petty playing the prominent organ accompaniment. The tracks have been hard to locate until Engler recently issued them on a CD, which also includes his recording of 'Bayou Baby'. Although quite different in sound to other Holly sessions, George Atwood told the author that he remembered playing bass on these tracks and confirmed that Bo Clarke was the drummer. Jerry Engler remains active as a songwriter and has released several CDs of his own material.

EPs

An American invention, the 7-inch, 4-track extended play album (or 'EP') was invented in 1953 to bridge the gap between the 45 rpm vinyl single introduced by RCA in 1949 and the 33⅓ rpm long-playing album (or 'LP') launched by Columbia a year earlier. For some reason, they never really caught on in the USA and were more or less obsolete by the start of the '60s. Brits, however, took the EP to their hearts and the format remained immensely popular until the mid-'60s.

Since so much Holly/Crickets singles and albums material was also issued on EPs during the '50s and '60s, especially in Britain, it is superfluous to write about the releases in any detail. However, some comments about the best-sellers among these releases may be appropriate.

In the UK, no EP charts existed before Holly's death. However, 1960's *The Late, Great Buddy Holly* reached the Top 5 on the *Record Retailer* EP chart. *Four More* by the Crickets made the Top 10 that same year, as did *Rave On* in 1961. In 1963, *Just For Fun*, featuring two tracks apiece by the Crickets and Bobby Vee, made the No.1 spot.

See also **LPs**.

DAVID ESSEX

An undoubted fan of Buddy Holly, David Essex first came to prominence in Britain when he played the lead in the 1973 movie, *That'll Be The Day*, a social drama that featured musicians such as Ringo Starr, Keith Moon and Billy Fury in quasi-acting roles. As to the varied soundtrack, it appears they were unable to get permission to use Holly's original recordings – despite the *Buddy Holly* album sleeve being used as a prop in the film! – and Bobby Vee covers were used instead.

A later Holly link came about in 1994, when Essex duetted on 'True Love Ways' with Catherine Zeta-Jones and scored a minor UK hit.

See also **JOHN DENVER**.

GODFREY EVANS – *See* **DENIS COMPTON**

EVERLY BROTHERS

From all we've read, it seems that Buddy Holly made several instant friends from among those artists he met on tours, and top of the heap were Eddie Cochran, Paul Anka and the pair named here, Don and Phil Everly. As Southerners from similar backgrounds, they forged an immediate bond that was sealed by their love of music. They were also close contemporaries: Buddy was born in September 1936, Don four months later, and Phil in January 1939.

Having sprung to fame at exactly the same time as the Crickets, the brothers often found themselves on the same bill. When they first went on the road together in 1957, it was Don and Phil who helped them get kitted out in better gear, and also suggested that, if Buddy needed to wear glasses, then he should just go all the way and get heavy frames. He took their advice and they soon became his trademark.

At one particular gig, landed with a pickup band that patently couldn't play, the Everlys performed with Buddy, Jerry and Joe playing back-up. Small wonder that, a few years later and with Buddy gone, the duo eagerly signed the group (at that time comprising Sonny Curtis, Jerry and Joe B.) to accompany them on a sell-out tour of Britain in April 1960.

In September 1958, Buddy and Phil Everly also teamed up to co-produce an unsuccessful single for a little-known New York singer called Lou Giordano called 'Stay Close To Me' (penned by Buddy) *b/w* 'Don't Cha Know' (penned by Phil). (NB Although both are credited to 'Everly', the latter was a different song to one recorded by the Crickets in 1960.) They also played on the record and sang backing vocals with Joey Villa of the Royal Teens (remember 'Short Shorts'?). Later, Phil was one of the pallbearers at Holly's funeral.

The Everly Brothers were among the first group of artists inducted into the Rock and Roll Hall of Fame in 1986.

'EVERYDAY'

(1) Recorded May 1957 at Norman Petty Recording Studios, Clovis, New Mexico
Personnel: Buddy Holly (acoustic guitar, vocals), Jerry Allison (knee slapping), Joe B. Mauldin (double bass), Vi Petty (celeste)
(2) Recorded Feb. 1958 prob. Fort Hesterley Armory, Tampa, Florida
Personnel: Buddy Holly (guitar, vocals), Jerry Allison (drums), Joe B. Mauldin (double bass)

One of the most simple yet effective of all of Buddy Holly's compositions, 'Everyday' was apparently recorded quite quickly with Buddy on acoustic guitar and Jerry slapping his knees to create a rhythm. Whether it was actually Vi Petty or her husband that played celeste is purely academic, but the use of such an instrument was certainly inspired. It was around in the studio for when the Norman Petty Trio were recording, and Buddy was keen to incorporate the sound on one of his gentler numbers. It works superbly, and the song has become a standard that has been included on just about every Holly/Crickets hits compilation ever since. Not too bad for the flip side of a recording ('Peggy Sue') that didn't manage a chart life of its own in the UK or US, although it was a Top 10 smash in Australia.

History might have been so much different, as Jimmy Bowen recalls that the song was one of a batch of Holly compositions passed to him to record. However, Buddy landed his contract almost immediately thereafter and claimed his songs back!

Holly did occasionally sing ballads on stage, and a very short fragment of 'Everyday' recorded live at a Florida concert has circulated amongst fans for a number of years. Meanwhile, the 1984 Picks' overdub of the Holly classic (see **OVERDUBS** and **PICKS** for more info) brings to mind the phrase 'if it ain't broke, don't fix it'.

As to covers, just about anybody who is anybody has recorded it at some time, with Don McLean, John Denver and James Taylor all taking their versions into the charts.

Holly also recorded a jingle for KLLL radio to the tune of 'Everyday' which has circulated among collectors for years (see **JINGLES**).

F

FAIR PARK COLISEUM

Fair Park Coliseum and the Cotton Club were the two main venues that Buddy and the boys played in Lubbock as a support act before their career took off. Of the two venues, the Cotton Club was 'down and dirty', while the larger Coliseum with its 10,000 capacity could cater for the bigger acts which regularly passed through Lubbock in those days. It was there that Buddy and his pals saw the early Elvis on stage in January 1955 – something that had an instant and profound effect on him and the others. Sadly, nothing was televised or taped from those days.

ADAM FAITH

There's no doubt that, for the first year of his hit parade career, Terence Nelhams *aka* Adam Faith (1940-2003) borrowed more than a little something from Buddy Holly, whether it was his elongated pronunciation of *'baby'* in 'Someone Else's Baby', the hiccup in 'Poor Me', or, with John Barry's help, the pizzicato strings of 'It Doesn't Matter Anymore' on 'What Do You Want'.

Having come up via skiffle and the 2I's coffee bar route, Faith was determined to break into the big time, even if he had to borrow a bit here and there at the outset. From heading the queue of Holly soundalikes, he gradually developed his own individual style. After seven years of non-stop hits, he diversified into all manner of projects from acting to management (Leo Sayer) to financial guru, and back to acting again. He described his roller-coaster life in his 1996 autobiography, *Acts of Faith*.

TERRY FARLAN

One of many artists to record a tribute album of Buddy Holly songs (in this case in 1969), Terry Farlan is a complete mystery. Who knows, perhaps he was a session man?

JIMMY LEE FAUTHEREE

Jimmy Lee Fautheree was born in Smackover, Arkansas in 1934, but later moved to Roswell, New Mexico and Dallas, Texas. When he came to the fore in the '50s, it was as one half of the popular country duo Jimmy & Johnny, who almost topped the *Billboard* C&W

chart in 1954 with 'If You Don't, Somebody Else Will' on Chess. Thereafter they became regulars on the *Louisiana Hayride* and their recordings appeared on a variety of labels including Decca, D, Capitol, Vin and Towne House.

What links Fautheree with Holly is the intriguing fact that, as far back as 1958, he recorded a single under the name 'Johnny Angel', which coupled a sax-based version of 'Baby It's Love' with 'Teenage Wedding' – the latter mentioning Buddy Holly by name (and this *pre-*February 1959!). Surprisingly, 'Baby It's Love' is one of the few Buddy & Bob recordings that hasn't inspired any covers. In later years, Fautheree admitted that he'd learnt the song from an acetate which someone had given him. As he often performed in Lubbock in the mid-'50's, it is surely likely that it came from Buddy & Bob themselves, who would have been keen to push material to a chart act.

Fautheree later recorded at Clovis, but with little commercial success. He eventually retired in the Dallas area and died in 2004. Some of his back catalogue (both solo and as Jimmy & Johnny) is available on Bear Family.

IRVING FELD

Irving Feld was the original driving force behind the General Artists Corporation of 5th Avenue, New York. GAC, like Alan Freed, were package show promoters in the early days of rock'n'roll, and many tours were run from their Chicago office. Sadly, their name is more associated with the fiasco of the 1959 *Winter Dance Party* tour these days. Shortly after this disaster, they changed direction and moved away from promoting. Feld later purchased what had been the legendary Barnum & Bailey's Circus and ran this for many years before passing away in 1984 at the age of 66.

FENDER STRATOCASTER

Buddy Holly is famous as one of the first rock'n'roll artists to champion the Fender Strat – a solid-bodied, electrified instrument – and was almost single-handedly responsible for its introduction into Britain. It was in 1954 that guitar manufacturer Leo Fender first launched the model which has since become legendary in the hands of Eric Clapton, Robert Cray, Hank Marvin and a host of others. In Buddy Holly's case, the dollars to purchase his first distinctive sunburst guitar came from brother Larry, but most fans wouldn't get to see it until they purchased the *Chirping Crickets* album and drank in the colour cover. As Joe Ely once put it, *'the aliens had landed in Lubbock'*. Sadly, Buddy didn't live to benefit from the mega-money era of the 'namesake models' that gave birth to the Waylon Jennings Tribute Telecaster, the Dick Dale Stratocaster, and even a Trini Lopez model.

Of course, Holly owned a variety of guitars even in his short lifetime. These are examined in more detail under **GUITARS**.

FILMS

We know that the Crickets would have loved to be in one of the many rock'n'roll film quickies that proliferated in the '50s, and in their 1957 interview with deejay Freeman Hover they admit to buddying up to their friend Eddie Cochran in an effort to get a part in a movie he was shooting. Around the same time, Buddy Knox, Jimmy Bowen and the Rhythm Orchids, who'd all started out together in Clovis, were lip-synching to their latest hits in *Jamboree* (released as *Disc Jockey Jamboree* in Britain). It's said that Norman Petty wasn't keen on the idea, plus the Crickets had all the work they could handle at that time, so the moment was lost.

Surviving film clips of Holly and the Crickets are few and far between, and probably amount to between ten and fifteen minutes in total. Essentially, they consist of the familiar ones of the group's appearances on the *Ed Sullivan Show* and *Arthur Murray's Party* (the latter broadcast in colour, though only monochrome footage survives). A few other snippets exist, such as Norman Petty's colour ciné-film of them on stage on their British tour, but this is strictly home movie stuff. Colour footage of Holly and other musicians relaxing backstage in Lubbock shot by Ben Hall also exists.

It was also a shock, having only seen photos of the crash site for years, to belatedly see moving images from 1959 crop up during a recent TV documentary. The only other find to surface of late is an intriguing fragment of Buddy, Jerry and Joe B. singing 'That'll Be The Day' around a mike on the *High Time* show on KPTV (Portland's local version of *American Bandstand*).

See also **PHOTOGRAPHS**.

FIREBALLS

The Fireballs (named after their standing-ovation performance of 'Great Balls Of Fire' at a high school talent contest) originated from Raton, New Mexico, a town about 150 miles north of Clovis, and their lead guitarist, George Tomsco, vividly remembers being introduced to

One of several Fireballs line-ups. *Back row, left to right:* Stan Lark, George Tomsco and Eric Budd. *Front:* Jimmy Gilmer.

Buddy Holly in Norman Petty's studio in September 1958 – the one and only time they met.

Buddy was back in Clovis for a business meeting with Petty, and Tomsco was suddenly confronted by an unknown musician playing his brand-new guitar. However, once he heard the sounds being coaxed from the instrument, his initial anger melted away! In interviews since, Tomsco has always said that he felt Holly's talent was God-given, and has always felt honoured that he and his group were used to overdub his recordings. In fact, there turned out to be a phenomenal amount of material for release, all of which Petty felt needed sweetening. This ranged from the earliest rough Buddy & Bob demos, to the final solo recordings Buddy left behind on his Ampex tape machine in New York. (Just how essential this overdubbing was is debatable, as most fans were crying out for any Holly material in any format. Was it really necessary to doctor, edit or otherwise mess with virtually each and every demo?)

The Fireballs duly decamped to Petty's studio and undertook many lengthy overdubbing sessions at varying times throughout the '60s. Mostly these involved George Tomsco on lead guitar, Keith McCormack on rhythm guitar, Stan Lark on bass and Eric Budd or Doug Roberts on drums. Sometimes backing vocals were also added.

In all, the group worked on about 45 recordings – a prodigious number by any standard. The majority of these overdubs enabled stereo masters to be produced from mono originals, except for the Buddy & Bob material, where mono masters were preferred (admittedly it would probably not have been wise to separate the sound on those earliest tracks). Years later, Bob Montgomery confessed he was amazed that those early efforts had ever been considered worth putting out in *any* format.

Over the years, fans have expressed surprise that the Crickets were not used on the overdubs and Norman Petty himself never said too much on that subject, although to be fair the Fireballs were hot in hit parade terms throughout the '60s and were constantly to be found at Clovis. They were also Petty's group, whereas the Crickets had moved on and were based in Los Angeles. Perhaps it was the convenience factor, although Jerry Allison has always maintained that all it would have taken for them to have got involved was a phone call. But all that's history now, and the Fireballs undeniably did a really good job in dealing with a wide range of material, almost all of which was never intended for release.

Many readers will have some Fireballs material in their collections, as they've had a long career as one of the great instrumental groups (they are credited with unknowingly helping to start the surfing sounds of the early '60s!), even if their only gold record was 1963's 'Sugar Shack' with Jimmy Gilmer on vocals. The group still perform, and have appeared at many Holly-related tributes in both Clovis and at the Surf Ballroom in Clear Lake, Iowa.

See also **GEORGE TOMSCO**.

JOHN FIRMINGER

A drummer extraordinaire whose friendship with the Crickets as individuals goes back too many years to remember, John launched the *Crickets File* magazine in 1979. This started off in a black & white format, but has since progressed to HD colour (well almost). The fanzine is now well on the way to its 100th issue. As if all that isn't enough, he's also promoted several UK concerts for both the Crickets and Sonny Curtis.

LESTER FLATT & EARL SCRUGGS

Legendary bluegrass duo who were a huge influence on Buddy Holly during his formative years, particularly with numbers such as 'I'll Just Pretend', which they'd recorded back in October 1952 and which would certainly have been a favourite of the Holley family. Coming from Lubbock, Buddy was largely brought up on the country influences of Flatt & Scruggs, Hank Williams and Rose Maddox to pick just three. Before he turned to the electric guitar, he picked on anything with strings from acoustic guitars to mandolins and banjos.

'FLOWER OF MY HEART' *(Buddy & Bob)*
Recorded 1954 or 1955 at Nesman Recording Studio, Wichita Falls, Texas
Personnel: Buddy Holly (guitar, vocals), Bob Montgomery (guitar, vocals), Sonny Curtis (fiddle), Larry Welborn (double bass), Don Guess (steel guitar)

One of a batch of five demos recorded by Buddy & Bob way back, but which it's never been possible to date with any accuracy. These recordings, together with some made at KDAV, first surfaced on the 1965 *Holly In The Hills* album complete with instrumental overdubs by the Fireballs. It's said that Bob Montgomery wrote this particular song for a school singing group and it is listed as 'Westerner Song of the Year' in the 1955 Lubbock High School yearbook.

It's not a composition that has inspired any covers, although Mike Berry, with the help of Sonny Curtis and Jerry Allison, used it as the opening number for *Buddy Holly – A Life In Music*, his recreation of Buddy's life story that was released on CD in the late '90s. The undubbed versions have never been released, and it's not known if they still exist.

FOLK MUSIC

In the publicity blurb for the MCA tribute CD, *Not Fade Away (Remembering Buddy Holly)*, Nick Kane, guitarist with the Mavericks states: *'Buddy's music is the kind that transcends lines. In a way it's folk music set to a rock'n'roll beat.'* Amen to that. And if there's any doubt, just trawl through the pages of this book and you'll find randomly mentioned the following folk-related artists whose lives or music touched Buddy's or *vice versa*: Harvey Andrews, George Atwood, Bobby Darin, Sandy Denny, John Denver, Bob Dylan, Nanci Griffith, Carolyn Hester, Trini Lopez, Don McLean, Joni Mitchell, the Nitty Gritty Dirt Band, Tom Rush and Steeleye Span.

'FOOL'S PARADISE'

Recorded mid-Feb. 1958 at Norman Petty Recording Studios, Clovis, New Mexico
Personnel: Buddy Holly (guitar, vocals), Jerry Allison (drums), Joe B. Mauldin (double bass)
Overdubbed February 1958: Vi Petty (piano), The Roses (backing vocals)

This was one of the many songs that were sent to Norman Petty by Southern Music Publishing, but it's the only Sonny LeGlaire & Horace Linsley composition that Buddy Holly or the Crickets ever recorded. Unusually, Sonny was a lieutenant in the US Army and she came up with the basic concept, which was then finished off by Linsley, a prolific composer whose works had been recorded by Eddie Fisher, Sarah Vaughan and a host of others.

The first time most of the listening public heard the Crickets' recording was as the flip side of 'Think It Over', which became a hit both in Britain and America. As a potential album track, it was overlooked for years before it finally appeared in the UK on the 1971 *Remember* LP.

'Fool's Paradise' is also noteworthy because it was the first time that Norman Petty used the Roses to overdub backing vocals instead of the Picks. Like the Picks, they went into the studio days after the session to overdub their parts under Petty's supervision. (Later in the year, the Roses went out on tour with the Crickets – the only time this happened.)

Several years ago, it transpired that outtakes from the original session had survived, and that three complete takes of 'Fool's Paradise' exist without the overdubs of either Vi Petty's piano or the Roses' backing vocals. As the third and final take was the one that was subsequently released, it means the song exists in four different forms (including the overdubbed version). Although the outtakes have long been available on various unauthorised releases, it remains a great pity that they have never seen an official release, although it is rumoured that this situation will be remedied soon.

'Fool's Paradise' has not inspired many covers where the singles market is concerned, but it was included on the Allisons' 1961 album, and much later by Don McLean on 1973's *Playin' Favorites*. The Crickets (with Gordon Payne) recorded it for 1993's *Double Exposure*, while more recently they teamed up with Mike Berry to perform it on their 2005 *About Time Too!* CD – actually the second time he has recorded the song. (Incidentally, the 'Fool's Paradise' in Eddie Cochran's discography is an entirely different song composed by Eddie and Hank Cochran.)

'FOOTPRINTS IN THE SNOW' *(Buddy & Bob)*
Recorded 1952 or 1953 at Buddy's home in Lubbock, Texas
Personnel: Buddy Holly (guitar, vocals), Bob Montgomery (guitar, vocals)

Only an acetate exists of Buddy and his childhood friend, Bob Montgomery, attempting the classic bluegrass song, 'Footprints In The Snow'. The number had been a country music staple since Bill Monroe's version reached No.5 on the *Billboard* 'Folk' chart back in 1946. British record collectors will know the song from the skiffle days of Johnny Duncan & The Blue Grass Boys, who had a Top 30 hit with it in 1957.

The tape certainly predates the *Holly In The Hills* material by Buddy & Bob, and both singers sound very young. It's certainly not a recording that demands to be released commercially; it is predominantly of academic interest to those dedicated fans who have to have everything by Holly. It surfaced a few years back on the 1995 4-CD Vigotone bootleg, *What You Been A-Missin'*, and more recently on the 2006 Rev-Ola CD compilation of Holly's earliest material, *Gotta Roll! The Early Recordings 1949-1955*.

US researcher Bill Griggs lists another version recorded by Buddy, Bob and two of their classmates which is thought to have been in the possession of Buddy's late mother, but whether this still exists or whether the Holley family hold other acetates isn't known.

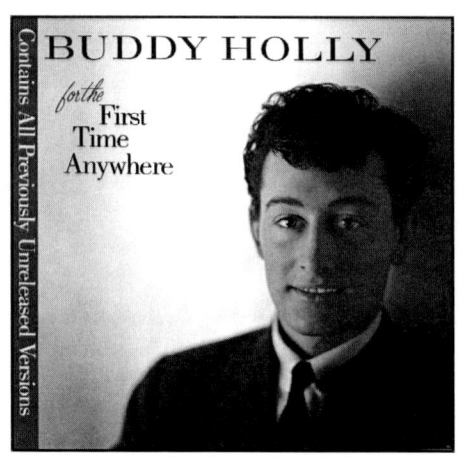

FOR THE FIRST TIME ANYWHERE *(LP)*
Rock-A-Bye Rock / Maybe Baby [first version] */ Because I Love You / I'm Gonna Set My Foot Down / Changin' All Those Changes / That's My Desire / Baby Won't You Come Out Tonight / It's Not My Fault / Brown-Eyed Handsome Man / Bo Diddley*

     One of the last great Holly albums, this 1983 MCA LP gathered together ten tracks which had never been released in their undubbed, pristine form, quite literally *'for the first time anywhere'*. That may sound boring to some, but for avid Holly fans this was a chance to finally hear certain recordings which had previously been obscured by overdubs, however well intentioned. Strictly speaking, unofficial tapes of various alternates, outtakes, etc had been circulating among Holly fans for years. However, it was now possible to hear these recordings mastered to a high standard.

     Furthermore, the photographs adorning the sleeve were also previously unseen, making the album an essential purchase. Other packages from MCA were promised, such as *Lost And Found* and *The Stereo Album*, but ongoing legal issues prevented them ever materialising. Thus *'the long waiting game'*, as an article about Holly releases was once titled, continued from the 1980s to the present. In the intervening years, an assortment of non-MCA releases has appeared including the 1995 4-CD Vigotone bootleg, *What You Been A-Missin'*, and 1986's *Something Special From Buddy Holly* on Rollercoaster. In 2007 the latter company released even more goodies on *Ohh! Annie!*, thereby ensuring that Holly's elderly fans will die happy.

LANCE FORTUNE

A British singer (real name Chris Morris), who came close to being tagged a 'one-hit wonder' when his 1960 Holly-ish sounding hit, 'Be Mine', made the British Top 10. With pizzicato strings and hiccup-like vocals, it may well have been Lance imitating Adam Faith imitating Buddy Holly.

The Four Teens.
Left to right: Joe B. Mauldin, Brownie Higgs, Terry Noland and Larry Welborn.

FOUR TEENS

The entry here ties in the fact that Joe B. Mauldin, bass player with the Crickets, actually started off playing bass with Lubbock group the Four Teens, whose lead vocalist, Terry Noland, later also had connections with Buddy Holly. Noland was subsequently replaced on vocals by Jimmie Peters. There's also a further link with Holly in that the Four Teens' guitarist, Larry Welborn, formerly played bass with Buddy & Bob and also appeared on the Crickets' hit recording of 'That'll Be The Day'.

Joe B.'s tenure with the Four Teens was only brief, but he is thought to have stayed long enough to cut a couple of tracks with them in Dallas in 1956, 'That Ain't Right' (a Noland composition) and a version of Presley's 'Hound Dog', released years later on Bear Family.

The group were quite successful and won a couple of talent contests in Lubbock, eventually appearing on the *Big D Jamboree* in Dallas (which in regional terms was a major success).

After Joe B.'s departure, the Four Teens cut 'Spark Plug' *b/w* 'Go Little Go Cat' for Challenge Records, a hit-making label, though sadly not in this instance. Needless to say it is now very collectable.

CONNIE FRANCIS

Born Concetta Rosa Maria Franconero in 1938, Connie Francis was a contemporary of Holly's but it seems unlikely they met, partly as her possessive father famously shielded her from appearing on the large rock'n'roll packages of the day (although, conversely, she did crop up in the occasional rock'n'roll flick).

So why is she mentioned here? Well, having always been an artist who made innovative recordings, and having released a string of 'genre' albums over the years (folk, country, Spanish, Jewish favourites, etc), Connie recorded a Holly tribute album in 1996 with assistance from Sonny Curtis and Stuart Colman. Essentially a collection of Holly/Cricket covers, *With Love To Buddy* also included a couple of Holly medleys for good measure. Cricket Sonny Curtis played lead and rhythm guitar throughout and added the harmony vocals to 'Love Is Strange'. The album is also notable for having a female singer interpret 'Peggy Sue'! Not, of course, as a gay anthem, but instead with new lyrics (courtesy of Sonny) which imply that Peggy Sue was the girl who stole the singer's man.

Connie has had a marathon list of gold records, but surprisingly hasn't yet made it into the Rock and Roll Hall of Fame. Meanwhile her private life has been laced with tragedy which saw her quit the music business for years.

FREDDIE & THE DREAMERS

Freddie Garrity (1936-2005) and his group sprang to fame in 1963 shortly after the Beatles, but unlike most of his contemporaries he didn't originate from Liverpool, but from Manchester. Sporting prominent horn-rimmed glasses, Freddie wasn't afraid to occasionally hiccup his vocals or cavort around the stage, which made him hugely entertaining to watch. He even tried to start his own dance craze with 'Do The Freddie', but it never seriously rivalled the Twist.

Freddie & The Dreamers had three years of real chart success in the mid-'60s including an American No.1, and included versions of Holly's 'Early In The Morning' and 'It Doesn't Matter Anymore' on their second UK album, *Sing Along Party*, as well as on the best-selling US Mercury compilation, *Freddie & The Dreamers*. Along with the (post-Holly) Crickets, they were also featured in the 1963 film, *Just For Fun*.

Sadly, Freddy had to retire from performing in the '90s and died from emphysema in 2005. Reference books often erroneously quoted a later birth date for him, and it was a surprise to learn that he had entered his 70th year.

ALAN FREED

While there were others, Alan Freed (1922-65) will forever remain famous as the white deejay who championed black music and broke rock'n'roll in the USA. Incredibly influential, he promoted live shows, appeared in movies and even led his own band.

A hot act thanks to their chart success with 'That'll Be The Day' and 'Oh Boy!', the Crickets were booked to appear on Freed's *Christmas Holiday of Stars* show in 1957, and on his *Big Beat Show* in 1958 – a star-studded package also featuring Jerry Lee Lewis, Chuck Berry, Frankie Lymon & The Teenagers, Larry Williams and many other big names of the day. Several photos of Alan Freed and Buddy Holly taken on the tour exist, one of them with Larry Williams. Freed also recorded an excellent radio interview with Buddy in the WNEW-TV studios on 23 September 1958, and this is available on the 2002 Rollercoaster CD EP, *That's What They Tell Me – That's What They Say*.

Sadly, in 1959 everything began to unravel. Freed admitted taking 'payola' (money in exchange for playing records) – at that time a widespread, and hitherto accepted practice – when other, equally obvious candidates simply denied the charges. A scapegoat for the industry, he was found guilty but only received a suspended sentence. Despite this, it all proved too much for him and he died prematurely, a broken man.

Freed's fascinating story is recounted in John A. Jackson's well-researched biography, *Big Beat Heat*, and far less accurately in the 1977 *American Hot Wax* movie. Still greatly revered for his contribution to the world of music, Freed was included in the first cohort of inductees to the Rock and Roll Hall of Fame in 1986.

The late, great Bobby Fuller.

BOBBY FULLER FOUR

If ever a singer aspired to emulate Buddy Holly and the Crickets, it was surely Bobby Fuller, and it's a supreme irony that his life ended prematurely and so tragically when he finally had the musical world at his feet.

Born near El Paso, Texas in 1943, all Bobby Fuller ever wanted to do was make music and, more specifically, West Texas rock'n'roll! And that he certainly did. He made his first studio recordings in 1961, and even briefly recorded at Clovis the year after ('Gently My Love' *b/w* 'My Heart Jumped', released on Yucca), but first came to prominence in 1966 with his Top 10 version of the Sonny Curtis classic, 'I Fought The Law'. He'd originally recorded the song for the small Exeter label in 1964, but it was his 1965 remake for Mustang that became the hit.

Having taken a 1961 song written by a Cricket high into the charts, he then went one better by recording a Buddy Holly number, 'Love's Made A Fool Of You', as a follow-up later that year. This was also a hit, though it peaked lower at No.26.

Still in the charts and following national TV appearances on *Shindig!* and *Shebang*, Fuller was found dead at the age of 23 in mysterious circumstances. It looked suspiciously like murder (gasoline asphyxiation), but for reasons that remain obscure the case was not investigated. His death was deemed a suicide, though his friends have never accepted that verdict.

Fuller never made any secret of his affection for Holly's music, and at one point sent a tape to Mr & Mrs Holley in Lubbock that they passed on to Norman Petty. It resulted in him travelling to Clovis to record, but without any commercial success. After his death it came to light that Petty had written to Fuller congratulating him on his hits and suggesting that he returned to Clovis again, but sadly this would never happen. Later, it became apparent that Bobby had recorded much of the Holly/Crickets songbook, either as completed masters or as demos, which resulted in a posthumous compilation album, *Memories of Buddy Holly*, being released in 1984.

Apart from these obvious connections with Holly, it's also worth mentioning that Fuller was managed by Bob Keane, who owned Mustang – the same Bob Keane who discovered Ritchie Valens and gave Sam Cooke his first commercial success.

BILLY FURY

Ronald Wycherly *aka* Billy Fury (1941-83) was a contemporary of Cliff Richard and Adam Faith, but unlike them was famously signed to pop guru Larry Parnes and branded with one of his silly names (Fury, Wilde, Power, Eager, Gentle, etc). However, Billy had a magnetism and sex appeal that raised him above many of his stablemates and propelled him to a lengthy chart career, as well as a couple of fairly successful '60s films, *Play It Cool* and *I've Gotta Horse*.

Direct links with Buddy Holly are thin, but later on in his career Fury turned to Holly's songbook and recorded 'Well... All Right', 'Maybe Baby', 'I'm Gonna Love You Too' and, with a similar feel, Tommy Roe's 'Sheila'. His career had peaked by the '70s, but he went back into films, notably playing a rock'n'roll singer in 1973's *That'll Be The Day*.

Fury was out of the limelight for some time, but revived his career in the early '80s. Sadly, his congentital heart condition caught up with him and he died in 1983 aged just 41. Fondly remembered by many, most of his recordings (like Holly's) remain in catalogue and a biography, *His Wondrous Story*, was released on DVD in 2007. This entry can't finish without a mention of his first album, *The Sound of Fury*, which was said by many to be the best British rock'n'roll album ever issued, and much of which was self-penned. He was a genuine great.

G

The irrepressible Snuff Garrett.

SNUFF GARRETT

A contemporary of Buddy Holly, Thomas 'Snuff' Garrett (born 1938) was originally from Dallas and had first met Holly and the others back in 1956 when he was a deejay in the Lubbock area. Perhaps it came from that early kinship, but having moved to California to head up the A&R wing of Liberty, he signed the post-Holly Crickets after their involvement with Coral came to an end in the early '60s. He went on to produce a string of British hits for them in 1963-64, but had noticeably less success in the USA.

Earlier, Snuff had also kept in touch with Buddy and it seems likely that he would have been involved with Holly's plan to set up a recording studio in Lubbock (see **PRISM RECORDS**). By a tragic coincidence, Garrett was broadcasting on KSYD in Wichita Falls on the day of the fatal plane crash and he had the heartbreaking job of doing a phone link-up with Jerry Allison, Joe B. Mauldin and Norman Petty. A tape of that emotional broadcast survives.

Of course, Garrett's career didn't just revolve around Holly and the Crickets, and he made many albums under his own name and with others, including *Flamenco Guitar* with Sonny Curtis. He was also the musical director on several movie soundtracks. He is now retired and thought to be resident in the Houston area.

PEGGY SUE GERRON – *See* **PEGGY SUE**

GIANT *(LP)*
Love Is Strange / Good Rockin' Tonight / Blue Monday / Have You Ever Been Lonely / Slippin' And Slidin' / You're The One / Dearest / Smokey Joe's Café / Ain't Got No Home / Holly Hop

Released in the USA in January 1969, this was one of the last great Buddy Holly album releases as far as fans were concerned, as it contained largely new material. It was immensely exciting to finally hear songs that we'd only heard rumoured to exist. We also discovered that 'I'm Just A Lonely Boy' was actually Clarence 'Frogman' Henry's 'Ain't Got No Home' (the original master tape had been incorrectly marked).

The drawback was that, as an album concept, it was extremely uneven, mixing early demos with recordings left behind on tape in the last months of the singer's life. So, the ballad 'Love Is Strange' (January '59) is literally followed by the garage-like run-through on 'Good Rockin' Tonight' (late '56).

To give Norman Petty his due, the heavy overdubbing was probably an attempt to make the album seem homogeneous and commercial in the market of the day, but on that score it was only partially successful. Chartwise, it was on the *Record Retailer* lists for a six-week period in the UK. There was also the irony of listening to an album produced by Buddy's former manager, when it was common knowledge that the singer had split from him in late 1958, and his music would have headed in a different direction.

JIMMY GILMER

The Fireballs entry mentions the huge US No.1 the group had with 'Sugar Shack' which featured Jimmy Gilmer's vocals. It was amusing to discover that Norman Petty's organ (or, to be more specific, Solovox) was added to the finished track – to the dismay of the group at the time – although it transformed the song and may have been the reason it went to No.1.

Gilmer went on to record a tribute album to Holly entitled *Buddy's Buddy*. It's an album that listeners either love or hate, as all the songs are given unusual arrangements – at times even the melodies are disguised – and thus they bear little relation to Holly's originals. He also took part in the Fireballs' overdubbing session for 'You're The One'.

Jimmy Gilmer left the music business in 1969 to go into artist management, but briefly returned to the stage in 2005, when he joined the Fireballs for their performance at the *Clovis Music Festival*.

LOU GIORDANO

Louis Patsy Giordano (1929-69) was a minor recording artist whom Holly and his pal Phil Everly took under their wings. They both produced and played on his 1958 Brunswick single, 'Don't Cha Know' b/w 'Stay Close To Me' – the latter an original Holly composition, and one of the few he never recorded himself. The record deal came about after he was introduced to Buddy and Phil by a mutual friend, Joey Villa of the Royal Teens. Sadly, neither side made any impression on the charts.

It is known that Buddy was still in touch with Giordano during early 1959, and maybe they would have undertaken more work together. It was also Giordano who phoned Buddy's wife, Maria Elena, on 3 February 1959 and told her not to switch on the radio.

For years, not much was known about Lou until his family was finally located in 1980. The singer often went under the name 'Lou Jordan', and besides doing stage and TV work had record releases on the Jubilee, Josie and 20th Century-Fox labels.

Lou passed away at the age of 40 following kidney failure. He should not be confused with the Boston, Massachusetts punk producer of the same name from the 1980s.

'GIRL ON MY MIND'

Recorded July 1956 at Bradley's Barn Studio, Nashville, Tennessee
Personnel: Buddy Holly (guitar, vocals), Sonny Curtis (guitar), Jerry Allison (drums), Don Guess (double bass)

This song was one of five recorded by Holly at his second session in Nashville in 1956. Unlike his previous visit, Buddy was able to bring along Sonny Curtis, Jerry Allison and Don Guess to help out. This time, all the songs – except for 'Ting-A-Ling' – were written by group members, and this one was down to bassist Don Guess. It has to be said that the song is a bit pedestrian, if somewhat hypnotic, though it's little surprise that it wasn't put out by Decca at the time. In fact, nothing from this session was released – hence Buddy's phone call to Paul Cohen (see **PAUL COHEN**). However, two years later, and with recordings by both Holly and the Crickets charting, Decca changed their minds and issued 'Girl On My Mind' as a single in the USA.

The first time British fans got to hear Buddy's Nashville recordings was through the posthumous release of a pair of Brunswick EP's in mid-1959: precious 7-inch packages that are today highly collectable.

In 1984, the Picks overdubbed backing vocals onto this recording (see **OVERDUBS** and **PICKS** for more info). (Incidentally – for completists only – the released take with the studio engineer announcing *'Take 3'* is now available on the 2007 Rollercoaster CD, *Ohh! Annie!*.)

Covers of the song are particularly hard to find, but a home recording by David Box from 1962 was released a few years ago by Rollercoaster on a Box retrospective.

GLASSES

It may seem surprising that the subject of a singer wearing glasses should feature here at all, but back in the '50s, Holly's stance was thought to be quite daring and he was the first overtly bespectacled rock'n'roll singer in town. As John Lennon once famously observed, *'He made it okay to wear spectacles on stage.'*

Pretty soon, Buddy wasn't the only artist with glasses – and some wore frames for effect, even if their eyesight didn't require it. One such was pianist Reg Dwight, who emerged in the early '70s as Elton John and parodied the whole genre with ever more outlandish styles. New wave artist Elvis Costello also got in on the act by wearing Holly-style glasses *and* daring to appropriate the name of the King.

As for Holly himself, he needed glasses and was said to have 20/800 vision in both eyes. He did briefly switch to contact lenses, but they evidently didn't work for him. In 1980, the pair of glasses Buddy had with him on the night of the plane crash were discovered in police archives and returned to his next of kin.

GLOTTAL STOP

The term 'glottal stop' is occasionally used to describe the vocal mannerism that Buddy Holly employed in such a unique way, although one needs to consult a dictionary to understand what that means. Better perhaps to stick to 'hiccup' as a description for the innovative Holly gimmick that first surfaced during the '50s when he cut his original demo of 'Love Me'. Certainly, Buddy's stuttering treatment of the initial *'Well'* in 'Rave On' was unprecedented in mainstream pop, introducing excitement and tension from the song's opening bars.

The author doesn't pretend to know how it originated, although it's been said that he used the hiccup to bring a smile to the face of Norman Petty behind the glass screen. Many would later try to copy Buddy's style, but for him the vocal trick seemed natural and effortless. Work your way through the Buddy Holly popular songbook from 'Everyday' to 'It Doesn't Matter Anymore' from his last studio session if you have any doubts.

ARTHUR GODFREY'S TALENT SCOUTS

In these days of wall-to-wall television and non-stop trawling for talent (currently *The X Factor, America/Britain's Got Talent, et al*), it's salutary to note that the Crickets also went down this route, although with far less hullabaloo and scant success.

Sometime in early 1957, before 'That'll Be The Day' had broken out, they tried to take a short-cut to fame by auditioning for *Arthur Godfrey's Talent Scouts*, one of several such shows of the era. On pre-Interstate roads, they'd motored north to Amarillo, Texas and, from memory, it's said they performed a Little Richard number, but never got asked back. They were in good company, for a year or two earlier Elvis had also failed to impress the Simon Cowell of his day. But many acts did get their big break on the show, and for every surprising failure there were successes like Patsy Cline, Johnny Burnette and Guy Mitchell.

JOHN GOLDROSEN

The pioneer biographer of Buddy Holly, whose 1975 book, *Buddy Holly: His Life and Music*, was rightly acclaimed as the first and last word on the singer and has stood the test of time remarkably well. What is particularly astonishing is that Goldrosen, a Harvard graduate, wasn't a professional writer at that point, but decided to take two years out to research the singer's life, about which, at the time, very little was known outside of what a few dedicated fans had uncovered. This meant John had to travel almost the length of the country from his home in Massachusetts to Texas and New Mexico in order to interview as many of Buddy's friends, family and fellow musicians as possible. Since those days, the book has been revised with the help of Holly expert John Beecher and republished as *Remembering Buddy*. John Goldrosen occasionally attends Holly tribute events in the Clear Lake area and remains the most unassuming of men, as well as one of the most inspirational.

'GONE'
Recorded late 1956 at Buddy's home in Lubbock, Texas
Personnel: Buddy Holly (guitar, vocals), Jerry Allison (drums), unknown (double bass)

This song first appeared with overdubs by the Fireballs on the 1964 *Showcase* album, almost eight years after Holly recorded it as a demo. In 1986, Rollercoaster issued the undubbed original, as well as a previously unknown alternate version on *Something Special From Buddy Holly*. In 2007, the same company came up with yet another milestone release, *Ohh! Annie!* which included both of these plus a third demo version. It's interesting to hear all of Buddy's attempts in the raw, although, in the author's opinion, the addition of an overdubbed guitar line on the *Showcase* version gives the number a tension that the sparse, undoctored versions lack. Of course, this is a personal opinion and views will differ.

But just who was the composer, Smokey Rogers, and just what was it that attracted Buddy to this rather sad, if beautiful song originally?

Well, the name is surely a giveaway: Rogers was a Western swing banjoist and singer born in 1927, who had had spells with Spade Cooley and Tex Williams – both famous names in the history of C&W. In 1949, he had a Top 10 hillbilly hit with 'A Little Bird Told Me', whilst his greatest success in commercial terms was as the composer of 'Gone', a million-seller for Ferlin Husky in 1957.

Interestingly, Holly's recording pre-dates Husky's hit by virtue of the fact he was already familiar with an earlier version recorded by Husky back in 1952 under the pseudonym 'Terry Preston'. In 1957, Buddy also backed Gary Tollett on his cover of 'Gone'.

'GOOD ROCKIN' TONIGHT'
Recorded late 1956 at Buddy's home in Lubbock
Personnel: Buddy Holly (guitar, vocals), Jerry Allison (drums)

This is a number that Holly and his friends would have been very familiar with as an R&B hit, as well as in even more rocked-up form by Elvis, who regularly featured it in his early shows and also recorded it for Sun in 1954. The boys doubtless saw him perform it on stage in Lubbock and it comes as no surprise to find it amongst the posthumous demos that have turned up for release (Jerry Allison has confirmed that he and Buddy cut it because they liked Elvis's version). It first appeared, heavily overdubbed, on the 1969 *Giant* album. Years later, in 1986, the undubbed version surfaced on the *Something Special From Buddy Holly* album on Rollercoaster.

The song was written in 1948 by Roy Brown, and any self-respecting rock'n'roll singer has not only sung it, but probably recorded it too (Perkins, Jerry Lee and Ricky Nelson to name just three). That said, it's quite ironic that the number only made the US Top 50 pop chart via Pat Boone, who was in every way the antithesis of raunchy rock'n'roll.

'GOTTA GET YOU NEAR ME BLUES' *(Buddy & Bob)*
Recorded 1954 or 1955 at Nesman Recording Studio, Wichita Falls, Texas
Personnel: Buddy Holly (guitar, vocals), Bob Montgomery (guitar, vocals), Sonny Curtis (fiddle), Don Guess (double bass)

Buddy & Bob recorded a demo of this early Bob Montgomery composition at Wichita Falls. It first appeared in overdubbed form on the 1965 *Holly In The Hills* album, while the undubbed version was included on the 1995 4-CD Vigotone bootleg, *What You Been A-Missin'*. On the latter, we get to hear a bit more country guitar-picking, and more of Sonny Curtis's fiddle too. It's the first really uptempo number that Holly recorded, and was the forerunner of what was to come. As with almost all the very early demos, this did not inspire any cover versions.

'GOTTA TRAVEL ON'

This classic story-in-song was said to have originated in the British Isles in the nineteenth century, but it took Billy Grammer from Benton, Illinois to take it almost to the top of the *Billboard* 'Hot 100' and earn himself a gold disc. It entered the chart a fortnight before the *Winter Dance Party* got underway and Waylon Jennings remembers that Buddy opened each show either with this number, or the bluegrass-flavoured 'Salty Dog Blues' (sadly, he never got to record either). Certainly, the words of the song (*'Well I've stayed around and played around this old town too long'*) seem so apt, that it's almost as though Buddy had a premonition of what was soon to happen.

Grammer himself went on to have a long career in country music, appearing on the *Grand Ole Opry* and scoring the occasional country hit throughout the '60s. Born in 1925, he is still alive at this writing. He reprised the number on the 2004 compilation, *Stay All Night: Buddy Holly's Country Roots*.

GRAND OLE OPRY

The symbol of live country music in the USA, but, although Buddy and his compatriots would have tuned in to the weekly broadcasts on WSM, it's not somewhere he yearned to appear. Indeed, the nearest he got to the venue was in 1956, when, in the space of just ten months, he visited Nashville three times to record at Decca's studios. But did he visit the Opry in his spare time, one wonders? Some of the musicians who played on the sessions such as Grady Martin, Floyd Cramer, Owen Bradley, and his brother Harold, certainly had connections there.

More likely venues for Holly to aspire to were the *Big D Jamboree* in Dallas (he appeared on it just once) and the *Louisiana Hayride* in Shreveport, Louisiana, both of which have separate entries in this book.

However, it needs to be mentioned here that, before he hit the big time, Buddy appeared on many shows as a support act for touring country stars such as Hank Thompson, Wanda Jackson and George Jones. Later on, his 'Peggy Sue' was briefly listed in the *Cash Box* Top 20 Country chart, while *Billboard* proclaimed that he was *'the latest rocker to hit the country charts'*. Buddy certainly had a lot of country in him (as well as rhythm & blues... and rock'n'roll... and soul).

RICK GRECH

Bass player Rick (sometimes 'Ric') Grech joined the Crickets in 1972 at the suggestion of his friend, Glen D. Hardin. A member of the touring band, he also appeared on several of the group's early '70s albums including *Bubblegum, Bop, Ballads & Boogies* (which, unusually for a Crickets album was recorded in Britain), *Remnants* and *A Long Way From Lubbock*.

Although thought of as British, Grech was actually born in Bordeaux, France in 1946, but spent his musical life based in Britain during a high-flying career that saw him linked with a roll-call of famous bands from Family to Blind Faith, and artists as diverse as Muddy Waters and Gram Parsons.

Although he ceased to be a Cricket on a continuous basis in 1974, he occasionally sat in with the group up until 1988. Sadly, Grech had a drug habit he couldn't shake and died prematurely of liver failure in early 1990 at the age of just 43.

REN GREVATT

A staff writer for years with *Billboard* magazine in the USA, Ren Grevatt first came to the notice of most overseas fans after penning the sleevenotes for the best-selling *Buddy Holly Story* album in 1959. He peppered his tract with a few interesting quotes, asserting that Holly was a wild, frantic rockabilly with a Tex-Mex sound – a good soundbite, though not strictly true. Grevatt later had the unenviable job of penning a similar eulogy to Patsy Cline four years later.

NANCI GRIFFITH

Classed as an honorary Cricket these days, Nanci Griffith first teamed up with the group during the mid-'90s, when they played back-up on several tracks on her 1997 *Blue Roses From The Moons* album and also accompanied her on her 1997 world tour, a highlight of which were the duets she performed with Sonny Curtis. She's formed a lasting link with the group that culminated in her performing 'Heartbeat' on the 2004 *Crickets And Their Buddies* album.

Born in Seguin near Austin, Texas in 1953, Griffith is on record as idolising Holly's music whilst growing up, and, although her main influences are in the folk field, she treasured the chance to team up with the Crickets when the opportunity arose.

She came to national prominence in the '70s after being discovered by Carolyn Hester, and her success led *Rolling Stone* magazine to acclaim her *'the Queen of Folkabilly'*. Having come to the fore with her interpretations of others' material, Griffith has increasingly turned to her own songs, and along the way has also picked up a couple of Grammies. It's a pleasure to include her name in this book along with the aforementioned Carolyn Hester, another folk artist who found Holly's work so inspirational.

BILL GRIGGS

A major name in the exploration of all things Holly. A native of Connecticut with a musical pedigree, Griggs relocated to Lubbock, Texas to pursue his love of rock'n'roll, West Texas music and Buddy Holly in particular. He has organised fan conventions and associated events over the years, and later founded the *Rockin' 50s* magazine. In 1997, he produced *Buddy Holly Day-By-Day*, a five-volume series of booklets cataloguing (as far as possible) how Buddy's life progressed from cradle to grave.

DON GROOM

An English drummer who had the unexpected thrill of sitting in with the Crickets on their November 1962 UK tour (which they jointly headlined with Bobby Vee). Jerry Allison had dropped out because he was on the reservist list for the US Air Force at the time. He had hoped to be granted leave, but at the last minute the Cuban missile crisis escalated and his request was denied. Consequently, he missed out on a major tour – much to his chagrin. While in Britain, the group also filmed an appearance for the *Just For Fun* movie, and again Don Groom was the man with the sticks.

Groom's other main musical association was as a member of Mike Berry's backing group, the Outlaws, and he also backed-up several other British artists later in the '60s. A few years ago, *Crickets File* revealed that he was playing with a jazz outfit in the Brighton area.

DON GUESS

During his Buddy & Bob days, and up until Joe B. Mauldin joined the Crickets, Holly was usually accompanied on bass by either Larry Welborn or Don Guess. When he was asked to put together a support band for a Sonny James tour and a couple of Hank Thompson tours in 1956, Guess was the natural choice for the slap-bass. Even as late as 1956, it was he who played on all of Holly's Nashville sessions – the only Lubbockite to be used throughout.

Nashville, January 1956.
Left to right: Thelma King (of Cedarwood Publishing), Sonny Curtis, Buddy Holly, Don Guess, Sonny's brother Dean Curtis and Thelma's sister Joanna McClanahan..

Guess was born in 1937, just north of Abilene, Texas. His family first moved to New Mexico, and then to Lubbock, where he became acquainted with Holly at high school through their shared interest in music. His older sisters sang in a gospel group and worked at a Clovis radio station, and it's almost certain that Buddy first heard of Norman Petty via Don, although several others have claimed it was through them.

Unfortunately, by the time Holly got his big break, Guess was playing elsewhere and concentrating on songwriting. Although he spent part of his life in music and cut occasional singles for local labels, he failed to make any real headway in the business. One of his most intriguing recordings was a tribute issued in the wake of Senator Robert Kennedy's death in 1968 entitled 'Kennedy, Lincoln, Martin Luther King'.

Things may well have been different had Buddy lived, as it seems certain that Guess was one of those he intended to link up with again in 1959, when he got his proposed new recording facility up and running in Lubbock (see **PRISM RECORDS**). As it was, Guess left the music business and turned to running a successful insurance business in El Paso. He died of cancer in 1992 at the age of 55.

GUITARS

Buddy began playing guitar as a child at the feet of his older brothers, Larry and Travis Holley. His first instrument was a second-hand Harmony guitar, bought for him by his father. Harmony were an old, established company and the biggest producer of guitars in the USA at the time. A photo from 1955 shows Buddy holding a Stratotone H44 model.

By the time Holly met up with Jerry Allison in his teens, he was toting an electric Gibson Les Paul Gold Top, but switched to a Fender Stratocaster as soon as he could borrow enough money from brother Larry, and that was the iconic model he would stick with and help to popularise.

Unsurprisingly for a proficient guitarist, Holly owned many different guitars over the years including a Gibson J45 acoustic (for which he made a hand-tooled leather cover and strap, personalised with his name), a Gibson J200, an Epiphone (which he usually played in his Buddy & Bob days), a Guild F50 Navarre, and even a Gretsch – the make that Eddie Cochran and Bo Diddley favoured. The above list is probably not exhaustive, and of course there's also the Hofner model that Buddy purchased during his UK tour and presented to Des O'Connor (see **DES O'CONNOR**).

Perhaps more interesting than any technical stuff is Waylon Jennings's comment that Buddy *'was a natural rhythm player'* and that he developed a technique which enabled him to play a mix of rhythm and lead (as on 'Peggy Sue'). It's also worth mentioning that Holly was also an adept banjo and mandolin player – instruments he'd often played as a child.

See also **FENDER STRATOCASTER**.

H

BOB HALE

Bob Hale was a 25-year-old deejay on KRIB in Mason City, Iowa when he came to emcee the *Winter Dance Party* show at the Surf Ballroom in Clear Lake on the evening of 2 February 1959. It was a routine job he'd done before: spin some discs, intersperse the music with a bit of patter and introduce the acts. The show went amazingly well and there was no hint of the tragedy that was to come, though a weather front had been predicted to sweep in around midnight. Holly evidently played drums behind some of the other headliners that night, as his drummer, Carl Bunch, was hospitalised with frostbite.

Needless to say, the memories of that fateful night are etched on Hale's mind forever. An ebullient individual, he still lives in and around the Mason City area.

Just an amusing postscript: in an earlier edition of this book, the author stated that Bob Hale was *'still alive'* – as though it were a surprise! While signing my copy at the Surf a few years ago, a laughing Bob added: *'Darned right I'm alive.'*

BILL HALEY

William John Clifton Haley (1925-81) was certainly the most unusual of rock'n'roll heroes, but nevertheless is still revered by many. Sightless in one eye and a good ten years older than his contemporaries, he came to fame from a country music background (Bill Haley & The Saddlemen). Unusually for a country act, he hailed from Michigan in the North, and shaped a new music that was a unique hybrid of country and R&B, and would take the world by storm in 1955. Certainly, he must have been doing something right, as copycat groups by the dozen soon sprang up.

But Buddy Holly and Bill Haley, the inventor of the 'kiss curl', are unlikely bedfellows, so why does he make an appearance here? Well, on 14 October 1955, Bill Haley & His Comets were booked to headline a show at the Fair Park Coliseum in Lubbock. Propping up the bill were Buddy & Bob (and Larry Welborn), still striving to get their foot on the ladder.

Although Haley turned up in good time, it transpired that the Comets and their instruments had been delayed and wouldn't make curtain-up. And so it came to pass that Buddy & Bob became Haley's

Comets for part of the evening until his band showed up – a story Haley later loved to recount.

Buddy in particular managed to impress Nashville talent scout Eddie Crandall, who was present in the audience and recommended him to Jim Denny, who in turn got him a contract with Decca. And the rest, as they say, is history.

After the Crickets became chart-toppers, they appeared with Haley and his Comets on Harry K. Smythe's 1958 *Big Gold Record Stars In Person* tour along with Jerry Lee Lewis and the Everly Brothers.

Haley continued to tour and make music until his health deteriorated in the '80s. He died in Harlingen, Texas of a heart attack at the age of 55. He was inducted into the Rock and Roll Hall of Fame in 1987, the year after Buddy Holly.

BEN HALL

Ben Hall was born near Wichita Falls, Texas, and during a lengthy career was the leader of a country band, a composer, a deejay, a manager, a record producer, and probably a couple of other things besides. He also wrote a couple of the best of the early numbers recorded by Holly, and Buddy and Sonny Curtis would occasionally sit in with Ben Hall & The Ramblers before 'That'll Be The Day' exploded.

'Blue Days, Black Nights', written by Hall, deserves a special mention, as it wound up as the 'A' side of Holly's first-ever single – both in Britain and America – although with little reaction aside from some good reviews. Buddy had approached him for material shortly before leaving for his first Decca session and Hall had given him the song. It was one of the four numbers that Buddy cut in January 1956, and is probably as good as anything else he got to record in Nashville (see **NASHVILLE SESSIONS**).

Another song, 'It's Not My Fault', was co-written by Hall with steel guitarist Weldon Myrick, and remained in the vaults for seven years until it was released in overdubbed form on the 1963 *Reminiscing* album.

Several years ago, it was discovered that Buddy and Sonny Curtis (on guitar and fiddle respectively) played on a couple of demos that Ben Hall had cut at local Lubbock radio stations: 'All For Loving You' at KSEL, and 'Rose Of Monterey' at KDAV. Both numbers were penned by Hall and are pleasant enough country fare, as well as obviously required listening for Holly completists. Both cuts may be found on the 1993 Rollercoaster CD, *Country Ways And Rockin' Days*.

From around 1958 to 1964, Hall ran his own record label, Gaylo, and also operated a modest recording studio in Big Spring, Texas. Among the many recordings made there was the Newbeats' 1964 Hickory smash, 'Bread And Butter'. In the 1980s, he moved to Nashville and ended up designing recording studios for others.

'HALLELUJAH I LOVE HER SO'
Recorded February 1958 prob. backstage at Fort Hesterley Armory, Tampa, Florida
Personnel: Jerry Lee Lewis (piano, vocals), Buddy Holly (guitar)

Ray Charles recorded two of Buddy Holly's all-time favourite songs at the same 1955 Atlantic recording session: 'Hallelujah I Love Her So' and 'Drown In My Own Tears' (composed by Henry Glover), both of which became huge R&B hits in 1956. However, Buddy never got to record either of them in the studio. But – and it's a neat coincidence – brief snippets of Holly and Jerry Lee Lewis jamming backstage on both songs have been found, though they are far too fragmentary and poorly-recorded to be considered for normal commercial release. The interest lies in knowing for a fact that this is the sort of material Holly loved.

GEORGE HAMILTON IV
Born in 1937, country singer George Hamilton IV was a close contemporary of Buddy Holly, whom he met when they toured together in the late '50s (they had mutual friends in Don and Phil Everly). Hamilton has been interviewed several times on the subject of Holly, and has always spoken most eloquently about him, stressing the contrast between his onstage charisma and his quiet offstage demeanour. After enjoying a lengthy career as a country hit-maker up to the late '70s, Hamilton became a member of the Nashville's *Grand Ole Opry* before turning to Christian music to spread his message. His son, George Hamilton V, has likewise gone on to enjoy a successful career in country music.

TOMMY HANCOCK
Hailing from the Lubbock area, Tommy Hancock was a fixture on the local music scene when Buddy, Sonny and the other boys were growing up. He led his own group, Tommy Hancock & The Roadside Playboys, but is probably better remembered as the owner of the Cotton Club, one of two niteries he ran in Lubbock. Sonny Curtis recalls that he played some gigs with Tommy's band during 1956, and thinks

Buddy probably did too.

For a bit of fun, Hancock also founded the Society for Unappreciated Musicians and, as guitar pickers, both Holly and Curtis became founder members, their membership cards entitling them to free admission at Tommy's establishments.

Later on, in 1958, Hancock teamed up with ex-Cricket Niki Sullivan and backed him on his first Dot release, 'It's All Over' *b/w* 'Three Steps To Heaven' (not the Cochran song).

Hancock's family is replete with talent, and his wife, Charlene Condray, together with their daughters, started a popular local group, the Texana Dames several years ago. They live in the Austin area and Tommy remains a larger-than-life character who, Sonny insists, has been a great influence on many of the musicians from the Lubbock area.

CLYDE HANKINS

A musician from the Lubbock area, Clyde Hankins briefly tried to teach Buddy guitar, but the youngster was in too much of a hurry and quit. Sonny Curtis claims that Hankins was the single biggest influence on his own guitar style. He occasionally recorded at Clovis, leading a jazz-style combo of which George Atwood was also a member. Amongst their recordings was an album titled *Swing Fever*, featuring tracks like 'Moonglow' and 'Margie', which was produced by Norman Petty and came out in 1959.

JACK HANSEN

For the majority of fans, the name of Jack Hansen is just that – a name only, and one that didn't crop up until talk of Holly's posthumous recordings arose and it became known that the overdubs of the December 1958 Apartment Tapes were carried out under the direction of Hansen in New York.

In fact, it was Hansen who'd helped to organise Holly's first Pythian Temple session for 'Early In The Morning' in June 1958. He was also involved in masterminding Holly's final studio recordings (the 'True Love Ways' session of October 1958), so he was probably the natural choice to work on the tapes in mid-1959 when the pressure was on to get a new release into the shops. 'Peggy Sue Got Married' *b/w* 'Crying, Waiting, Hoping' came out on 20 July 1959 in the US, and a month later in Britain.

Hansen died in 1977.

CHARLES HARDIN

In case anyone isn't aware, Buddy Holly was christened Charles Hardin Holley, and many compositions from early 1957 were listed under the name 'Charles Hardin', rather than under his real name. It was important for a time that Holly's name didn't appear on record, as, from the start of 1956, he was contracted to Decca and, more importantly, his music publishing was tied up with Cedarwood in Nashville – complications he needed to circumnavigate for a while.

GLEN D. HARDIN

Glen D. Hardin hails from the small town of Wallington, just outside Lubbock, where he was born in 1939. He knew Buddy and Sonny Curtis from way back, although he never got to make music with them in the '50s. His link here is mainly through his association with the post-Holly Crickets, whom he met up with again in the '60s when Jerry Allison lured him to California, where the group were then based.

Hardin is a consummate musician and his CV is amazing, although it's only possible to give a flavour of it here. His most notable association must surely have been his time with Elvis, when he played keyboards and doubled as musical arranger from 1970 to the end of 1975. One of his favourite memories is of preparing the arrangement for 'The Wonder Of You', a gold record and one of Presley's personal favourites. In monetary terms, it only earned Glen a one-off fee, but it increased his musical stature, and ultimately his earning capacity, no end.

After leaving Elvis (he felt things were getting very stale), Hardin spent time with Gram Parsons and Emmylou Harris as a founder member of her legendary Hot Band before teaming up with John Denver in an association that was to last for almost ten years.

In amongst these edited highlights, he still managed to link up with the Crickets intermittently over the years and was responsible for composing several of their songs including the 'Peggy Sue'-like 'Teardrops Fall Like Rain' (which he co-wrote with Jerry Allison).

Several other artists have recorded his material over the years including Rick Nelson, Dean Martin and Bobby Vee. Never really comfortable as a front-man, Hardin has contributed an awful lot to the overall music scene, even if his name is little more than a footnote to many. In recent years, he has performed on the Elvis *TCB* tours.

'HAVE YOU EVER BEEN LONELY'
Recorded late 1956 at Buddy's home in Lubbock, Texas
Personnel: Buddy Holly (guitar, vocals), Jerry Allison (drums), unknown (double bass)

Tucked away amongst the staple tunes of the era that Holly recorded are a few that were no doubt attempted as much to please his mother as anything else. Top of that list was probably 'Wait Till The Sun Shines, Nellie', while the one shown here runs that close. Certainly, he attempted it at least three times during the one session, and the overdubbed version, first saw the light of day on the 1969 *Giant* album.

Uniquely, it captures Buddy shouting *'Mother!'* after the song has finished. It seems he couldn't wait for her to hear it. (How different to the mores of today, where, if the word 'mother' were used on record, it would no doubt be as an expletive!)

Those three takes – some were only partial attempts – were first heard in undubbed form on the 1986 Rollercoaster LP, *Something Special From Buddy Holly*, but since then the 2007 *Ohh! Annie!* CD on the same label has seen the songs issued in superior sound, and with one take being technically listed as *'previously unreleased'*.

Peter De Rose (1900-53) who wrote the music, penned a number of memorable songs in his time including 'Deep Purple', but this one was probably his biggest, first charting in 1933 at the hands of Ted Lewis & His Band, and again in 1948 for Ernest Tubb. In the '60s, Teresa Brewer and the UK's Caravalles both enjoyed minor pop hits with it too, but the quirkiest hit version was surely when the voices of the late Patsy Cline and the late Jim Reeves were combined to take the song into the Top 5 of the Country chart in 1982 – around two decades after their deaths!

HAWAII

This book isn't meant as a travelogue, but it's worth mentioning in passing that the Crickets, Paul Anka, Jerry Lee Lewis and Jodie Sands stopped over on the island of Hawaii on their way to and from Australia during January/February 1958, playing concerts in Honolulu on both occasions. At the time, the island wasn't part of the Union (it joined the following year) and the stopovers were partially brought about by the need to refuel the aircraft in those far-off days.

That whole period was terribly intensive as far as the Crickets were concerned: they had just come off a successful tour with the Everly Brothers, and immediately went to Bell Sound in New York for a recording session ('Rave On' and 'That's My Desire'), followed by an appearance on the *Ed Sullivan Show*. Busy days.

Some particularly fine colour photos exist of Buddy and the Crickets in Hawaii.

'HEARTBEAT'
Recorded late May 1958 at Norman Petty Recording Studios, Clovis, New Mexico
Personnel: Buddy Holly (guitar, vocals), Tommy Allsup (guitar), Jerry Allison (drums), George Atwood (double bass)

This classic song was composed by Buddy's long-time friend Bob Montgomery (although Norman Petty's name was also added to the credits) and has endured in popularity over the years. Lead guitarist Tommy Allsup recalls how Buddy wanted to get a Spanish feel to the guitar sound on the recording and demonstrated to him how he wanted it to sound. Although Joe B. usually played bass, Buddy pulled in the older George Atwood for this particular number, and Jerry Allison recalls with great amusement that his particular contribution in the studio that day was to play the cowbells!

Quite why the record performed so poorly in the US charts is difficult to say, but it only reached a lowly No.82 and turned out to be the last chart single Holly would have in his homeland during his lifetime. Happily, it fared much better in the UK, charting in 1959 and again in 1960 after being reissued, reaching No.30 on both occasions.

In retrospect, 'Heartbeat' is surely the most hackneyed of titles, *ten* different compositions by the same name having entered the British charts by the time the new Millennium arrived. However, of all those different songs, it's surely the Holly one that is the most memorable and certainly the one that has inspired most covers. This is definitely the case in the UK, where four acts have so far charted with the Holly song. Chronologically these were the England Sisters (who covered the 1960 reissue of 'Heartbeat' and beat Buddy into the charts), Buddy Holly, Showaddywaddy in the '70s, and Heartbeat Country and Nick Berry in the '90s (British fans will know that the song 'Heartbeat' is synonymous with the incredibly successful and long-running TV drama series of the same name, starring Berry). The most successful of these was the latter, which reached No.2 in 1992.

It's also worth a mention that 'Heartbeat' was the first song that rockabilly great Larry Donn ever recorded, while Willie Logan did a fine instrumental version for his *The Legend Lives* CD series.

For collectors there aren't too many alternative Holly versions to complicate life, though the Picks did overdub backing vocals onto the cut in 1984 (see **OVERDUBS** and **PICKS** for more info) – which is somewhat ironic, as by the time 'Heartbeat' was recorded, Norman Petty was using the Roses to do all the backings.

CAROLYN HESTER

The acclaimed modern folk singer Carolyn Hester was born in Waco, Texas in 1937 and made her first album, *Scarlet Ribbons*, under Norman Petty's direction at Clovis during July 1957. According to the author's personal correspondence with George Atwood, the musicians who played on the album were Atwood himself on stand-up bass, Mike Mitchell on drums and Hester's father, Gordon, on harmonica. Atwood also recalled Buddy playing acoustic guitar on a few of the tracks, though Hester insists she was the only guitarist on the album.

One of her favourite songs is Holly's 'Lonesome Tears', which she first recorded in the early '60s and still occasionally features on stage. Frustratingly, a 1958 Clovis session where she cut four tracks with Holly on guitar and Jerry Allison on drums remains both unheard and unissued, although the tapes almost certainly exist. One of the titles – to stimulate Holly fans – is reputedly a folk-oriented interpretation of 'Take Your Time' with Buddy on acoustic guitar. In the mid-1960s, Hester also recorded 'Rave On' at Clovis, but that is likewise unissued.

Buddy met up with Carolyn in New York during 1958, and it seems possible that she might have been one of the first artists to use Holly's proposed Lubbock recording studio (see **PRISM RECORDS**). In an interview a while back, she mentioned that Buddy had performed one of her songs, 'Black Is The Color Of My True Love's Hair', on at least one occasion during his British tour. Photos of Hester and Holly together are also known to exist.

Hester went on to record for the Dot label among others and, after helping to spearhead the 1960s folk revolution from her base in New York's Greenwich Village, eventually moved to California, where her daughters now run a Los Angeles nightclub.

Apart from the early contact with Holly, Carolyn Hester was also one of the first singers to encounter a youthful Bob Dylan, who she claims had heard her sing 'Lonesome Tears'. He later played harmonica on her third album before his own career began to take off. Hester's career remains ongoing at the present time.

See also **CHRISTMAS RECORDS**.

HICCUP – *See* **GLOTTAL STOP**

HIGH TIME

This was an early evening TV show broadcast weekly on Channel 12 KPTV from Portland, Oregon, which enjoyed a three-year run from mid-1957 to mid-1960. From what we read, it was similar in format to Dick Clark's *American Bandstand*, with local teenagers being invited to participate, free tickets being snapped up from the moment they were made available. During its run, the show featured an array of guest stars from Liberace to Paul Anka and anyone in between.

The Crickets, who were on tour at the time, appeared on the show on 22 October 1957 (*The Biggest Show of Stars for 1957* played the Portland Paramount that evening before heading for Vancouver). In the past few years, a brief film clip of the boys singing 'That'll Be The Day' around the *High Time* microphone was shown in a documentary about the TV station.

HOLLEY FAMILY

The Holley family of the '50s comprised Buddy's parents Lawrence Odell Holley (1901-85) and Ella Pauline Holley (1902-90), and their four children: Larry (born 1925), Travis (born 1927), Pat (1929-2008) and Buddy (1936-59).

They were quite a musical family. Both older brothers played guitars and other instruments, and encouraged their younger sibling to follow suit. One of the delights for anyone visiting Lubbock must be the chance to see and hear Travis and Larry Holley, complete with their guitars, giving an impromptu performance of down-home country singing.

Contrary to the impression given in the *Buddy Holly Story* biopic, Buddy's parents also encouraged him in his musical endeavours. Indeed, his father later also gave several other local singers a helping hand, though he wasn't a manager in the full sense of the word.

Buddy brother, Larry Holley, has spent his working life in the family tiling business, but later on combined this with running his own small record labels, Cloud 9 and Holly House. In 2008, he published his autobiography entitled *I Don't Know How I Did It*. Understandably perhaps, it concentrates on his own life, and there are only a few references to his more famous younger brother.

Larry's daughter, Sherry, looked to be following Buddy into a full-time music career after bringing out several recordings of her own, with help from her dad. Foremost among these was her 1992 Cloud 9 tribute album, *Looking Through Buddy's Eyes*. A single pulled from it, 'The Cost Of Loving You' b/w 'Not Fade Away' on the Comstock label, was a minor hit in Europe during the '90s. These days, she is mainly directing her talents into producing sculpture and artwork.

Since Buddy's days, a whole new generation of the Holley family has grown up in and around the Lubbock area, and all are noticeably proud of their famous antecedent, Charles Hardin 'Buddy' Holley.

MARIA ELENA HOLLEY – *See* **MARIA ELENA**

HOLLIES

Allan Clarke and Graham Nash had played together from their Manchester schooldays in the late '50s, so it was no surprise that, with the Liverpool Sound beginning to emerge, they got in on the act and formed a group. Some say their name was foisted on them without forethought, but lead singer Clarke has explained that, with the Christmas season then looming and with Buddy Holly being a particular favourite of theirs, the name 'The Hollies' simply picked itself.

It would take up unnecessary space to summarise the group's record-breaking career here, which is ongoing, although Graham Nash departed in 1968 to join Stephen Stills and Dave Crosby in the USA, and there have been other personnel changes since. However, the tenuous connection with Buddy Holly escalated when they put together a Holly tribute album, *Buddy Holly*, in 1980 (since reissued on CD), bravely employing their own arrangements to fit their unique harmonies. Surprisingly, the album didn't chart, though a medley from it briefly dented the UK Top 30.

Another Holly-related project emerged in the '90s, with Graham Nash returning to help out on a majestic duet blending Buddy's lead vocals with the harmonies of the Hollies on 'Peggy Sue Got Married' – a work of art that deservedly became the opening track on the 1996 MCA Nashville tribute album, *Not Fade Away (Remembering Buddy Holly)*. Bringing things up to date, Nash also appeared on 'Think It Over' on the 2004 *Crickets And Their Buddies* album. Maybe this connection has yet more surprises in store!

BUDDY HOLLY

As the bulk of this book concerns the singer himself, to add much here would be pedantic and not a little repetitive. So we will make do with a few personal stats: Buddy was born on 7 September 1936 (combined Labor Day and Dollar Day) and was christened Charles Hardin Holley. He lived in and around the city of Lubbock – 'the Hub City of the South Plains' – during his adolescence and completed his schooling at Lubbock High School. A photo exists of him in cap and gown from the awards ceremony at the end of his final year.

According to his driving licence, he was 5 feet 11 inches tall, so occasional descriptions of him as a gangling 6 feet 3 inches should be ignored. His weight was constant at 145 pounds, while both his eyes and hair were brown. He had exceptionally poor eyesight, forcing him to wear glasses from an early age, although at one time he briefly experimented with contact lenses.

Music was Buddy's life from the start, though he did briefly work as a carpenter's assistant, and also helped his brother Larry in the family's tiling business. A best-selling, innovative recording star, he married Maria Elena Santiago from New York City in Lubbock on 15 August 1958, and relocated to New York shortly afterwards.

He headlined the *Winter Dance Party* tour from its opening date on 23 January 1959 in Milwaukee, Wisconsin through to 2 February at the Surf Ballroom, Clear Lake, Iowa. Along with Ritchie Valens, the Big Bopper and pilot Roger Peterson, he was killed in a plane crash in the early hours of 3 February 1959 while flying to his next engagement in Moorhead, Minnesota. Married for just six months, he left a widow, but no children.

Holly's impact on popular music is inestimable. His innovative, driving brand of rock'n'roll, often utilising complex harmonies and melodies, inspired the Beatles, the Rolling Stones and many others – and continues to do so to this day. As Waylon Jennings once remarked, *'Don't ask where music would have taken Buddy Holly; the real question is where Buddy Holly would have taken the music.'*

Although recognition was initially slow in coming, Holly has for many years been universally acknowledged as one of the all-time rock 'greats'. Indeed, of all the original '50s rockers, probably only he and Elvis Presley have succeeded in retaining complete credibility into the twenty-first century. His life has inspired books, stage musicals and a full-blown film biography. In 1980, he was commemorated by his hometown with a life-size statue which forms the centrepiece of the West Texas Walk of Fame in downtown Lubbock. In 1986, he was included in the first group of inductees into the Rock and Roll Hall of Fame, and has been similarly recognised by the Rockabilly Hall of Fame. His image has appeared on postage stamps in at least two countries (see **POSTAGE STAMPS** for details), and in 2000, he even had a newly-discovered asteroid (No.16155 to be specific) named in his honour. Buddy Holly may be gone, but he is certainly not forgotten.

'HOLLY HOP'
Recorded late 1956 at Buddy's home in Lubbock, Texas
Personnel: Buddy Holly (guitar, vocals), unknown (guitar), Jerry Allison (drums)

We know that Buddy Holly was a consummate guitarist, but it's equally true that he never went into the recording studio with the specific intention of recording an instrumental. Indeed, none were released during his lifetime. But thanks to the abundance of posthumous releases, several instrumentals survive – two of them from the same 1956 demo session.

The one listed here was belatedly labelled 'Holly Hop' ('Holley Hop' would probably have been more correct) with Buddy's mother, Ella, nominally credited as composer while the singer's affairs were being sorted out. It may have been a theme that Buddy played on his KDAV appearances: it's really a simple guitar workout, but still moves along nicely. It was first heard – overdubbed of course – on the 1969 *Giant* album, while Rollercoaster issued the sparser, undubbed version on *Something Special From Buddy Holly* in 1986.

Bobby Vee included an instrumental version of 'Holly Hop' on his 1999 Holly tribute album, *Down The Line*, making him the only artist of note to cover it.

See also **INSTRUMENTALS**.

US version

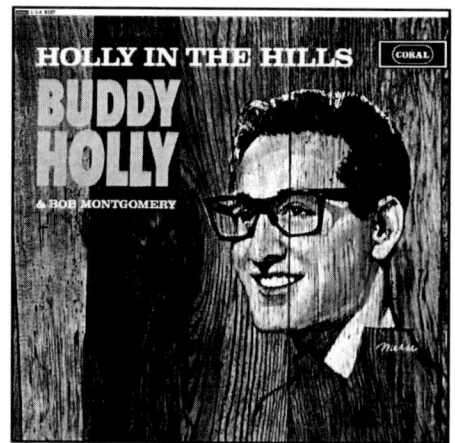
UK version

HOLLY IN THE HILLS *(LP, US only)*
I Wanna Play House With You / Door To My Heart / Fool's Paradise / I Gambled My Heart / What To Do / Wishing / Down The Line / Soft Place In My Heart / Lonesome Tears / Gotta Get You Near Me Blues / Flower Of My Heart / You And I Are Through

HOLLY IN THE HILLS *(LP, UK only)*
I Wanna Play House With You / Door To My Heart / Baby, It's Love / I Gambled My Heart / Memories / Wishing* / Down The Line / Soft Place In My Heart / Queen Of The Ballroom / Gotta Get You Near Me Blues / Flower Of My Heart / You And I Are Through [*early pressings mistakenly included *Reminiscing* instead of *Wishing*]

First released in January 1965, *Holly In The Hills* never amounted to much in an America preoccupied with the Beatles and the British Invasion. In the UK, however, it was a different story. Since his death, Holly had remained incredibly popular in Britain, scoring no fewer than sixteen posthumous hits up to the end of 1964. The unexpected appearance of *Holly In The Hills* in June 1965 reawakened fans' interest and took it to No.13 on the *Record Retailer* 'Top LPs' chart.

We were vaguely aware that Buddy's music had country roots and were also familiar with his early Decca sessions, but had never heard this sort of material before. These early recordings were much more country-oriented, and the song titles obscure. It was intriguing and thought-provoking stuff, even if not particularly commercial.

The twelve tracks on the British album could be broken down into one studio recording ('Wishing', which had already been a hit single in the UK), two great rock'n'roll-styled demos ('Down The Line' and Presley's 'Baby Let's Play House'), plus nine country-styled duets by Buddy & Bob, with Bob Montgomery handling the majority of vocals. Later, we would discover that many of the tracks emanated from KDAV and had been originally cut onto 78 rpm acetates.

The reason why the tracks on the UK release differed from the US version is quite interesting. Apparently, after hearing the US album, Buddy's erstwhile manager, Hi-Pockets Duncan contacted Norman Petty to offer him acetates of 'Queen Of The Ballroom', 'Baby It's Love' and 'Memories'. Like the other cuts, these were then overdubbed and included on the UK release. They weren't issued in the USA until the 1970s.

To the real fan, the album was and remains a revelation regardless of technical quality, and, although heavily overdubbed, it couldn't obscure the inclusion of a country fiddle on most tracks. Unlike the majority of tracks overdubbed by the Fireballs, most of the Buddy & Bob recordings have not appeared in their original form, officially or otherwise. While the material was far removed in style from the Holly/Crickets hits of '57 and '58, fans accepted the album as bringing a fresh insight into Buddy's earliest musical attempts, while introducing us to Bob Montgomery for the first time.

'HONKY TONK'
Recorded late 1956 at Buddy's home in Lubbock, Texas
Personnel: Buddy Holly (guitar, vocals), unknown (guitar), Jerry Allison (drums)

Although rock'n'roll as a genre was multi-layered, some of those layers were delightfully simple, and Bill Doggett's 1956 instrumental smash, 'Honky Tonk', is the perfect example.

At the end of '56, when Holly and Jerry Allison were busy laying down several garage-type demos, 'Honky Tonk' was still on the tail-end of its chart run, so it was only natural for them to practise it so they could play it live. It is the only full-length instrumental that Holly ever recorded (see also **'BUDDY'S GUITAR'** and **'HOLLY HOP'**), although of course it would normally never have seen the light of day, had it not been for his premature demise.

With Jerry's help, Buddy manages to transform the saxophone-led workout into one that sounds equally good on the guitar, while their exuberant whoops add to the track's excitement. Here again we have two versions of what is essentially the same recording: we first heard it in overdubbed form on the 1964 *Showcase* album, but later, the much earthier undubbed track appeared on the 1986 Rollercoaster album, *Something Special From Buddy Holly*.

FREEMAN HOVER

Back in the late '50s, interviews with rock'n'roll stars were far briefer affairs than today and usually revolved around asking an artist what their next record was, or where they were appearing next. The era of in-depth (and interminable!) interviews hadn't yet evolved into the art form it later became. In fact, aural evidence of some extant '50s interviews sometimes reveals an interviewer who was plain bored or, as in one Gene Vincent interview, downright hostile.

But that was far from the case where Freeman 'Freddy' Hover was concerned, and one of the most delightful interviews from those days – it lasts a full seven minutes – is the one he conducted with Holly and Jerry Allison in a Denver hotel room for KCSR, Chadron, Nebraska. Hover had travelled some 300 miles specially to interview the headliners on the *Biggest Show of Stars for 1957* package. Eddie Cochran was also present throughout, and a separate interview with him has subsequently also been released. It's fun too, with Buddy, Jerry and Jimmy Bowen laughing in the background. Both interviews are included on the CD *Cochran Mighty Mean*, released in 1995 by the UK's Rockstar label.

A delightful individual, Hover is now retired and lives near to Tucson, Arizona.

JACK HUDDLE

Jack Huddle (1928-73) was active in the post-war entertainment business around Lubbock, hosting both a children's programme (*Children's Theater*) and a talent show (*Around Lubbock*) on KDUB-TV. It's known that Buddy & Jack and Sonny Curtis appeared on the latter at various times.

Huddle was also a singer, and in 1957 went to Clovis to record a Jim Robinson composition called 'Starlight' and his own 'Believe Me'. Initially issued on Norman Petty's Petsey label, the tracks were leased to Kapp shortly after for national distribution. Backing on the record was supplied by Buddy Holly (who contributes some great guitar-work on 'Starlight'), Jerry Allison on drums and probably George Atwood on bass. The Bowman Brothers sang backing vocals on 'Believe Me'. It's of academic interest only, but over the years the tracks have been released both with and (on a bootleg) without the addition of echo.

Tina Robin covered 'Believe Me' for Coral in 1958 and, intriguingly, her version contains an extra verse.

Sadly, Huddle died early of a heart attack a few weeks before his 45th birthday.

FERLIN HUSKY

Buddy Holly fell in love with Ferlin Husky's original recording of 'Gone' when it appeared in 1952 under the pseudonym of 'Terry Preston' (at the time, Husky felt his real name was too strange to use professionally). Buddy was once booked to appear on a show that Husky was headlining and sang 'Gone' during his set, not realising that Husky and 'Terry Preston' were one and the same.

Recording under his real name (and as 'Simon Crum', a comic *alter ego*) Husky became a huge country star, accumulating over forty country hits between the '50s and the '70s. Never comfortable in a rock'n'roll setting, it's interesting to re-watch his big-screen performance in the 1957 *Mister Rock And Roll* movie: he seems more bemused and embarrassed than the audience!

I

'I FORGOT TO REMEMBER TO FORGET'
Recorded 1956 at KLLL, Lubbock, Texas
Personnel: Buddy Holly (guitar, vocals), others unknown

While searching for inspiration for a song back in 1955, songwriter Stan Kesler reputedly overheard somebody apologise by saying, *'I just forgot to remember'*. All Kesler needed was an unusual phrase such as that and the song almost wrote itself. After hearing Elvis Presley's version (as Sun 223 it topped the *Billboard* C&W chart in 1955), Buddy recorded a demo of it at KLLL and the acetate was played on air several times. But later, with his Decca contract looming, Buddy thought playing it might compromise his chances and the disc was rendered unplayable. However, it still exists and one wonders whether it might still be possible to salvage something of it.

'I FOUGHT THE LAW' *(post-Holly Crickets)*

A standout composition from the Sonny Curtis songbook that has inspired numerous covers over the years, 'I Fought The Law' first appeared on the *In Style With The Crickets* album in 1961, the first (and last) post-Holly Crickets album on Coral. It was actually released as a single, but failed to chart.

However, you can't keep a good song down, and it was eventually picked up by the Bobby Fuller Four and released on the small Exeter label in 1965. Re-recorded for Mustang the following year, it reached the US Top 10. Since then, it has become a perennial, with versions by everyone from Sam Neely (another Texan) to the Clash and Tom Petty. Unlikely as it may seem, even the Dead Kennedys and the iconic Iggy Pop recorded versions. It's fair to say the composition has entered our musical consciousness, and as a story-in-song it's a number that we haven't heard the last of yet.

'I GAMBLED MY HEART' *(Buddy & Bob)*
Recorded 1954 or 1955 at Nesman Recording Studio, Wichita Falls, Texas
Personnel: Buddy Holly (guitar, vocals), Bob Montgomery (guitar, vocals), Sonny Curtis (fiddle), Don Guess (double bass)

A simple country-styled number that Buddy & Bob made a demo of in the early days, which surfaced in 1965 on the *Holly In The Hills* album. Composer credits were originally to Bob Montgomery, but later amended to both Holly and Montgomery. The only version of the song is the one overdubbed by the Fireballs, in mono. It is not known whether the undubbed version still exists.

'I GUESS I WAS JUST A FOOL'
(1) Recorded December 1955 at Nesman Recording Studio, Wichita Falls, Texas
Personnel: Buddy Holly (guitar, vocals), Sonny Curtis (guitar), Jerry Allison (drums), Don Guess (double bass)
(2) Recorded early 1956 at Norman Petty Recording Studios, Clovis, New Mexico
Personnel: Buddy Holly (guitar, vocals), Sonny Curtis (guitar), Jerry Allison (drums), Don Guess (double bass)

Another demo that is believed to have been cut several times, and, although only two versions have been released, a third definitely exists. A self-composed country-styled number this first surfaced as a posthumous release on the 1964 *Showcase* album, but, unlike the other six cuts from the same session, it wasn't overdubbed at all. A similar but slightly looser version appeared on the 1995 4-CD Vigotone bootleg, *What You Been A-Missin'*, but is easily identifiable from the background chatter.

'I Guess I Was Just A Fool' was erroneously listed as 'I Tried To Forget' in paperwork by Jim Denny, and this has led to endless rumour and confusion in the past.

'I KNOW I'LL HAVE THE BLUES AGAIN'
A number co-written by one John Mackey (of whom little is known) and Buddy Holly, with royalties split 90%–10% respectively. Published by Nor-Va-Jak, the percentage split would seem to indicate that Holly was only nominally involved, but a lead sheet does exist and the song was copyrighted in 1957. The Whitesidewalls, a Holly tribute band, performed the song some thirty years ago as part of their set.

'I TRIED TO FORGET' – *See* 'I GUESS I WAS JUST A FOOL'

'I WANNA PLAY HOUSE WITH YOU'
This was the original, albeit incorrect title applied to 'Baby Let's Play House' when it was released on the 1965 *Holly In The Hills* album.
See **'BABY LET'S PLAY HOUSE'**.

FRANK IFIELD

Born in Coventry, England in 1937, singer/yodeller Frank Ifield was raised in Australia and was one of the support acts on the bill when the Crickets played Sydney on their 1958 tour.

Ifield returned to the UK at the end of the '50s and went on to have a string of chart hits including three consecutive No.1's just before the arrival of the Beatles. He is on record as saying that he is a great fan of Buddy Holly's music, and indeed his hiccup-laden 1960 hit, 'Gotta Get A Date', was quite obviously influenced by Holly. Later on, he also recorded 'True Love Ways'.

'I'LL JUST PRETEND' *(Buddy & Bob)*
Recorded 1952 at Buddy's home in Lubbock, Texas
Personnel: Buddy Holly (mandolin, vocals), Bob Montgomery (guitar, vocals)

A recording which dates from Buddy's schooldays, this acetate is notable for the fact that Buddy plays mandolin (as he does on 'Take These Shackles From My Heart') and sings harmony, while Bob Montgomery handles lead vocals and plays acoustic guitar. The song was a recent Flatt & Scruggs release, composed by West Virginia songwriter Jessie Mae Martin. Buddy's version was later issued by his brother Larry in 1986 on an untitled 7-inch EP on the Holly House label. (Incidentally, it's said that the first song that Buddy sang before a live audience as a juvenile was the bluegrass favourite, 'Did You Ever Go Sailing'.)

'I'M CHANGIN' ALL THOSE CHANGES'
(1) Recorded early 1956 at Norman Petty Recording Studios, Clovis, New Mexico
Personnel: Buddy Holly (guitar, vocals), Sonny Curtis (guitar), Jerry Allison (drums), Don Guess (double bass)
(2) Recorded July 1956 at Bradley's Barn Studio, Nashville, Tennessee
Personnel: Buddy Holly (guitar, vocals), Sonny Curtis (guitar), Jerry Allison (drums), Don Guess (double bass)

One of the five numbers Buddy and the boys got to cut in Nashville in their second stab at fame, this one was much closer to rockabilly than to country. Initially credited as a Jim Denny composition, it was later correctly attributed to Buddy.

The released master is Take 4 and, as with all three Nashville sessions, was recorded in mono. It first appeared in the USA on the Decca album, *That'll Be The Day*, released in 1958 in an attempt to cash in on Holly's hit parade success (although, of course, Coral and Brunswick were subsidiaries of Decca).

Several months before the Nashville session, Holly also cut a demo of this and some other songs at Clovis. It's readily identifiable, as it's far shorter than the Decca version. Having been overdubbed by the Fireballs, the Clovis demo appeared in stereo on the 1963 *Reminiscing* album, while the undubbed mono original finally made an appearance in 1983 on the *For The First Time Anywhere* album.

So, there are three different versions with two different lead vocals, for those that wish to count. A seventeen-second fragment of what appears to be Take 3 from the Nashville session also exists.

Holly acolytes Bobby Vee and Mike Berry are among a select few artists to have covered the number.

'I'M GONNA LOVE YOU TOO'
Recorded July 1957 at Norman Petty Recording Studios, Clovis, New Mexico
Personnel: Buddy Holly (double-tracked guitar, vocals), Jerry Allison (drums), Joe B. Mauldin (double bass)

Recorded during the extended session that produced 'Listen To Me' and 'Peggy Sue', this track is famous for including the sound of a male cricket chirping (female crickets apparently do not chirp!) during the fade-out. Bizarrely, it had crept into the echo chamber and was preserved for all time on record.

Coupled with 'Listen To Me', 'I'm Gonna Love You Too' was issued as the 'A' side of a single in the US, where it crept into the bottom of the *Cash Box* chart; in Britain, however, it appeared on the flip, so never charted in its own right. Nevertheless, it was the song that Buddy chose to lip-synch to on Kent Walton's *Cool For Cats* ATV show while on tour in the UK in 1958.

The two songs are also linked in another way, as both feature Holly's first attempts to double-track his vocals – a fairly innovative technique back then. Composer credits list Jerry Allison, Joe B. Mauldin, Niki Sullivan and Norman Petty: this was a time when ideas were being thrown into the musical pot by everyone.

Blondie recorded a powerful version of 'I'm Gonna Love You Too' in 1978 as a follow-up to their British hit, 'Picture This', although sadly it didn't chart. The song has been covered quite a few times by the likes of Mike Berry, Adam Faith, Billy Fury, Gary Busey (in the *Buddy Holly Story* biopic) and Denny Laine (on his 1977 *Holly Days* album).

Unusually, there is just the one Holly recording of the song – no overdubs, no out-takes, no alternates, no nothing.

'I'M GONNA SET MY FOOT DOWN'
Recorded early 1956 at Norman Petty Recording Studios, Clovis, New Mexico
Personnel: Buddy Holly (guitar, vocals), Sonny Curtis (guitar), Jerry Allison (drums), Don Guess (double bass)

A Buddy Holly composition which was recorded as a demo at Clovis sometime between the January and July 1956 Nashville sessions. Quite a potent number, it was released posthumously on the 1963 *Reminiscing* album, suitably overdubbed by the Fireballs for a stereo release. It surfaced in undubbed, mono form in 1983 on *For The First Time Anywhere*, while in 1984 the Picks added backing vocals to the Fireballs version (see **OVERDUBS** and **PICKS** for more info). It's bewildering to think that the Picks were overdubbing vocals over a track that already had instrumental overdubs! A slightly confusing state of affairs, but the point to be stressed is that, although there are three different versions of this available, the lead vocals are one and the same. Needless to say, cover versions are thin on the ground, but the legendary Carl Perkins included an excellent interpretation on his 1969 Columbia album, *Carl Perkins On Top*.

'I'M JUST A LONELY BOY'
Although once rumoured to be an unreleased Holly song, this is no more than an erroneous title for 'Ain't Got No Home'.
See **'AIN'T GOT NO HOME'**.

'I'M LOOKING FOR SOMEONE TO LOVE'
Recorded February 1957 at Norman Petty Recording Studios, Clovis, New Mexico
Personnel: Buddy Holly (guitar, vocals), Jerry Allison (drums), Larry Welborn (double bass), Niki Sullivan, Gary Tollett and Ramona Tollett (backing vocals)

This was a demo track that was worked on at Clovis at the same time as 'That'll Be The Day' and, having been assigned the earlier master number, may well have briefly been considered for the 'A' side. But, when the record appeared in the shops, we all knew which was the hit side.

It's said that, during the drive from Lubbock to Clovis, the group tried unsuccessfully to come up with a lyric to replace, *'Drunk man, street car, foot slipped: there you are'*, a phrase from a pre-war road safety campaign which Buddy's mother often quoted to her children. Unable to find any inspiration, they left it in, and it's probably the most memorable verse of the song. The snappy phrasing certainly helps the track move along.

Being a demo, it was recorded live in the studio and the

accompanying vocals were courtesy of Gary and Ramona Tollett, who had been rehearsing the track with Buddy. So, this is the one and only version we have: no alternates, no out-takes and no overdubs.

For such a wonderful number, covers are surprisingly thin on the ground, although Mike Berry, Skeeter Davis and Denny Laine (instrumentally) are three who have included it on albums.

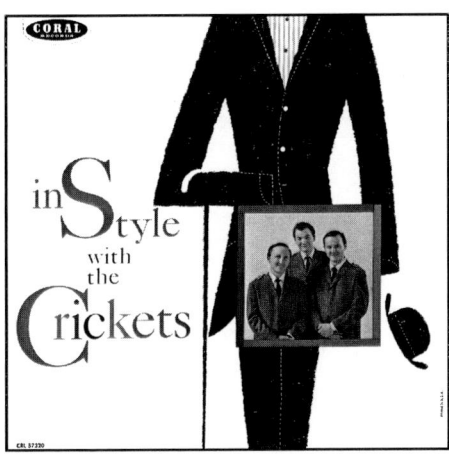

IN STYLE WITH THE CRICKETS *(LP)*
More Than I Can Say / Rockin' Pneumonia And The Boogie Woogie Flu / Great Balls Of Fire / Ting-A-Ling / Just This Once / Deborah / Baby My Heart / When You Ask About Love / Time Will Tell / A Sweet Love / I Fought The Law / Love's Made A Fool Of You

Released in December 1960 in the US and early 1961 in Britain, this was the first (and only) Coral album recorded by the Crickets without any participation by Holly. The tracks were the product of as many as seven different recording sessions in Clovis, New York and Los Angeles between December 1958 and February 1960.

Readers today will be amazed to know of the amount of misinformation that record companies peddled back in the '50s and '60s, and this album release is a prime example. Perhaps in an attempt to gloss over any changes from the Crickets' hit-making days, the original sleevenotes listed them as being a trio comprised of Jerry Allison, Joe B. Mauldin and Sonny Curtis – whereas Earl Sinks, who isn't mentioned at all, performed lead vocals on *every* track on the album bar two!

The other mystery must be why this album didn't achieve the commercial success it deserved, though several of the tracks registered as hit singles in the UK. In the USA, *In Style* never even bubbled under the *Billboard* 'Top LPs' chart. In Britain, *Record Retailer* listed it in their Top 20 for weeks, where it peaked at No.13. Although the vinyl album was deleted back in the '60s, it was reissued on CD by MCA – with extra tracks – as part of their 'Rockin' Reissue' series a few years ago.

JOHN INGMAN

In 1985, Vi Petty invited John Ingman and Jerry MacNeish to document the contents of Norman Petty's tape and publishing vaults. This led to them opening the original Norman Petty Recording Studios at 1313 West 7th Street in Clovis to visitors in September 1986 and launching an annual *Norman & Vi Petty Music Festival*. Ingman tells of his involvement in this project in the excellent 2008 Rollercoaster compilation, *Clovis Rocks: Stars of the Clovis Music Festival*.

John has been thanked in the *Acknowledgements* as the man that has done more than anyone to help complete the *A to Z* you are holding. He has contributed to countless books, magazines and LP/CD projects, and for several years ran Ingman Music Research, which published the *Crickets Fact File* (the only book ever devoted to the music of the post-Holly group) and *AOK – Record Labels of West Texas & New Mexico*. These publications are still available.

INSTRUMENTALS

During the '50s and '60s in Britain the weekly *New Musical Express* regularly ran an annual poll to discover the best vocalist, best group and best instrumentalist. Of course, Buddy Holly did consistently well in the singing department, but he also managed to finish high up on the 'Best Instrumentalist' list and give the likes of Duane Eddy a run for his money.

Although Holly never went into a recording studio with the specific intention of cutting an instrumental for commercial release, we do get plenty of chances to hear his guitar prowess on over a hundred different recordings outside of his hit singles. Of course, it doesn't automatically follow that Buddy's biggest hits contain his best guitar work. 'You've Got Love', initially just a track on *The Chirping Crickets* album, contains one of his greatest-ever solos and readers will doubtless be able to nominate their own favourites. Some of his session work – for example Jack Huddle's 'Starlight' – is also superb. In passing, it should also be noted that Holly isn't present on guitar on every title he ever recorded, as in the early days it was sometimes Sonny Curtis, or later Tommy Allsup, who played lead on a handful of his classic recordings.

So what are we left with? Well, three instrumentals ('Holly Hop', 'Honky Tonk' and 'Leave My Woman Alone') have crept out on various posthumous releases, and all are discussed in more detail under their separate entries. However, only one of these, 'Honky Tonk', could be truly described as a full-length effort.

The Holley family also own a short mandolin instrumental by Buddy recorded in the early '50s which has never been issued in any form.

Also worthy of special mention is the almost nine minutes of rehearsal tape of Bo Diddley's 'Mona', with Holly's vocals off-mike while his acoustic guitar and Jerry Allison's drumming are picked up loud and clear. This first appeared on the 1995 4-CD Vigotone bootleg, *What You Been A-Missin'* and still awaits a legal release. Incredibly, it may at long last have one by the time you read this!

INTERVIEWS

Over the years, several interviews with Buddy Holly and the Crickets have come to light. In the main, these make interesting listening, providing us with a brief glimpse into the world of rock'n'roll back then – a strange new world that was being created before our eyes (and ears). Predictably, these interviews tend to be lightweight, feelgood affairs, usually quite brief, and don't lend themselves to much retrospective analysis fifty years on. (There is one rare exception to this, and readers are directed to the entry on Snuff Garrett for more on his particularly emotional on-air interview with the Crickets and Norman Petty from 3 February 1959, which took place just hours after the plane crash.) Rock'n'roll was surely ephemeral, or so it was thought, and no-one imagined that it would develop its own history in perpetuity. But it most certainly has done, which is why you are reading these words today.

But enough amateur philosophy, just what are these interviews and where do they come from? Well, in 2002, nine such interviews were collected together by John Beecher on the Rollercoaster CD EP, *That's What They Tell Me – That's What They Say*, and constitute close to 100% of the extant interview clips. Of these, seven are American (with Bob Chesney, Dick Clark, Alan Freed, Freeman Hover, Dale Lowery, Ted Randal and Ed Sullivan), one Canadian (with Red Robinson) and one Australian (with Pat Barton). Sadly, although the Crickets spent a month in the UK during 1958 and several interviews appeared in print, none were recorded.

'IT DOESN'T MATTER ANYMORE'
Recorded October 1958 at Pythian Temple Studio, New York
Personnel: Buddy Holly (vocals), Al Caiola (guitar), Sanford Bloch (bass), Ernest Hayes (piano), Doris Johnson (harp), Clifford Leeman (drums), Boomie Richman (tenor sax) plus string section

This Paul Anka composition was recorded at Holly's final studio session and is arguably the most famous of the four titles from that date, by virtue of the fact that it would become a poignant, worldwide posthumous hit for Holly (it made No.1 in both Britain and Australia, and No.13 in the *Billboard* 'Hot 100').

Despite being backed by an eighteen-piece New York orchestra, Buddy wasn't phased and managed to get the number down in a couple of takes. In interviews, producer/arranger Dick Jacobs later recalled that Anka brought the song to the session late on, for which he had to improvise an arrangement on the spot. Jacobs's arrangement, which unusually featured pizzicato strings, proved nothing less than inspired and was later heavily copied by others.

Interestingly, Jerry Allison, Joe Mauldin and Norman Petty were all present in the studio, but only as spectators. It was also the only Holly session to be recorded in stereo, although both mono and stereo masters were created for release.

Over the years, dozens of artists have recorded Anka's composition (as has Anka himself), and Linda Ronstadt briefly charted with it during the '70s, but it has to be said that Holly's version remains the definitive one and is unlikely to be bettered.

'It Doesn't Matter Anymore' was one of a long line of unfortunate song titles that came to be regarded as particularly ironic when viewed with hindsight. Holly had started his recording career by singing *'that'll be the day when I die'*, so perhaps we shouldn't have been too surprised when he ended it in a similar fashion!

But can the cruel irony of Holly's last recording really be topped by anyone else? Well, a few others surely ran it close: 'Three Steps To Heaven' by Eddie Cochran, 'What Am I Living For' by Chuck Willis and 'I'll Never Get Out Of This World Alive' by Hank Williams. The fact that Williams's hit was already on the US Country charts when news of his death broke surely makes it hard to top, although the flip side of Willis's single, 'Hang Up My Rock And Roll Shoes', makes it seem that the singer perhaps really did sense his own mortality. Let's change the subject.

'IT'S NOT MY FAULT'
Recorded early 1956 at Norman Petty Recording Studios, Clovis, New Mexico
Personnel: Buddy Holly (guitar, vocals), Sonny Curtis (guitar), Don Guess (double bass)

A song composed by Ben Hall and onetime band member and steel guitar legend, Weldon Myrick, this was yet another Holly recording that surfaced posthumously on the 1963 *Reminiscing* album, dutifully overdubbed by the Fireballs. It was made legally available in 1983 on the *For The First Time Anywhere* album, and without the extended instrumental ending is considerably shorter. In 1984, the Picks overdubbed backing vocals onto the dubbed master (see **OVERDUBS** and **PICKS** for more info) to create a third version.

Hall is on record as saying that he wrote the song specifically for Buddy, and never sang it himself.

'IT'S SO EASY'
Recorded May 1958 at Norman Petty Recording Studios, Clovis, New Mexico
Personnel: Buddy Holly (acoustic guitar, vocals), Tommy Allsup (guitar), Jerry Allison (drums), Joe B. Mauldin (double bass), The Roses (backing vocals)

We weren't to know, but this would be the last release by Holly and the Crickets, and it remains a perennial mystery as to why it wasn't a big hit, given the plusses it had going for it. First of all, it's a great track and was a *Billboard* chart pick. The group had been featuring it daily whilst on tour, and in October 1958 appeared on *American Bandstand* to plug it nationally (they lip-synched to this song and, a few days earlier, 'Heartbeat').

Despite this, it never charted in the USA, and its performance in Britain was somewhat patchy (it wasn't listed in the main UK charts, although it made No.19 in the *Record Mirror* singles chart and No.22 in the *World's Fair* 'Juke Box' chart). However, Australia kept the faith and it went Top 10 over there. The additional irony is that Jerry 'Ivan' Allison's solo single, 'Real Wild Child' – which was released on the same day – spent five weeks on the US chart, even though it only peaked at a relatively lowly No.68. It's been suggested that Holly had maybe had his day, that his career wasn't just in the doldrums but perhaps in terminal decline, but that's something that can never be proved either way.

Written by Holly, 'It's So Easy' featured Tommy Allsup on lead guitar (Allsup has since revealed that he strung his instrument differently to achieve the sound he wanted) and backing vocals by the Roses (which Allsup confirms were recorded live on the day, not overdubbed later, as was the usual practice). Both instrumentally and vocally it's a great recording and, despite its lack of chart action at the time, it still made its way onto the *Buddy Holly Lives (20 Golden Greats)* album, which lived up to its description by going gold in 1978.

'It's So Easy' was re-recorded by the post-Holly Crickets with Gordon Payne, and they often perform it on stage despite its poor chart performance. Linda Ronstadt, however, discovered the magic formula and took it to No.5 in the *Billboard* 'Hot 100' in 1977 – one of three Holly/Crickets numbers that she had big hits with during the '70s (the other two were 'It Doesn't Matter Anymore' and 'That'll Be The Day'). Many other versions have also made it onto wax since 1958, and even Buddy's chum Waylon Jennings turned out a powerful early rendition.

'IT'S TOO LATE'
Recorded July 1957 at Norman Petty Recording Studios, Clovis, New Mexico
Personnel: Buddy Holly (guitar, vocals), Jerry Allison (drums), Joe B. Mauldin (double bass)
Overdubbed October 1957: The Picks (backing vocals)

This was a No.3 R&B hit in 1956 for Chuck Willis and a particular favourite of Buddy's brother, Larry. So, when the Crickets were casting around for material to complete their first album, this was earmarked for inclusion alongside the hits. The group take it at the same pace as the Willis original, although the use of the echo chamber on the Crickets' version adds to the potent atmosphere. Curiously, it was nearly three months before the Picks overdubbed their backing vocals – probably because John Pickering had meanwhile taken up employment in Houston. The original undubbed version has survived, but only on a damaged acetate. Surprisingly, the song has inspired a dearth of covers, although of course Roy Orbison recorded it at Sun.

IVAN

Ivan was the middle name of Crickets drummer Jerry Allison, who released a couple of singles as 'Ivan' in 1958. One of them, 'Real Wild Child' (on Coral) entered the *Billboard* 'Hot 100'. It came about after they'd toured Australia with antipodean star Johnny O'Keefe and fell in love with the song (originally entitled 'Wild One'), which was a nightly highlight of his stage act. The flip saw Allison doing an amusing cod vocal on 'Oh, You Beautiful Doll', modelled on the vocal gimmickry of comedian Sam Hirt. Holly plays guitar on both songs, but, by the time Jerry recorded the follow-up, 'That'll Be Alright', the group had split and Buddy had moved to New York.

Despite his success, there was never any desire on Allison's part to become a solo act, and in her 2007 memoir, Jerry's ex, Peggy Sue, recalls the embarrassment he felt when having to lip-sync the number on TV to promote it.

See also **JERRY IVAN ALLISON** *and* **'REAL WILD CHILD'**.

J

DICK JACOBS

Dick Jacobs had enjoyed a lengthy and illustrious career before his path ever crossed that of Buddy Holly back in 1958. He'd been staff arranger for both the Jimmy Dorsey and Tommy Dorsey orchestras before becoming musical director/arranger for artists like Perry Como, Eddie Fisher, and countless others. As it turned out, he was also responsible for both of Buddy's Pythian Temple sessions (see **'EARLY IN THE MORNING'** and **'TRUE LOVE WAYS'**).

Jacobs was a very innovative and creative individual, and, from a lengthy 1984 interview with Jay Berman and others, it transpired that he and Holly were formulating plans to work together more (possibly even experimenting in other styles) when fate intervened. After Buddy had recorded his last six compositions ('Peggy Sue Got Married', etc) in December 1958, he gave the tapes to Jacobs to write appropriate arrangements. Additionally, Tommy Allsup claims that Buddy was thinking of teaming up with bandleader/arranger Neal Hefti for a Christmas album, the title of which would have been *Deck The Halls With Hefti Holly*! Sadly, all these plans came to nothing.

After a fruitful nine-year association with Jackie Wilson in the '60s and early '70s, during which he arranged and produced most of his Brunswick material, Jacobs died prematurely in 1988 following a serious stabbing attack a few years earlier. Curiously, he is not mentioned at all in Coral/Brunswick boss Bob Thiele's 1995 memoir, *What A Wonderful World*.

WAYLON JENNINGS

Waylon Arnold Jennings (1937-2002) is an important name when the annals of Buddy Holly are under discussion, as he was involved with him both at the start and finish of his career, coming within a hair's breadth of being a crash victim himself prior to giving up his seat to the Big Bopper.

Like Holly, Jennings was immensely proud of his West Texas roots and was always quick to mention that he was from the tiny community of Littlefield, just a few miles outside Lubbock on Highway 84. Broadcasting on KLLL from the age of twelve, he had become a deejay by seventeen – which is indirectly how he came to link up with Holly.

Waylon Jennings snapped at the Laramar Ballroom, Fort Dodge, Iowa on 30 January 1959.

Some time later, when he was starting to become famous, Buddy readily agreed to record some radio jingles for him at KLLL. He was also the first to recognise Waylon's musical talent, and in 1958 he organised and produced his first recording session ('Jole Blon' and 'When Sin Stops'), flying the great King Curtis in from New York to Clovis to play sax.

After splitting up with the Crickets that October, Holly hired Jennings to play electric bass in his back-up band on the *Winter Dance Party* tour in January 1959. Just before the tour, they cut an impromptu number at the KLLL studio called 'You're The One', which like many other tracks would one day receive a posthumous release.

As we now know, Jennings was deeply affected by the trauma of February 1959 and it was to be several years before he started to climb the country ladder. In 1963, he recorded a 'Three Stars'-style tribute called 'The Stage', while many years later he penned a much more understated tribute to Buddy titled 'Old Friend'.

Over the years, he has also recorded a lot of the Holly songbook and in 1996 participated in the MCA 40-year Nashville tribute album, *Not Fade Away (Remembering Buddy Holly)*, sensitively singing 'Learning The Game' to Mark Knopfler's guitar accompaniment. Having been an 'unofficial' Cricket on that final tour, Jennings invited the Crickets to join his touring show from 1978 to 1983, during which time they got to play larger venues than they'd seen for many a year.

Married to country singer Jessi Colter for over thirty years,

Waylon Jennings was elected to the Country Hall of Fame in 2001, but succumbed to diabetes-related problems the following year at the age of 64. Their son, Shooter Jennings, played his father in the Johnny Cash biopic, *Walk The Line*, and is now a country recording star himself.

Anyone wishing to find out more about Waylon Jennings can easily do so, as, before health issues overtook him, the singer had already collaborated on a 1991 video biography, *Renegade Outlaw Legend*, as a precursor to his 1996 book, *Waylon* (see *Selected Bibliography*). And, when investigating Waylon's music, please don't overlook his fertile period as a member of the Highwaymen (Jennings, Nelson, Cash and Kristofferson, should anyone not know).

JINGLES

There are really two groups of jingles that need to be mentioned under this heading.

Firstly, there are the personalised 'That'll Be The Day' jingles which the Crickets cut in July 1957 as a 'thank you' to several individuals who'd helped them get their break. They are certainly great fun to listen to, as they are exuberant and infectious, and the recipients were the main individuals who had helped them most: Bob Thiele (Coral), Murray Deutch (Southern Music) and deejay Bill Randle (WERE, Cleveland). Snippets of these jingles have cropped up in various Holly documentaries over the years, while all three recently appeared in their entirety on the El Toro 3-CD, *Not Fade Away: Buddy Holly – The Complete 1957 Recordings*.

Secondly, there are the jingles, or promotional spots, which Holly and the Crickets made for individual radio stations during '57 and '58. Many of these are simply brief endorsements, while some were sung to a Holly tune (for instance, one of the jingles that Buddy recorded at KLLL in September 1958 was sung to the tune of 'Everyday', while the other was based on 'Peggy Sue'). However, all have the same message to listeners: *'Tune our way!'* Some of these were also included on the El Toro 3-CD. Whether or not all such jingles have survived is not known.

JITTERS

In the first few days of February 1959 a temporary confusion arose as to what would become of the Crickets in the immediate aftermath of the tragedy. Although the original Crickets (after their break-up with Holly) had already recorded at Clovis in November 1958 with Earl Sinks on lead vocals, there was another group coming off the *Winter Dance Party* tour (Waylon Jennings, Tommy Allsup, Carl Bunch and temporary vocalist Ronnie Smith) who could potentially consider themselves Crickets.

It soon became apparent to the shell-shocked survivors of the tour that the Crickets name was inextricably bound to Clovis, and a temporary, but quite apt name – the Jitters – was suggested. But it went nowhere: everyone just needed to get back home to Texas and to reality. Thus, the name that never was ebbed away as quickly as it had arisen.

BEN JOHNSON

Buddy's pastor back in Lubbock, who had the mixed experience of officiating at the marriage of Buddy and Maria Elena (at Buddy's parents' house) on 15 August 1958, and six months later on 7 February 1959 conducting the funeral service for the singer at the Holley family's church, the Tabernacle Baptist on 15th Street.

Reverend Johnson passed away in 1969.

GEORGE JONES

Country singer George Glenn Jones was born in Saratoga, Texas in 1931, and is mentioned here as someone who Buddy would have run across in 1956 when they both appeared on the same bill with Hank Thompson. Jones had already had country hits on the Starday label by then, while Buddy – still in his pre-Crickets days – was billed as 'Buddy Holly & The Two-Tones'.

Jones had something of a stronger link with the Big Bopper, and after signing with Mercury (also the Bopper's label), he went on to record several of his compositions – notably 'White Lightning', which he took to the No.1 spot on the *Billboard* C&W chart. For a while, he recorded rockabilly under the twin aliases of 'Hank Smith' and 'Thumper Jones', while later on his well-publicised personal problems earned him the nickname of 'No Show Jones'. But certainly all would agree that he is one of the greatest ever voices in country music.

MALCOLM JONES

One of the pioneer names of Holly research for many years was Malcolm Jones, who together with John Beecher compiled and annotated the 1979 6-LP/cassette *Complete Buddy Holly* box set: a compilation that still stands as a benchmark against which any future release must be judged. A few years earlier, in 1975, Jones had single-handedly put together a 5-LP/cassette Holly box set for World Records called *The Buddy Holly Story*, which, with its accompanying booklet, was at the time probably the finest Holly/Crickets collection ever put together. He was also responsible for the first British release of the overdubbed stereo masters by Buddy.

Jones had joined EMI in 1967 as A&R manager and signed Joe Cocker, Procol Harum, Marc Bolan and Dave Edmunds for the label. He was responsible for the success of many artists in Britain including Gloria Gaynor, Johnny Bristol and Neal Sedaka, whose career he helped to revive. Sadly, he died prematurely in 1990.

K

RONNIE KEENE

Ronnie Keene & His Orchestra and their vocalist, Lynn Adams, were on the bill of the Crickets' 1958 UK tour. The author interviewed Keene a few years back and he had fond memories of that particular tour, but also realised from the audience reaction to the Crickets that the days of the big band were numbered. He mentioned that there were only fourteen pieces in the orchestra – others have quoted double that number when reminiscing about the tour.

Described as *'Britain's newest musical sensation'* (they had a great publicist!) they opened each half of the night's bill with such big band favourites as 'Woodchoppers' Ball' and 'One O'Clock Jump', and also backed Lynn Adams, Gary Miller and the Tanner Sisters on their numbers.

Keene never made it into the recording studio as a bandleader, but he did get to appear weekly on TV during the run of the very popular *6.5 Special* show (1957-59).

KING CURTIS

The hugely talented black saxophonist King Curtis (1934-71) was an in-demand backing musician throughout his career, but it's perhaps surprising to learn that the gritty horn man who played on live Harlem dates with Sam Cooke was, in fact, a soft-spoken Texan from Fort Worth called Curtis Ousley.

The Crickets first met Curtis while touring, and it's of little surprise that Buddy hired him to play on one of his sessions. Logistically, it was quite a feat, with Holly driving his new Cadillac upstate to Amarillo to collect Curtis from the airport, then heading for Clovis. In the lengthy sessions that followed, Curtis's saxophone ended up on two Holly cuts ('Reminiscing' and 'Come Back Baby') and, perhaps more significantly, Waylon Jennings's first-ever recordings ('Jole Blon' and 'When Sin Stops'). 'Reminiscing' became a posthumous UK Top 20 hit for Holly in 1962.

With a bit of Hollywood licence thrown in, Curtis is portrayed in the *Buddy Holly Story* biopic as backing Holly on the *Winter Dance Party* tour. That certainly did *not* happen, but it's a good bet the two men would have collaborated further had fate not intervened.

Buddy Knox on stage in Nanaimo, BC, Canada in 1960.

Ousley went on to become a successful recording artist in his own right in the '60s, but sadly his life was prematurely curtailed when he was stabbed to death outside his New York apartment at the age of just 37. He was posthumously inducted into the Rock and Roll Hall of Fame in 2000.

MARK KNOPFLER

Mark Knopfler, who was born in Glasgow in 1949, had an incredible career as the inspiration behind Dire Straits – a career that would form a bridge between the '70s and the '90s. Wielding a Fender Stratocaster, he has always been quick to acknowledge Holly as an early influence, even if his own repertoire never travelled down the same route. However, he linked up with Waylon Jennings in Nashville to produce a wonderful interpretation of 'Learning The Game' for MCA's 1996 Holly tribute album, *Not Fade Away (Remembering Buddy Holly)*. Drawn to country music, he had UK chart albums in 1990 with Chet Atkins (*Neck And Neck*) and the Notting Hillbillies (*Missing... Presumed Having A Good Time*).

BUDDY KNOX

Born July 1933 in Happy, Texas, a small panhandle town halfway between Lubbock and Clovis, Buddy Wayne Knox was a contemporary of Buddy Holly. They met at Clovis during '56, when they were both busy rehearsing and cutting demos. At the time, Knox was in a group called the Orchids with Jimmy Bowen on double bass and Donnie Lanier on lead guitar. At Roy Orbison's suggestion, they approached Norman Petty about making a record.

Knox had written 'Party Doll' as far back as the late '40s(!) and this, along with Bowen's 'I'm Stickin' With You', came out on the local Triple-D label in 1956. Picked up for national distribution by Roulette, both sides were issued as separate singles: 'Party Doll', credited to Buddy Knox & The Rhythm Orchids, shot to No.1 in the US charts, while 'I'm Sticking With You', credited to Jimmy Bowen & The Rhythm Orchids, reached a respectable No.14.

It's known that Buddy Holly and Jerry Allison played on one or two Knox recordings, and it had been speculated that this was on 'All For You'. However, it has since been established that it was Sonny Curtis who played guitar on that particular track. Jerry Allison has also confirmed that Holly and the other Crickets helped out on Knox's 'Swinging Daddy' and 'Whenever I'm Lonely', and that the songs were cut in Seattle in 1957 when they were both on a big package tour together.

Knox's seminal 'Party Doll' is sometimes cited as the first rockabilly chart hit, and was the first of several hits for him on the Roulette label. During his time at the top, he appeared on all the big tours, on TV (the *Ed Sullivan Show*) and also in the *Jamboree* rock'n'roll movie. However, his career soon diverged from Jimmy Bowen's, when Knox was drafted and ended up at the Fort Hood army base with Elvis. His last Roulette hit, 'I Think I'm Gonna Kill Myself', featured both Sonny Curtis and Jerry Allison and charted despite being banned in some areas on account of its somewhat tasteless title.

Parting company with Roulette in the early '60s, Knox joined Liberty, but his chart career was on the wane and he moved into music publishing. In 1968, however, he signed a new contract with United Artists and went into the studio with producer Bob Montgomery, who helped him to modernise and polish his rockabilly style. The title track of his first album, *Gypsy Man,* written by Sonny Curtis and featuring his impressive acoustic guitar-work and Jerry's drumming, was a C&W hit that year, earning him respect from a new generation of fans. Sadly, despite a number of other critically acclaimed recordings in the late '60s and '70, Knox failed to connect with the mass audience and eventually moved to Canada to pursue business interests.

However, he never stopped performing and his act perennially included a lengthy medley of Buddy Holly's songs, which were well suited to his gentle slip-sliding style. Later still, in 1980, he returned to Lubbock and, in the very shadow of Buddy Holly's statue, recorded Lee Jackson's 'I Named My Little Girl Holly'.

Unfortunately, Knox suffered increasing health problems later in life and passed away from cancer in February 1999, a few months short of his 66th birthday. He is remembered by all as one of life's gentlemen.

See also **JIMMY BOWEN**.

L

DENNY LAINE

Denny Laine, born Brian Hines in 1944, has had a lengthy career in music, but is probably best known as the plaintive lead voice on the Moody Blues' mid-'60s hit, 'Nights In White Satin'. By 1972, however, he had moved on and was heavily involved with McCartney's Wings – an involvement that would see him working with the ex-Beatle on several Holly-related projects. For the most part these were fairly ephemeral, with Laine joining Paul and his posse for the annual *Buddy Holly Week* bash – a celebration that was particularly close to Macca's heart. But one Holly project was more permanent, and involved Laine holing up in Scotland with McCartney long enough to record a whole album of the Texan's songbook, released in 1977 as *Holly Days*. It didn't dent the charts, but was notable for avoiding the stereotypical hits in favour of lesser-known numbers such as 'Look At Me', 'Lonesome Tears' and 'Moondreams'. An album worth seeking out at record fairs.

'LAST NIGHT'

Recorded March 1957 at Norman Petty Recording Studios, Clovis, New Mexico
Personnel: Buddy Holly (guitar, vocals), Jerry Allison (drums), Joe B. Mauldin (double bass)
Overdubbed October 1957: The Picks (backing vocals)

From the pens of Joe B. Mauldin and his original group, the Four Teens, this beautiful song first appeared on the *Chirping Crickets* album. Recorded within weeks of 'That'll Be The Day' and overdubbed by the Picks shortly after, it quickly became a firm favourite with fans and is a perfect example of a Crickets ballad: *'Slowly, with a strong beat'*, as the sheet music put it.

A surprisingly good-quality, undubbed version appeared on the El Toro 3-CD, *Not Fade Away: Buddy Holly – The Complete 1957 Recordings*, and is one of only a few undubbed Holly/Crickets cuts to surface in reasonable quality.

Being an album track, it hasn't inspired many cover versions, although Jimmy Bowen & The Rhythm Orchids cut it in New York around the same time as the Crickets.

'LEARNING THE GAME'

Recorded December 1958 in Apartment 4H, The Brevoort, 11 Fifth Ave, New York
Personnel: Buddy Holly (acoustic guitar, vocals)

Surely one of Holly's finest-ever songs, and the last one he committed to tape in his New York apartment. Although only one minute and forty seconds long in its original, undubbed state, three other versions (with the same lead vocal) have been released. Thanks to studio additions, all of these extend to over two minutes. Chronologically they are the 1960 Jack Hansen overdub (a mix of instruments/backing vocals), the 1962/63 Norman Petty overdub by the Fireballs (instrumentation only), and the 1984 backing vocal overdub (of the Norman Petty/Fireballs version) by the Picks (see **OVERDUBS** and **PICKS** for more info).

The simple yet sincere words and enduring melody surely don't need that much by way of additional adornment, which is why the original, undubbed version – first heard on the 1979 *Complete Buddy Holly* box set – is the classic one and the benchmark for the others. Chartwise, the Jack Hansen version crept into the bottom of the UK charts in 1960 to clock up Holly's sixth posthumous hit in Britain.

Although not routinely covered, a particularly fine duet by Mark Knopfler (guitar) and Waylon Jennings (vocals) came out on the MCA Nashville tribute album, *Not Fade Away (Remembering Buddy Holly)*, in 1996. Since then, Albert Lee (on vocals and piano) has also recorded a touching version accompanied by a lone cellist.

ALBERT LEE

A great British guitarist who has been linked with the music of Holly and the Crickets throughout his career, albeit mostly in a roundabout way. Many years ago, Lee recorded a scintillating version of 'Real Wild Child' (which didn't chart) and also doubled as the title track of one of his few solo albums. In the '70s, he was recruited by Rick Grech and joined the Crickets for a couple of years, appearing on their two country-rock albums, *Remnants* and *A Long Way From Lubbock*. He's returned to the fold intermittently when he hasn't been playing with the Everly Brothers, or latterly Hogan's Heroes or Bill Wyman's Rhythm Kings. Most recently, he joined the Crickets for their 2004 *Crickets And Their Buddies* album and contributed a superb solo vocal on 'Learning The Game'.

LEIBER & STOLLER

Probably the most significant rock'n'roll songwriting team of the '50s, Jerry Leiber and Mike Stoller created the smouldering 'Baby I Don't Care' for Elvis Presley. Suitably impressed after seeing the song performed in *Loving You*, the Crickets decided to record it as a track for the *Buddy Holly* album. The only other number from the Leiber & Stoller songbook that Holly is known to have tackled is the Robins' 1955 hit, 'Smokey Joe's Café', which was discovered among the January 1959 Apartment Tapes.

Leiber & Stoller were inducted into the Rock and Roll Hall of Fame in 1987.

JOHN LENNON

A big Holly/Crickets fan, John Lennon (1940-80) would have a bit more time to move the music forward before he too came to a tragic and premature end. There is not too much to add here, although it's often said an occasional party-piece of his was to do an exaggerated rendition of 'Peggy Sue' – a number he later recorded for his solo *Rock'n'Roll* album with producer Phil Spector. In fact, Lennon is one of the few who could impersonate Holly's 'Rave On'-style hiccupping without sounding forced or silly. Several good examples found their way onto disc, and as good as any is the stretched syllable which opens 'Dear Yoko' on the 2004 album, *Acoustic*.

John Lennon has been inducted into the Rock and Roll Hall of Fame twice: firstly as a member of the Beatles in 1988, and later as a solo artist in 1994.

See also **'MAILMAN, BRING ME NO MORE BLUES'**.

JERRY LEE LEWIS

The 'Ferriday Fireball' was born in Louisiana back in 1935 and is still rocking as this book was going to press. It's said that personal friendships were never the Killer's strong point, but he and Holly were thrown together at a time when both were high in the American hit parade and Lewis has been touchingly complimentary when speaking of Buddy over the years.

They shared the bill on several US packages during early 1958, and even toured Australia together (*'Buddy was the star of that one'* according to Lewis). A couple of superb photos of them jamming exist (the better of the two depicts Jerry Lee at the piano with Holly playing

Backstage jam at the War Memorial Auditorium,
Fort Lauderdale, Florida on 25 February 1958.
Left to right: Jimmy Velvet, Jerry Lee Lewis, Don Everly and Buddy Holly.

guitar while Don Everly and Jimmy Velvet look on – see above). Some exceedingly brief snippets of them playing together are also in circulation, but the tape quality is dire.

There are also believed to be some live radio show recordings in the Australian National Sound Archive of Paul Anka, Holly and Lewis. But that was only 51 years ago, so they may yet be unearthed!

While some artists have covered Holly's material *ad nauseam*, Jerry Lee seems to have steered clear of it, though he famously charted with the Big Bopper's 'Chantilly Lace', and also recorded 'Real Wild Child', which he would have seen Johnny O'Keefe performing while on the Australian tour.

As is only to be expected, the Killer was included in the first group of artists to be inducted into the Rock and Roll Hall of Fame in 1986.

'LISTEN TO ME'
Recorded June or July 1957 at Norman Petty Recording Studios, Clovis, New Mexico
Personnel: Buddy Holly (double-tracked guitar, vocals), Jerry Allison (drums), Joe B. Mauldin (double bass)

The reason why many of you are reading this book is probably exemplified by a track such as this. Apparently simple, the song contains two-part overdubbed vocals *and* guitar, which in those far off days was a revolutionary technique that had seldom been heard on a rock'n'roll record (some mainstream vocalists – notably Patti Page – had been doing it for years, but Holly also double-tracked his guitar).

Written by Buddy, it's a beautiful composition that surely owes something to the musical technique of Mickey & Sylvia, whom he was so fond of. It is therefore something of a mystery that it did not chart in the USA, though it did reach No.16 in Britain, where the Crickets were touring at the time. Incidentally, Buddy's spoken interlude in 'Listen To Me' (the first time we'd heard him talking!) seemed to be curiously devoid of any Texas twang. We would have to wait for interview snippets to hear the humour of the man.

In 1984, the Picks overdubbed backing vocals onto this recording (see **OVERDUBS** and **PICKS** for more info), but in the author's opinion these detracted from the simplicity of the original.

It's also not a song that has been covered much – indeed, it has rarely been included in compilations of Holly material. However, the Searchers brought out a memorable version in the early '60s, and Gary Busey bravely attempted an acoustic rendition in the *Buddy Holly Story* biopic.

LITERATURE (BIOGRAPHIES)

It was years before a fully-fledged biography of Buddy Holly made an appearance, perhaps because the information base just wasn't in place in the early years and any attempt at biography would have contained a paucity of information. A secondary reason was that rock'n'roll biography as a genre hadn't yet been invented and books such as this would only gradually begin to make their appearance.

Dave Laing's 1971 UK biography, *Buddy Holly*, wisely concentrated on analysing the singer's musical legacy, and the biographical content was dispensed with in a few pages. Lifelong rock'n'roll fan and music pundit Rob Finnis also penned an insightful magazine-length biography for *Let It Rock* in the '70s, whilst about the same time Ralph and Elizabeth Peer's US biography of the singer *'in words, photographs and music'* focused almost wholly on sheet music. Probably the most detail we read in those years outside of Bill Griggs's *Reminiscing* magazines were the booklets contained in the World Records and MCA box sets.

But all of the foregoing had to be gauged against the first full-blown Buddy Holly biography by John J. Goldrosen, an unknown name but an obvious champion of Buddy's music, who came from nowhere to give us the definitive account of Holly's life and times. His book, *Buddy Holly: His Life In Music*, hasn't yet been bettered, although it was expanded in later years with John Beecher's help and republished as *Remembering Buddy* – this time with the benefit of a detailed 'Session File' section.

Since then, several journalists have entered the fray and (in the case of Philip Norman at least) have penned highly-readable biographies – although one felt the books were written in the hope that a newspaper would pick up the serialisation rights. Thus, the portraits painted were black and white, producing heroes and villains, rather than rounded characterisations. A selection of such biographies is contained within the *Selected Bibliography* section at the back of this book, with the exception of *The Legend That Was Buddy Holly* by Richard Peters, which was surely written by someone with scant knowledge of the singer or of his music.

LITERATURE (FICTION)

This header highlights some of the fictional books and articles that have used Buddy Holly as a character within their stories – a practice that seems to have been more prevalent years ago than of late. Below are a few examples that the author has stumbled across.

Words of Love by Philip Norman (who also wrote a heavyweight Holly biography) was a collection of short stories first published in 1989, with a title story based around the last few hours of Buddy Holly's life. Strictly speaking, it was a work of *faction* – a mixture of fact, fiction and a dash of poetic licence. It also formed the basis for a successful one-off TV drama about the singer.

Buddy Holly Is Alive and Well On Ganymede by Bradley Denton and *Not Fade Away* by Jim Dodge are both works of fantasy, while *Buddy* was the title of a series of books by children's author Nigel Hinton telling the story of Terry, a Holly-obsessed Teddy boy father struggling to bring up a young son as a single parent. It ended up as a children's TV series with Roger Daltrey from the Who in the main role and spun off into a film musical, *Buddy's Song*, starring Daltrey and Chesney Hawkes.

In 1975, a playlet titled *Jungle Music* appeared in the *City* magazine. This featured all manner of rock'n'roll figures (alive and dead) as characters: Buddy Holly was the Leader of the Laundromat, Little Richard the Chaplain and – wait for it – Pat Boone was the Prison Guard!

Possibly stranger still was a short story featured in *Penthouse* magazine under the one-word title, *Touring*. It was a ghostly tale, well told, of Elvis, Buddy and Janis Joplin appearing together on stage at the Armory, Moorhead (the next venue after Clear Lake) on 3 February 1959 – all of them somehow unaware that they had passed over! Obviously a fantasy, but entertainingly told.

The above list is by no means exhaustive, although it is also tempting to include the Ellis Amburn 'biography', *The Legend That Was Buddy Holly*, under this heading. *Memories of Buddy Holly* by Jim Dawson & Spencer Leigh (see *Selected Bibliography*) also listed several other works of fiction which feature Holly, either directly or otherwise.

'LITTLE BABY'
Recorded December 1957 at Norman Petty Recording Studios, Clovis, New Mexico
Personnel: Buddy Holly (guitar, vocals), Jerry Allison (drums), Joe B. Mauldin (double bass), C.W. Kendall Jr (piano)

Tucked away on Buddy Holly's first solo album, this is the sort of track that has a touch of genius about it that defies analysis. So simple in concept, the song was a collaboration between Buddy and Big Beats pianist C.W. Kendall, whose inspired playing really sets off the number so well. (Norman Petty is also listed as co-composer, but one assumes this was a business arrangement.) In 1984, the Picks overdubbed backing vocals onto this recording (see **OVERDUBS** and **PICKS** for more info).

Again, it's a song that hasn't been covered much, but in fairness it would be hard to better the original. Jimmy Gilmer's version, recorded at Clovis and included on his *Buddy's Buddy* album, was a rare attempt at reworking the number.

LITTLE RICHARD

Born in 1932, Richard Wayne Penniman was, in his day, the most outrageous of performers and arguably had as much of an impact on his fellow artists as on his audiences. Back in 1956, nobody had never heard – or seen – anyone quite like him in mainstream popular music. Certainly, the Crickets were in awe of the man, and almost from Day One performed his songs alongside their own. Buddy recorded several of Richard's hits including 'Slippin' And Slidin' ', 'Send Me Some Lovin' ', 'Ready Teddy' and 'Rip It Up' (the latter as an early demo). On stage, he also played 'Tutti Frutti' and 'Long Tall Sally', though they were never captured on tape. The post-Holly Crickets too continued to feature his material and for years never left the stage without performing 'Keep A-Knockin' '. It's also known that the title of 'Well... All Right' was inspired by the phrase with which Richard habitually punctuated his act.

Apart from covering Little Richard's material, Buddy and the boys were hugely taken with the man himself and the story is told (and was confirmed by Richard in his biography, *Quasar of Rock*), that Buddy took him to his home when they were both in Lubbock for a show. That may sound innocuous nowadays, but in the Deep South in 1956, it was quite an unusual action on Holly's part. Segregation was still the name of the game in those parts and mixing of the races was the exception, not the norm. Oddly, only one picture of Holly and Richard together has ever surfaced.

A total original and a much-loved performer, Little Richard was among the first group of artists to be inducted into the Rock and Roll Hall of Fame in 1986.

WILLIE LOGAN

A contemporary blues guitarist from Scotland who has released a series of albums entitled *The Legend Lives*. He's shown here as the second album in the series focused on the Buddy Holly songbook, and it's a good album even if the titles he chose to record were rather predictable. But it was a nice touch to include an additional number, 'Girl In Every Song', which was inspired by, and composed around Holly's melodies. This album is mentioned here because there are not too many good-quality instrumental albums of Holly's music out there. One can think of Hank Marvin's *Hank Plays Holly* and Tommy Allsup and Jerry Allison's Clovis-recorded *Buddy Holly Songbook*, but little else outside the bargain bin variety.

'LONESOME TEARS'
Recorded May 1958 at Norman Petty Recording Studios, Clovis, New Mexico
Personnel: Buddy Holly (guitar, vocals), Tommy Allsup (guitar), Jerry Allison (drums), Joe B. Mauldin (double bass), The Roses (backing vocals)

The classic 'B' side of the Crickets' 'It's So Easy' single, 'Lonesome Tears' featured Holly on rhythm guitar and vocals, and Tommy Allsup on lead. Allsup has stated in recent interviews that the Roses actually sang backing vocals live on this session, rather than being overdubbed later, as was the normal practice – which makes sense, as to the author's knowledge an undubbed version has never surfaced.

This Holly composition first surfaced in 1965 on the US version of *Holly In The Hills*, but didn't appear in the UK until the release of *Remember* in 1971.

Although 'Lonesome Tears' has inspired few covers, folk singer Carolyn Hester has recorded it on two occasions: firstly in the early '60s (released in 1995 on the Bear Family 2-CD, *Dear Companion*) and again for her 1999 CD, *From These Hills*. Meanwhile, Denny Laine's 1977 *Holly Days* album features him and Paul McCartney performing it as an instrumental duet – an unusual treatment.

'LOOK AT ME'
Recorded December 1957 at Norman Petty Recording Studios, Clovis, New Mexico
Personnel: Buddy Holly (guitar, vocals), Jerry Allison (drums), Joe B. Mauldin (double bass), C.W. Kendall Jr (piano)

Written by Holly and Jerry Allison (but co-credited to Norman Petty), this is an underrated recording which first appeared on the 1958 *Buddy Holly* album. Allison plays very effective 'cardboard box percussion', while the rolling piano of Big Beats pianist C.W. Kendall lifts it out of the ordinary into something a little bit special.

A surprise release in Britain in 1961, it wasn't a hit, although deeper charts in *World's Fair* listed it as creeping into the Top 100. Interestingly, this release (backed with 'Mailman, Bring Me No More Blues') had heavy tape echo added by Decca in London, and it certainly enhances the track.

A handful of artists have covered the song on albums. Bobby Vee didn't include it on his popular *I Remember Buddy Holly* album from 1961, but redressed the balance on 1999's *Down The Line*, which also contained other less well-known Holly numbers such as 'Holly Hop' and 'Blue Days, Black Nights'. Tommy Roe, whose music likewise owed a lot to Buddy Holly, also covered the song, as did Ronnie Smith, who cut his version at Clovis.

TRINI LOPEZ

Despite being christened 'Trinidad', Trini was actually a native of Dallas, Texas, where he was born in 1937. In an interview segment on his *Legacy: My Texas Roots* album, he recalls meeting Buddy Holly for the first time in Wichita Falls in the mid-'50s, and then later at Clovis (when, for a short time, he was lead vocalist with the Big Beats).

Lopez came close to becoming a member of the Crickets after Buddy died, when he was invited to join the re-formed group in Los Angeles in 1960. It seems that he was actually primed and ready to start touring with them, but, running out of money fast, he had to start gigging around to survive. He got a job in a bar singing mainly folk music, later progressing to P.J.'s nightclub in Los Angeles where he was discovered by producer Don Costa. Signed by Frank Sinatra's newly formed Reprise label, he scored a No.3 US hit with 'If I Had A Hammer' – the first of a lengthy run of hit singles. He went on to record well over forty albums.

LOUISIANA HAYRIDE

In the early '50s, there were several centres below the Mason-Dixon line which acted as magnets for musical talent from the cluster of states that surrounded them. Although they started off being headlined by the biggest country acts of the day, many would soon be peddling rockabilly or rock'n'roll to their listeners as Elvis opened the floodgates for others to follow through.

Dallas had the *Big D Jamboree*, on which Holly and Sonny Curtis appeared – just once – back in '55 or '56. Further east, and over the state border in Louisiana, Shreveport too exuded its own pull. Elvis may have been rejected by Nashville's *Grand Ole Opry*, but he wasn't shown the door by the *Hayride* and signed a contract to play there for a full year before national fame whipped him away in 1956.

He also famously advised Buddy & Bob to try their luck there, and the boys naively travelled down to Shreveport, only to find the *Hayride*'s door firmly closed to them: they weren't expected, and Elvis wasn't in town! But it was all part of trying to get established, even if at the time it must have seemed like quite a setback.

'LOVE IS STRANGE'
Recorded January 1959 in Apartment 4H, The Brevoort, 11 Fifth Ave, New York
Personnel: Buddy Holly (acoustic guitar, vocals)

This Mickey & Sylvia song, a huge US pop hit in 1957, was a favourite of Buddy's, and fortunately he left behind a version for posterity on his Ampex tape recorder in his New York apartment prior to setting out on the *Winter Dance Party* tour. Strikingly, the original, undubbed version lasts barely one and a half minutes and doesn't contain an instrumental break: it's just a straight run-through with Holly accompanying himself on acoustic guitar. We're told that the slight bump near the start of the undubbed tape is probably Tommy Allsup turning up and knocking on the door! If so, it certainly doesn't phase Buddy, who completes a beautiful reading of the song.

However, the first time his fans heard the number – on the 1969 *Giant* album – it sounded very different. It seemed that there had been a whole orchestra in the studio, although the sumptuous backing was actually Norman Petty playing a primitive type of synthesizer called an ondioline, plus the Fireballs injecting some rhythm. With Holly's vocals repeated and an instrumental break inserted, the end result was a master literally twice the length of the original. In 1984, the Picks added backing vocals to the overdubbed recording (see **OVERDUBS** and **PICKS** for more info), which in this instance worked well.

In 1969, 'Love Is Strange' was released on 45 rpm in a picture sleeve in both the US and the UK, but only with minimal success. In the USA, the single bubbled under the *Billboard* 'Hot 100' at No.105, and peaked at a lowly No.94 in *Cash Box*. In Britain, the single failed to chart, although the album from which it was pulled, *Giant*, reached No.13, showing that even ten years down the line Holly's fans hadn't disappeared.

Other covers have fared better: the Everly Brothers took it to No.11 in the UK in 1965, while ten years after Mickey & Sylvia, Peaches & Herb took it back into the US Top 20. In 1987, the song was given a totally new lease of life when Mickey & Sylvia's version was used on the soundtrack of *Dirty Dancing*. Holly's interpretation, meanwhile, has inspired its own series of covers including those by John Mueller (one of the very best Holly tribute artists) and Bobby Vee on his 1999 *Down The Line* album.

The composer details for 'Love Is Strange' are convoluted to say the least. Basically, Bo Diddley wrote the song, but copyrighted it in the name of his then wife, Ethel Smith. Some time later, he sold the song to Mickey Baker and Sylvia Vanderpool. To add to the confusion, Bo had based his composition around a very distinctive guitar riff which his lead guitarist, Jody Williams, had previously used on Billy Stewart's 'Billy's Blues'. This precipitated a lawsuit, but ultimately the Court of Appeal held that the two records were *'not substantially or materially similar'*. Ironically, 'Love Is Strange' has at various times been credited to all the above-named artists except Williams.

'LOVE ME'
(1) Recorded December 1955 at Nesman Recording Studio, Wichita Falls, Texas
Personnel: Buddy Holly (guitar, vocals), Sonny Curtis (guitar), Jerry Allison (drums), Don Guess (double bass)
(2) Recorded January 1956 at Bradley's Barn Studio, Nashville, Tennessee
Personnel: Buddy Holly (vocals), Sonny Curtis (guitar), Grady Martin (guitar), Don Guess (double bass), Doug Kirkham (percussion)

This was one of a couple of Sue Parrish compositions that Buddy recorded during his first trip to Nashville, and, is one of the four songs he had included on the audition tape that persuaded Paul Cohen at Decca to offer him a contract.

The recording we are familiar with is Take 10 from the Nashville session, and on the 2007 Rollercoaster CD, *Ohh! Annie!* we hear the studio engineer calling out the take number. In 1984, the Picks overdubbed backing vocals onto it (see **OVERDUBS** and **PICKS** for more info).

Buddy's demo was issued on the 2006 Rev-Ola CD, *Gotta Roll! The Early Recordings 1949-1955*. It's interesting to hear him open this version with a stretched *'Well'*, foreshadowing the dynamic start to 'Rave On'.

The Nashville cut ended up as the flip side of 'Blue Days, Black Nights', Holly's first-ever record release. It didn't chart, and the world had to wait a while for 'That'll Be The Day' to bring the singer to our attention. Although 'Love Me' obviously had shades of Elvis about it, the first Decca session that year had stifled Buddy somewhat and it would need the freedom of Norman Petty's Clovis studio to bring about the conditions that unleashed his full potential.

Although it's a pretty reasonable rockabilly-styled number, 'Love Me' has not inspired any covers to speak of.

'LOVE'S MADE A FOOL OF YOU'
Recorded June 1958 at Norman Petty Recording Studios, Clovis, New Mexico
Personnel: Buddy Holly (guitar, double-tracked vocals), Tommy Allsup (guitar), Bo Clarke (drums), George Atwood (double bass)

This composition by Buddy Holly and Bob Montgomery was written specifically with the Everly Brothers in mind (as was 'Wishing'), and during the early summer of 1958 Buddy went into the studio with Tommy Allsup to cut demos of both to pitch to Don and Phil. As bad luck would have it, the Everlys' choice of material was controlled by the Acuff-Rose publishing house and the duo never got a chance to record either title. With Holly never getting round to doing anything with the songs either, they were destined to moulder in the Clovis vaults for several years, hogtied by the legalities that dogged much of his musical catalogue in the '60s.

But surface they eventually did, albeit not together. 'Love's Made A Fool Of You' came out on the 1964 *Showcase* album, although in the UK it was also released as a single and became the last 'new' Holly song to make the Top 40. (Incidentally, Holly had posthumous singles continuously in the UK charts every year from 1959 to 1964 – a monumental achievement in hindsight.) It's a minor point only, but the hit version sported handclaps which had been dubbed on just prior to its release.

In 1984, the Picks overdubbed backing vocals onto the LP version (see **OVERDUBS** and **PICKS** for more info).

On the undubbed version, which was issued on the 1995 4-CD Vigotone bootleg, *What You Been A-Missin'*, the instrumental fade-out lasts several seconds longer, but otherwise the cut differs very little.

But wait, it gets even more complicated, for the *original* hit version of the song wasn't by Holly at all, but by the post-Holly Crickets. It was the group's first-ever single without Buddy's involvement and went on to reach the UK Top 30 in April 1959. The two versions sound almost like different songs: Buddy's is more of a folk-styled reading, while the Crickets lay down a backbeat to add tension and, with Earl Sinks on lead vocals, turn in a very powerful performance.

It was certainly the Crickets' version that went on to inspire the Bobby Fuller Four's huge American hit in 1966, while rockabilly revival outfit Matchbox also charted with it in Britain in 1981. (A few years earlier, they had resurrected the Crickets' 'When You Ask About Love' and took it into the British Top 5, and they no doubt hoped this number would fare equally well. Unfortunately, it was not to be, and the record peaked at a lowly No.63.) The song has also been covered by folk greats Tom Rush and Sandy Denny, and also punk-style by Classic Ruins on the 1989 Holly tribute album, *Everyday Is A Holly Day*, released by the French new wave label, New Rose. More recently still, the Crickets returned to their studio in Lyles, Tennessee and reinterpreted it yet again, this time with Johnny Rivers on lead vocals.

LPs

The 33⅓ rpm long-playing album (or 'LP') was launched by Columbia Records in 1948. To a public used to having to change 78s every few minutes, the luxury of being able to listen to music for over 20 minutes without a break was sheer luxury, and the format quickly caught on and was well established by the second half of the '50s.

The most famous Holly/Crickets album releases are discussed elsewhere in the book under their individual entries, whereas the broad heading here allows us to include more generalised comments. Frankly, if every subsequent album and its track listings from 1957 onwards were listed, there would be little room left for anything else: worldwide, the ongoing figure runs into hundreds – maybe thousands – of compilations, especially if we aggregate all the vinyl and compact disc releases. Additionally, there have also been a burgeoning number of unauthorised and bootleg releases over the years – all of which is startling when one reflects that only *two* albums were released during the singer's lifetime. And, as was standard practice, these were both collections of singles ('A' and 'B' sides) augmented by a few fillers (a misnomer of course, as few numbers in the Buddy Holly songbook – and certainly none on the two albums mentioned below – could remotely qualify as such). For some younger readers this must sound confusing, as we're looking back to the time when downloads didn't exist and even compact discs were decades away.

The first album was *The Chirping Crickets*, which came out in late 1957 in America. British fans had to wait almost six months to purchase their copy, by which time the group were already part-way through their spellbinding British tour. The pattern with other releases was invariably the same, with the American ones being issued weeks or months before British subsidiaries followed suit. But fans buying the Crickets album were confused by the cover depicting four smiling musicians, because there were only three of them on stage and not too much chirping was going on! We'd learn later that rhythm guitarist Niki Sullivan had already quit, and that Norman Petty's groups, either the Picks or the Roses, were responsible for the majority of the vocal harmonies we heard on record.

Sullivan died in 2002, but is fondly remembered because of his involvement with a handful of Holly's most classic recordings (also see separate entry for **NIKI SULLIVAN**).

Then, within months, a second LP – the solo album, *Buddy Holly* – hit the shops, and the main puzzle this time around was the cover photo of Holly *sans* his trademark glasses, although the sound, except for the backing vocals, was unchanged.

The musicians on both LPs were, with the occasional exception of Sullivan, one and the same. Of the two, it was the Crickets album that proved to be the bigger hit, but the solo one sold steadily over a period. Still popular today, both are available on CD, most recently as a '2-on-1' format.

See also **EPs**.

LUBBOCK

So unworldly was the average young British record fan in the '50s, that when the sleevenotes of the Crickets album reported the group as hailing from 'Bullock, Texas', we assumed the mistake lay with our atlases. Over the years, however, we have become far more familiar with Lubbock and its whereabouts, and many of this book's readers will have visited the so-called 'Hub City of the South Plains'.

Settled in 1890 and incorporated in 1909, the city was named after Thomas S. Lubbock, a former Texas Ranger and Confederate officer. His brother, Francis R. Lubbock, was Governor of Texas during the Civil War. From small beginnings, the city has grown rapidly to become a bustling metropolis boasting some 200,000 inhabitants (over a quarter-million if we include the rest of Lubbock County) at the centre of a major cotton-growing region. Certainly, the place today is far different than it was when Buddy Holly was born there in 1936, when a letter addressed simply to a name and a Route number would been delivered to its recipient!

Although most musicians who emanated from the Lubbock area – for example Waylon Jennings and Joe Ely – had to break away to make their names, it seems something in the air kept drawing them back to their West Texas roots. Holly for one never denied where he came from, and we know that he had plans to return and open a recording facility that would have drawn more talent into the city itself (see **PRISM RECORDS**). Sadly, all such plans died with the singer, and it seemed for some time that he had almost been forgotten in his hometown.

However, some seeds had taken root which culminated first with a statue of the singer being erected in 1980 and then a West Texas Walk of Fame springing up around it. Finally, and with the new Millennium approaching, a long-awaited museum facility came into being that features a permanent exhibition dedicated to its most famous musical son.

LUBBOCK RADIO

It seems that the most popular Lubbock station when the 1950s hove into view was KSEL, which featured a mixed format ranging from popular and country music to weekly wrestling commentaries. One of the presenters from those days was Pappy Dave Stone, who quit to set up KDAV in 1953, taking fellow deejays Ben Hall and Hi-Pockets Duncan with him. It was at KDAV that Buddy & Bob subsequently got a chance to appear on the *Sunday Party* show, while Buddy also occasionally sat in with Ben Hall & The Ramblers.

In 1958, the Corbin brothers launched KLLL (popularly known as 'K-triple-L'), with a young Waylon Jennings as one of its wannabe disc jockeys. It must have been a transitional period for the world of local radio, as in the same year the more staid KSEL decided to jump aboard the national bandwagon and banned rock'n'roll from its airwaves. In his time, Buddy Holly had occasional involvements with all three stations.

There were also other radio stations in Lubbock, such as the long-established KFYO, however Holly had no known connections with them.

ROD LUCIER

A brief correction to earlier editions: Rod Lucier has often been named as the promoter of the *Winter Dance Party* tour, whereas he was in fact the owner of the Armory in Moorhead, Minnesota – the venue the package was supposed on play on 3 February, 'the day after'. As sponsor of the date, he had to make the decision whether or not to go ahead with the show. He elected to advertise for local talent, and it was through his actions that a 15-year-old Bobby Vee got his big break. And, as they say, the rest really is history.

ROBIN LUKE

Robin Luke was born in Los Angeles in 1942, but moved to Hawaii in 1954. A one-hit wonder by virtue of his monster smash, 'Susie Darlin' ', which reached No.5 on the *Billboard* chart in August 1958, he was booked to appear on both the *Perry Como Show* and *American Bandstand*. It was backstage at the latter show that he first met Buddy Holly, whom he vividly recollects teaching him the chords to 'Peggy Sue'. Nevertheless, Luke never envisaged a long-term career in music and, after several unsuccessful follow-ups, returned to his studies and eventually gained a Doctorate in Business and Marketing.

M

ROSE MADDOX

In the late '40s and early '50s Roselea Arbana Brogdon *aka* Rose Maddox was lead singer with the immensely popular hillbilly outfit, the Maddox Brothers & Rose. Constantly touring, they were by all accounts frequent visitors to Lubbock during the early '50s, and among the many fans hanging around the stage door was a youthful Buddy Holly. Some years later, Rose bumped into the singer in Southern Music's offices in New York. He reportedly told her: *'Rose, I was the Lubbock stage door kid who took your advice. Without your help and encouragement I may never have become a professional musician.'*

'MAILMAN, BRING ME NO MORE BLUES'
Recorded April 1957 at Norman Petty Recording Studios, Clovis, New Mexico
Personnel: Buddy Holly (guitar, vocals), Jerry Allison (drums), Joe B. Mauldin (double bass), Vi Petty (piano)

Holly went into the Clovis studio in April '57 primarily to cut 'Words Of Love' for his next single, but while there he also tackled this unusual number (*'Moderately, with a blues beat'*), which had been specially written for him by record producer Bob Thiele – the music mogul who had put his head on the block for Buddy to get 'That'll Be The Day' released. At the same time, Thiele also pitched 'Mailman' to one of his other Coral artists, Don Cornell, but by then Cornell's hit parade days were on the wane and his record failed to chart.

First released on the 1958 *Buddy Holly* album, Holly's version was also released as a UK single in 1961, on the flip of 'Look At Me'. Both sides had echo added by Decca in London. This definitely enhances the impact of the recording and makes it something for the more avid collector to seek out.

The song hasn't inspired many covers, although Mike Berry included it on his *Buddy Holly – A Life In Music* album a few years back. But the strangest version surely has to be John Lennon's vocal on the Beatles' jam during the *Get Back* sessions in 1969 (when, coincidentally, they also made an informal recording of Holly's 'Not Fade Away').

MARIA ELENA

A receptionist at the Southern Music Publishing Company in New York, Maria Elena Santiago first met Buddy Holly, Jerry Allison and Joe B. Mauldin when they visited the office to see Murray Deutch. Famously, Buddy and Maria fell in love. After a courtship lasting some nine months, they married in Lubbock in August 1958 before returning to their rented New York apartment in the Brevoort building. Thereafter, the story is pretty well known if we accept the romanticized version of Buddy's life as depicted in the musical and the film.

After Buddy's death Maria Elena remarried twice and raised a family. At the present time, she lives near Dallas, Texas.

HANK B. MARVIN

Although he was by no means the only one to emulate American artists, it certainly looked like the Drifters/Shadows guitarist Hank B. Marvin owed more than a little to Buddy Holly and the Crickets from the outset. He seemed to materialise on the scene virtually overnight, complete with heavy-framed spectacles and an identical Fender Stratocaster to Holly (yet to his credit, he never appeared to be mimicking the Texan even when playing his songs). Even his stage name (he was born Brian Rankin in 1941) seemed to borrow something from Joe B. Mauldin.

But it's probably unfair to single Hank out here. Cliff Richard was also a known Holly fan who occasionally wore heavy specs, but based his act more on Elvis (though we shouldn't forget that he had a UK Top 10 hit with 'True Love Ways' in 1981). Not only that, the Shadows' bass guitarist, Bruce Welch, was also a big fan and later acted as musical consultant to the *Buddy* musical, which is approaching its twentieth year as these notes are being written.

After his days as a full-time Shadow ended, Marvin further indulged his love of Holly's music by recording the *Hank Plays Holly* album in 1996 with the help of several members of his family and earning a gold record for his efforts.

JOE B. MAULDIN

Joseph Benson Mauldin was born in Lubbock on 8 July 1940 and joined the Crickets in 1957, having previously been the bassist with the highly rated local group, the Four Teens. Younger than the other Crickets by a stretch, he'd dabbled in music at school, but it wasn't till he turned to the stand-up bass that he at last found his *métier*. (He briefly tried out a bass guitar, as photos of him from the July 1958 *Summer Dance Party* attest, but has stuck to stand-up ever since.)

It's a surprise to look back and realise that Joe wasn't with the Crickets when 'That'll Be The Day' was cut, either at Nashville or Clovis, but musical relationships are often subject to changes and chance, and when Larry Welborn decided to move on to other things, Joe B. was quickly drafted in. The arrangement was solid from the start, and Joe B. stayed with Buddy and Jerry for the next eighteen months until a well-catalogued parting of the ways came about in the autumn of 1958.

Joe continued with the re-formed Crickets from 1958 onwards and played on several singles they cut for Coral in the late '50s and at the start of the '60s, but bailed out when bookings dropped off and Jerry Allison and Sonny Curtis decided to head for Los Angeles.

With the group at a crossroads, Joe turned his back on music for several years and ran a trucking business. Further disruption occurred when he was called up to do a two-year stint in the US Army 1965-67, after which he went to work at the Goldstar studio with Phil Spector.

But the lure of being a Cricket proved too strong and, after rejoining the group in 1977 for a one-off show at London's Kilburn State Theatre, he has remained a member ever since.

See also **CRICKETS**.

'MAYBE BABY'
(1) Recorded March 1957 at Norman Petty Recording Studios, Clovis, New Mexico
Personnel: Buddy Holly (guitar, vocals), Niki Sullivan (vocals), Jerry Allison (drums), Joe B. Mauldin (double bass)
(2) Recorded September 1957 at Tinker US Air Force Base, Oklahoma
Personnel: Buddy Holly (guitar, vocals), Niki Sullivan (guitar), Jerry Allison (drums), Joe B. Mauldin (double bass)
Overdubbed October 1957: The Picks (backing vocals)

'Maybe Baby' has to be one of the most potent of all Crickets recordings and, like so many of their classic hits, it has stood the test of time. It was one of four tracks that the group recorded on the road at Tinker US Air Force base near Oklahoma City, where Norman Petty had been appearing around the same time with his trio. (It was a pre-planned session, and Petty had brought mobile recording equipment with him.) While the Picks usually overdubbed backing vocals within days of sessions, this time it would be some two weeks before they did so, and months before the record itself was put out.

It quickly became a worldwide hit and the second gold record for the group after 'That'll Be The Day'. The anomaly was that it only reached No.17 on the *Billboard* pop chart, yet climbed to No.4 on the R&B chart! But with rock'n'roll taking over, the US charts started to take on an increasingly ludicrous look with some records being listed simultaneously as pop, R&B *and* country hits! (Who *really* thinks 'Maybe Baby' is an R&B number?)

What most fans didn't realise until 1966 came around, was that Buddy and the Crickets had originally cut 'Maybe Baby' at Clovis with a swing beat, but were unhappy with the outcome and had no plans to put it out as a single. According to Jerry Allison, it was Dale Hawkins who suggested that they switch the rhythm pattern, which ultimately led them to re-cut the number.

The original 'swing' version gathered dust in the vaults until it was released on 45 rpm in Britain in 1966, with 'That's My Desire' on the flip. Both sides of the single, with backings added by the Fireballs, managed to brush the British charts without actually reaching the Top 50, but at least it proved to fans that the well of recordings hadn't yet dried up. Alternative overdubs of the 'swing' version were made at the same time, but have never been issued.

The original, undubbed master of the 'swing' version finally surfaced in 1983 on the *For The First Time Anywhere* album, and Niki Sullivan's harmony vocals, previously obscured by overdubs, can be heard here to good effect.

An audio recording of the Crickets singing 'Maybe Baby' live on the *Off The Record* TV show in Britain in 1958 also exists and will no doubt be released one day.

As for covers, literally dozens of artists including Billy Fury, the Nitty Gritty Dirt Band, Skeeter Davis, Brian May, Connie Francis and the Hollies have recorded 'Maybe Baby' over the years, although surprisingly no-one has ever taken it back into the charts. The post-Holly Crickets have recorded the song twice (on 1990's live *Sunday Night At The London Palladium* and 1993's *Double Exposure*), but this doesn't begin to compare with the number of times they've performed it on the bandstand.

As with 'Everyday', this is one of those Holly compositions that, although deceptively simple in construction, results in two minutes of musical magic.

SIR PAUL McCARTNEY

The former Beatle was born in 1942, and any form of CV here would be ballast. All the Fab Four were confirmed Crickets fans and included a smattering of the Texans' music in their repertoire, even in their earliest days as the Quarrymen. Indeed, their first real attempt to make a record was a demo of 'That'll Be The Day'. So, the links were there from the start for all to witness, but it was only in later life that Macca was able to really indulge his love of Holly's music in a practical way by acquiring the singer's music publishing (he purchased the US rights to the entire Nor-Va-Jak catalogue in 1975).

Thereafter, McCartney took a decision to inaugurate an annual *Buddy Holly Week*, and it's something that has run for many years since 1976. In 1977, 1979 and 1995, he brought the Crickets to England for fondly remembered concerts, and in 1985 he financed the superb *Real Buddy Holly Story* documentary for BBC-TV's *Arena*, an extended version of which later appeared on a commercial video.

He produced and played on Denny Laine's 1977 *Holly Days* tribute album, and in 1988 he both produced and played piano on the title track of the Crickets' *T-Shirt* album. Doubtless there will be more to come in future.

ECHO McGUIRE

In the *Buddy Holly Story* biopic, Buddy leaves Lubbock and his girlfriend in a fictional scene that probably never happened the way it did on screen. In reality, Echo McGuire and Buddy are said to have been close in their teens, but their lives were always heading in different directions. (Religion appears to have been one such difference: Holly was a Tabernacle Baptist, while Echo worshipped at the Church of Christ – an important difference in Lubbock in those days.)

Holly duly engaged in his music-making activities, while Echo went to Christian teacher training in Abilene, and then on to Nebraska, where she met her future husband, Ron Griffiths.

Until relatively recently, Echo had been just a name and a faded photograph until Holly biographer Philip Norman tracked her down in 1996, and we learnt that the relationship had been a deep one on both sides. In later years, many more photos of the two of them together have surfaced.

DON McLEAN

Born in 1945, singer-songwriter Don McLean was an acolyte of folk guru Pete Seeger and, on the face of it, the least likely of individuals to end up being linked with Buddy Holly. But in 1971 he single-handedly did more than anyone else to bring his name back before the American public by writing and recording 'American Pie' and taking it to the top of the charts worldwide.

Although he hasn't recorded a full-length tribute album of Holly's music, he has tackled several Holly titles over the years – which is an honour, given that the bulk of his output is self-penned. He recorded 'Fool's Paradise' and 'Everyday' for his 1973 *Playin' Favorites* album, and 'It Doesn't Matter Anymore' for 1979's *Chain Lightning*. In 1973, his live version of 'Everyday' reached the UK Top 40. During the '80s, McLean turned his hand to tackling other artists' hits with an album entitled *For The Memories*, on which he included a version of 'Maybe Baby'.

McLean's music is multi-layered and he has never been compromised by his links with Holly, or anyone else for that matter. He has also played occasional Holly tribute concerts over the years.

See also **'AMERICAN PIE'**.

DUTCH McMILLIN

Elbert Raymond 'Dutch' McMillin (1916-95) is given a name-check here, Holly's third and final Nashville session (November 1956) featured an alto saxophone, and for years the player was assumed to have been the better-known 'Yakety Sax' man, Boots Randolph. In fact, both Boots and Dutch were used extensively on Nashville country sessions for years, although McMillin didn't arrive in America until he was in his teens and never regarded music as his sole occupation. Despite his lower profile, he nevertheless became a regular sessionman and appears on material recorded by everyone from Hank Locklin and Marty Robbins to Perry Como.

JOE MEEK

Robert George 'Joe' Meek (1929-67) was born in Wales and has to be among the most tragic figures mentioned in these pages. Rather like Norman Petty, with whom he became friends, Meek came to music production and management via the hard graft of studio engineering, and in the '50s was responsible for the unique sounds on Humphrey Lyttleton's 'Bad Penny Blues' and Ann Shelton's 1956 British chart-topper, 'Lay Down Your Arms'.

It was also around this time that he developed an unhealthy preoccupation with Buddy Holly that would contribute to his eventual undoing. Meek had a keen interest in spiritualism and frequently organised séances. At one such session in January 1958, one of the participants wrote down the message: *'February 3. Buddy Holly dies.'* Shocked to the core, Meek attempted to warn Buddy by sending messages to his record company and music publisher. It is not known whether he received it, but 3 February 1958 duly passed without mishap. Nevertheless, Meek was convinced that the message he had received had substance. When the Crickets visited the UK in March 1958, he went to see Holly in person to pass on the warning. Buddy was seemingly unperturbed and calmly thanked Joe for his concern, but less than a year later the prediction tragically came true.

Meek's career took off in 1960, when he moved into production and opened his own independent London studio – in a terraced house(!) in Holloway Road – from where he either leased recordings to major labels, or put them out on his own Triumph label.

But Buddy Holly was never far away. Deeply affected by his death, Meek held numerous séances to contact Holly's spirit and felt that the deceased singer was helping him with his work. Certainly, many of his productions around that time had a definite Holly 'feel' - for example Lance Fortune's 1960 Holly-like hit, 'Be Mine'.

A particularly notable example was 'Tribute To Buddy Holly', written by Geoff Goddard – another committed spiritualist – which was reportedly inspired by a dream after a séance with Joe. Recorded by Mike Berry, it became a big hit in the UK and on the Continent.

Despite his Holly fixation, Meek's output was extremely wide-ranging and much of what he produced has stood the test of time well. Visit any British record shop and you'll probably be confronted with compilations of his work. Sadly, as the '60s progressed, his success began to wane and he became increasingly paranoid about being spied on and ostracised by the music industry.

On the eighth anniversary of Buddy Holly's passing, in the midst of a period of emotional turmoil, the notoriously volatile Meek shot his landlady, Mrs Violet Shenton, then turned the gun on himself.

Anyone wishing to learn more about this legendary UK producer should seek out John Repsch's sensitive biography, *The Legendary Joe Meek, The Telstar Man* (see *Selected Bibliography*) or see the 2008 biopic, *Telstar*.

'MEMORIES' *(Buddy & Bob)*
Recorded August 1955 at KDAV, Lubbock, Texas
Personnel: Buddy Holly (guitar, vocals), Bob Montgomery (guitar, vocals), Sonny Curtis (fiddle), prob. Don Guess (double bass)

Written by Bob Montgomery, this pretty song is one of a batch of informal recordings that Buddy & Bob left behind from their mid-1955 demo sessions. It first saw the light of day amongst similar material on the UK version of the 1965 *Holly In The Hills* album, albeit heavily overdubbed by the Fireballs. The undubbed version surfaced in 1995 on the 4-CD Vigotone bootleg, *What You Been A-Missin'*. In his Holly discography, *Buddy Holly – His Songs and Interviews (The Technical Stuff)*, Bill Griggs lists a second version of 'Memories', which remains unissued.

MICKEY & SYLVIA

There is no doubt that Buddy Holly had a penchant for the music of this duo from the time he first heard their hit recordings to the day when the Crickets appeared on the same 1957 tour bills as them. By all accounts, Mickey (Baker) and Sylvia (Vanderpool) didn't get along too well together, but that didn't stop them recording some potent music before they finally went their separate ways in the early '60s. Baker was also constantly in demand as a session guitarist for Atlantic, as well as for Columbia's R&B subsidiary, OKeh.

As we know, Buddy left behind home tape recordings of two Mickey & Sylvia songs, 'Dearest' and 'Love Is Strange' (both Bo Diddley compositions, incidentally), and again one wonders exactly what he would have done with those demos had he lived.

See also **'DEAREST'** *and* **'LOVE IS STRANGE'**.

'MIDNIGHT SHIFT'
Recorded January 1956 at Bradley's Barn Studio, Nashville, Tennessee
Personnel: Buddy Holly (vocals), Sonny Curtis (guitar), Grady Martin (guitar), Don Guess (double bass), Doug Kirkham (percussion)

This was surely one of the best recordings from the 1956 Nashville sessions and the wonder is that it wasn't chosen for a single release at the time. However, it did come out in Britain as a posthumous 45 on Brunswick in 1959 and briefly reached the Top 30.

Attributed to 'Earl Lee' (*aka* Luke McDaniel) and Jimmie Ainsworth, it's believed to have been written solely by the former, who was a minor singer-songwriter of the era. Although it seems to lean towards the popular 'Annie' records (see **HANK BALLARD & THE**

MIDNIGHTERS), this has always been denied.

In 1984, the Picks overdubbed backing vocals onto this recording (see **OVERDUBS** and **PICKS** for more info), which in this instance worked well.

For closet Holly fans, an epiphany took place in 2007 when Rollercoaster Records put out their *Ohh! Annie!* CD and gave us not only Take 4 (the usual master recording), but also the superb and wilder unissued Take 10, plus a curtailed Take 11, when a wrong note cuts the track short. Needless to say, all of these are essential listening.

Although it wasn't covered at the time, Commander Cody & His Lost Planet Airmen recorded the song in 1971, while Sonny Curtis also put it out in 1990 on his *No Stranger To The Rain* album on the Ritz label.

MIDNIGHTERS – *See* **HANK BALLARD & THE MIDNIGHTERS**

GARY MILLER

It's a tad ironic that Neville Williams *aka* Gary Miller (1924-68) should have been on the same bill as the Crickets on the 1958 UK tour, as it was rock'n'roll music that would virtually wipe singers such as him from the nation's airwaves. In fact, Miller's '50s hit parade successes were almost all American covers, and the emerging '60s would be a bleak time for him chartwise. Nonetheless, it appears that he and the Crickets got along well, and there are several good photos of them together on tour.

MITCH MILLER

Born in 1911, Mitchell William Miller was a musical name to conjure with in post-war America. The Mitch Miller Orchestra & Chorus enjoyed a string of chart (and numerous gold) records throughout the '50s. In addition to that success, he also had the mixed blessing of being head of A&R at Columbia Records when rock'n'roll was coming in, and famously turned down several acts who went on to carve out illustrious careers – most notably Elvis Presley.

When the Norman Petty Trio charted on Columbia with 'The First Kiss' in 1957, Petty wasted no time in pitching a dub of the Crickets' 'That'll Be The Day' to Miller, with predictable consequences.

Now long-retired, Miller has had his critics over the years for consistently taking a populist approach by giving the public what he thought they wanted. Despite some industry misgivings, he was awarded a lifetime Grammy Award in 2000, though it was a long time coming.

'MODERN DON JUAN'

Recorded November 1956 at Bradley's Barn Studio, Nashville, Tennessee
Personnel: Buddy Holly (vocals), Harold Bradley (guitar), Grady Martin (guitar), Don Guess (double bass), Floyd Cramer (piano), Farris Coursey (drums), Dutch McMillin (alto sax)

Written by bass player Don Guess and Buddy's old partner Jack Neal, this came out in the US as a Decca single in late 1956, but had little impact outside Texas, where it made it onto local jukeboxes. In Britain, the cut turned up posthumously on one of a pair of 1959 EPs that saw most of the Decca material at last getting a UK airing.

Dutch McMillin plays an effective saxophone on both this cut and 'Rock Around With Ollie Vee' (Holly's second attempt at the song). It seems that the released take of Don Juan was either 6 or 7 (the engineer appears to say *'Take 76'*!). Interestingly, in 1983 Jack Neal told John Ingman that Buddy phoned him from Nashville asking his permission to record the song, as one of the other numbers wasn't working out.

In 1984, the Picks overdubbed backing vocals onto this recording (see **OVERDUBS** and **PICKS** for more info), and that version is commonly available these days. Indeed, it seems that the bulk of Holly releases currently available in the UK feature those later Picks overdubs.

'MONA'

Recorded poss. December 1957 at Norman Petty Recording Studios, Clovis, New Mexico
Personnel: Buddy Holly (acoustic guitar, vocals), Jerry Allison (drums)

Composed by Bo Diddley, 'Mona' was the flip of his 1957 Chess single 'Hey Bo Diddley', and Buddy and his fellow Crickets would have been very familiar with the song. Certainly the Everlys remember it as a particular favourite when they were all together on tour. Holly experts feel the likeliest rehearsal date would have been December 1957, and the cut might have been a possible choice for the *Buddy Holly* solo album.

It seems Bo was inspired to write the song after watching a 45-year-old exotic dancer in a Detroit club where he was appearing: she obviously moved well for her age!

Apparently recorded with a tape delay echo, the whole thing lasts around nine minutes before the tape runs out, and the only frustration is that Holly's vocals are off-mike throughout. This recording has still not seen an official release, but may finally appear in 2009.

'MONETTA'

Buddy was in the habit of scribbling down potential lyrics wherever and whenever he could in the hope that they would eventually result in a completed song. One such fragment of his handwriting was auctioned off a few years back. The simple lyrics consisted of an opening verse, *'Monetta – I betta – I getta – sweet kisses from you'*, and an equally direct second verse, *'Monetta – my petta – please letta – my dreams come true'*. Undated, it was one set of lyrics which apparently never made it past the 'ideas' stage. However, in recent years Sonny Curtis actually finished off the song and even sang it during a BBC Radio Merseyside interview with broadcaster Spencer Leigh!

BOB MONTGOMERY

The 'other half' of the Buddy & Bob duo, Bob Montgomery was actually born quite a way south-east of Lubbock in Lampasas, Texas in May 1937. However, his family moved to Lubbock in 1949 and he ended up together with Buddy in the same class at Hutchinson Junior High. Sharing a mutual love of music, they quickly paired up and before long were playing informal gigs around town and broadcasting over the local airwaves. Much of their music was in the bluegrass style, but eventually rock'n'roll would exert a much greater pull on Buddy.

After finishing school, Bob worked in a local TV repair shop in Lubbock before linking up with Norman Petty in Clovis, where he acted as an engineer and session musician before going on to make records in his own name. He cut an unissued version of 'Down The Line' in 1958, and also had singles released on Brunswick and Warner Brothers.

In the early '60s, Montgomery put his recording days behind him and relocated to Nashville, where he worked for Warner Bros. as a songwriter and producer. After moving to United Artists, he signed former Cricket Earl Sinks in 1968 and produced his first session for the label. In 1969, he formed the House of Gold with Bobby Goldsboro, which became a major music publishing concern, and also produced hits for many artists in the country, pop and even R&B fields.

Of course, we know him best through his association with Holly, both on the recording front (Buddy & Bob), and as composer of some of the best songs Buddy Holly ever recorded: 'Heartbeat', 'Wishing' and 'Love's Made A Fool Of You'.

In the '70s, Montgomery produced several of the Crickets'

Buddy and Bob at the grand opening of a local store, 1953.
Buddy is playing a banjo loaned to him by his brother Larry.

albums including *Bubblegum, Bop, Ballads & Boogie*, which was recorded in England. He was justifiably awarded a star on the West Texas Walk of Fame in Lubbock a few years back, and is now enjoying a well-earned retirement in Queensland, Australia.

See also **KEVIN MONTGOMERY** *and* **MARTY ROBBINS**.

KEVIN MONTGOMERY

Kevin Montgomery is the son of Bob Montgomery. He has continued the Buddy Holly link and frequently tours with Tommy Allsup performing Holly's music. He also participated in the 1996 *Not Fade Away (Remembering Buddy Holly)* MCA tribute, duetting Everlys-style with Mary Chapin Carpenter on 'Wishing', a song composed by his father and Buddy Holly.

'MOONDREAMS'

Recorded October 1958 at Pythian Temple Studio, New York
Personnel: Buddy Holly (vocals), Al Caiola (guitar), Sanford Bloch (bass), Ernest Hayes (piano), Doris Johnson (harp), Clifford Leeman (drums), Boomie Richman (tenor sax) plus string section

This was a ballad that Norman Petty had penned the year before and would record at Clovis more than once with his trio. Buddy had played on some of those sessions and presumably liked the haunting beauty of the melody, as he decided to cut it at what would turn out to be his final studio outing.

It was something of an epic recording session, given that it took place in the prestigious Pythian Temple where Bill Haley had previously recorded 'Rock Around The Clock', and was the first (and, in the event, only one) to feature a full string section. Although they didn't participate, Norman Petty, Jerry Allison and Joe B. were also present in the studio.

The proceedings were recorded on an Ampex 4-track recorder, which enabled separate mono and stereo masters to be made of the tracks recorded that day. 'Moondreams' was first issued in the US in 1960 on *The Buddy Holly Story (Volume II)*, whilst in the UK it came out in the same year as the flip side of 'True Love Ways' (a Top 30 hit).

Over the years, it has also appeared with the *'1-2-3'* count-in, while in 1984 the Picks added some effective backing vocals (see **OVERDUBS** and **PICKS** for more info).

This singular song has inspired few covers, but Denny Laine did a vocal version with the help of Paul McCartney on his 1977 *Holly Days* album.

'MOONLIGHT BABY' – *See* 'BABY WON'T YOU COME OUT TONIGHT'

Joe, Jerry and Buddy shortly after purchasing their bikes in Dallas, 1958.

MOTORCYCLES

Buddy owned a Cushman Eagle motor scooter when at school, but he carried the dream of getting himself a high-powered dream machine at some future point. The opportunity suddenly presented itself in mid-1958 when he, Jerry and Joe were returning to Lubbock from an Alan Freed tour with money to burn. Flying in to Dallas, and with Lubbock 300 miles away, they decided to purchase new bikes for themselves and ride home in style. (It's not recorded whether Joe B. had any misgivings about this. Some time before, he had been involved in a serious accident when riding his scooter and had been off school for months as a result.)

After famously being given the cold shoulder at a Harley dealership, the boys decided to try a nearby bike shop run by Ray and Betty Miller. Each of them ended up with a new machine: Holly's was a powerful maroon-and-black 1958 Aerial Cyclone, while Jerry and Joe picked out different model Triumphs. The total bill came to $3,200.

For years after his death, Buddy's bike was used by his dad, before eventually being bought by Jerry, Joe and Sonny and presented to a grateful Waylon Jennings on his birthday in 1979. Jennings only rode it a few times, and for years it ended up on display in the Johnny Cash museum in Nashville. Trivia collectors may wish to note that it also appeared on TV in an episode of *The Dukes of Hazzard*!

In 1995, a lengthy article on the Crickets' motorcycles appeared in the specialist *Classic Bikes* magazine.

ARTHUR MURRAY'S PARTY

Shortly after Niki Sullivan quit the Crickets in December 1957, they appeared live on *Arthur Murray's Party*, a regular weekly show aired by CBS and hosted by Arthur and Kathleen Murray. They were one of many guests on the show that day and performed 'Peggy Sue' live on air against a background of somewhat immobile dancers – the clip is regularly shown whenever a Holly documentary is screened. The programme was broadcast in colour, but only a monochrome copy survives. An incomplete version, missing part of the instrumental break, was included on a Dick Clark *Best Of Bandstand* video and later used in several TV documentaries.

'MY TWO-TIMIN' WOMAN'
Recorded 1949 at Buddy's home in Lubbock, Texas
Personnel: Buddy Holly (guitar, vocals)

This is the earliest known recording by Buddy Holly, committed to acetate and never intended to be heard beyond the confines of his own home. The lyrics were quite risqué for Lubbock at that time. Buddy accompanies himself manfully on the acoustic guitar and sings the Hank Snow song (in a high register, as befits his age), which was a popular country single at the time. Perhaps he was drawn to the number because of the lengthy instrumental segment, which he faithfully recreates. It's obviously not a recording that would normally warrant a commercial release, but Larry Holley put it out on his own Holly House label in 1986, though it's mainly of academic interest. It later transpired that this had been edited, when the complete, unedited recording – complete with the scratchy first verse – surfaced on the 2004 Rev-Ola CD, *Gotta Roll! The Early Recordings 1949-1955*.

N

NASHVILLE SESSIONS

Buddy's first real shot at fame came towards the end of 1955, when he was still playing in and around Lubbock with Bob Montgomery. With the popular music scene exploding, most record companies were busy casting around for talent, hoping to discover the next million-selling artist. Having impressed Marty Robbins's manager, Eddie Crandall, when appearing on a Lubbock bill with Bill Haley, Holley (the 'e' was still there) got the chance he had been yearning for when Decca offered him a contract – although agent Jim Denny disappointingly made it clear that the company only wanted him, and not his pal Bob. It was a solo act that Decca wanted, not a duo. It must have been a bittersweet moment for both men, although both ultimately went on to greater things.

Although Buddy first went to Nashville in late January 1956, Decca didn't send out his contract until mid-February. When he received it, it was made out in the name of Buddy *Holly*, which he adopted as his stage name from that point onwards. At least, that's how the story goes. Whether it was as straightforward as that we'll probably never know.

During the course of 1956, Holly made three visits to Nashville which yielded twelve completed recordings, including two attempts at 'Rock Around With Ollie Vee'. The selections came from a variety of sources: Holly himself, Sonny Curtis, Don Guess, and Lubbock-based songwriters Sue Parrish and Ben Hall. The 'odd song out' was 'Ting-A-Ling', which had been a R&B No.1 in 1955 for the Robins.

All the sessions were overseen by famed country producer Owen Bradley, and among a galaxy of emerging Nashville names accompanying Buddy were Floyd Cramer, Grady Martin and Harold Bradley, Owen's brother. In commercial terms, the sessions were a failure, yielding no hits and leaving Buddy in hock to Decca for the foreseeable future. Years later it would be interesting to hear the concerted efforts that Buddy went to in an effort to extricate himself from the contract (see **PAUL COHEN**). Inevitably, the Decca recordings were all eventually released in an effort to capitalise on the Crickets' subsequent huge success.

A summary of the sessions follows below.

First visit to Nashville, January 1956.
Above, left to right: Sonny Curtis, Buddy Holly, Don Guess and Sonny's brother Dean.
Below, left to right: Sonny, Buddy, Thelma King (of Cedarwood Publishing), Don, Thelma's sister Joanna McClanahan and Dean Curtis.

First visit – 26 January 1956
Love Me / Don't Come Back Knockin' / Midnight Shift / Blue Days, Black Nights
Personnel: Buddy Holly (vocal), Sonny Curtis (guitar), Grady Martin (guitar), Don Guess (bass), Doug Kirkham (percussion)

Famously, producer Owen Bradley wouldn't allow Buddy to play his own lead guitar on the session. Also, Jerry Allison was still attending school and was unable to be present. 'Blue Days, Black Nights' b/w 'Love Me' became Holly's first single, released in the USA and, surprisingly, in the UK too.

Second visit – 22 July 1956
Rock Around With Ollie Vee [guitar version] */ I'm Changin' All Those Changes / That'll Be The Day* [original version] */ Girl On My Mind / Ting-A-Ling*
Personnel: Buddy Holly (guitar, vocal), Sonny Curtis (guitar), Don Guess (bass), Jerry Allison (drums)

This time, all the musicians were from Lubbock and no Nashville sessionmen were involved.

Third visit – 15 November 1956
Rock Around With Ollie Vee [sax version] */ Modern Don Juan / You Are My One Desire*
Personnel: Buddy Holly (vocal), Harold Bradley (guitar), Grady Martin (guitar), Don Guess (bass), Floyd Cramer (piano), Farris Coursey (drums), Dutch McMillin (alto sax)

With Jerry Allison unable to go, all the musicians were Nashville sessionmen with the exception of Don Guess. 'Modern Don Juan' b/w 'You Are My One Desire' were issued as Buddy Holly's second single, but only in the USA.

JERRY NAYLOR

From Chalk Mountain near Stephenville, Texas, where he was born in March 1939, Jerry Naylor Jackson was the Crickets' lead singer who – it briefly seemed – might have gone on to replace Buddy Holly on a permanent basis. (For the record, although he never performed with Holly, they did briefly meet in 1955.)

Naylor provided backing vocals for the 1961 Liberty LP *Bobby Vee Meets The Crickets*, which led to him joining the Crickets when they moved to the label. He sang lead vocals on several classic tracks including 'Don't Ever Change' and 'My Little Girl', and toured Britain with the group in 1962, but suffered a heart attack in early 1964. He rejoined the Crickets for their January 1965 Clovis sessions – their last recordings for Liberty.

Naylor was a regular on *Shindig!* during the late '60s, when he was still hoping to crack the pop charts. He had just one minor 'Hot

100' hit, 'But For Love', but it was a smash in the 'easy listening' market and earned him a Grammy nomination.

Thereafter, he moved into country music and enjoyed a string of hits in the '70s and '80s including a cover of 'Rave On'. His biggest hit was his first, 'Is This All There Is To A Honky Tonk', which reached the *Billboard* Country Top 30 in 1975. He also became a TV producer and hosted the *Continental Country* radio show for years, winning awards along the way. Sadly, he was forced into temporary retirement by a serious car crash in 1982.

As if the foregoing wasn't varied enough, Naylor also crossed over into Christian music before spending much of the '80s as one of President Ronald Reagan's Federal Commissioners on the National Commission for Employment Policy.

In the more recent past, he was instrumental in putting together a *Rockabilly Legends* tribute on DVD with the help of Kris Kristofferson and Red Robinson. Packaged with the DVD was a new Jerry Naylor CD entitled *A Tribute To My Friends* containing versions of songs which his contemporaries from the '50s had made famous. Among a lot of Southern rockabilly were Jerry's versions of Holly's 'Think It Over' and 'Everyday'.

He was inducted into the West Texas Walk of Fame in 1998, and the national Rockabilly Hall of Fame two years later.

JACK NEAL

A fine guitarist and pianist, Jack Neal was born in Fort Worth, Texas in 1934 and was introduced to Buddy while working as a carpenter's assistant with Buddy's dad, Lawrence, in the Lubbock area in the early '50s. As we know, the duo of Buddy & Jack was created soon after, but was succeeded by Buddy & Bob in 1954. However, Neal never really stopped performing, albeit mostly in a semi-professional way. Around 1980, he put out a single, 'Silent Hours' *b/w* 'East Of Dallas', and he has also re-recorded 'I Saw The Moon Cry Last Night', one of the two gospel numbers that he and Buddy first recorded back in 1953 (the other one was 'I Hear The Lord Callin' For Me'). These days he lives over the border in New Mexico.

RICKY NELSON

Born in Teaneck, New Jersey in 1940, Eric Hilliard 'Ricky' Nelson was one of the all-time greats of rock'n'roll, with a hit-making career that stretched from 1957 to 1973. He was frequently drawn to Buddy Holly's material and cut versions of 'True Love Ways' and 'Rave On'. Sonny Curtis also occasionally played guitar for him during the '60s.

It's even said (or is it apocryphal?) that the last number he ever sang on stage was 'Rave On'. After the show in Guntersville, Alabama, Nelson and his band boarded their plane to fly to Dallas. As they were nearing their destination, a fire broke out on board and the DC-3 crashed near De Kalb, Texas on 31 December 1985, killing him and his musicians, although both crew members survived.

It's often said that Holly's death was the last time that news of a tragedy was made public before the next of kin were informed. Not so. The first that Nelson's family heard about the crash was when they turned on the radio and heard Ricky's songs being played.

He was posthumously inducted into the Rock and Roll Hall of Fame in 1987.

NESMAN STUDIO

Situated close to the Oklahoma border at 3108 York Avenue, Wichita Falls, Texas, the small Nesman recording studio was the brainchild of Lewis Nesman. It was also close to local radio station KSYD, where Holly's friend, Snuff Garrett, was a local jock. So it's hardly surprising that the studio was used by Holly and his contemporaries throughout 1955 until they discovered Norman Petty's studio in Clovis virtually on their doorstep (figuratively speaking, at least: Clovis is only 100 miles or so from Lubbock, whereas Wichita Falls is nearer 200).

Among various songs Buddy cut at Nesman are the four demos he submitted to Pappy Dave Stone, which resulted in him being offered a Decca contract: 'Moonlight Baby' (*aka* 'Baby Won't You Come Out Tonight'), 'I Guess I Was Just A Fool', 'Don't Come Back Knockin' ' and 'Love Me'.

NEW YORK

Several years ago, a Buddy Holly documentary featured Jim Croce's 'New York's Not My Home' as the accompanying music, and somehow that seemed very appropriate, as surely the Texan that was Buddy Holly wouldn't have remained in the Big Apple permanently? It's a rhetorical question and one we can't answer, although we do know that, in his last months, Buddy had drawn up plans for a recording facility back in Lubbock (see **PRISM RECORDS**). But, from the autumn of 1958, shortly after getting wed, he and Maria Elena had set up home in the Brevoort building (Apartment 4H, to be precise) on Fifth Avenue, just on the edge of Greenwich Village.

Certainly, Buddy's recording company, Coral, were based in New York; so were Southern Music, who handled his publishing; and more and more of his recording sessions were also taking place in New York rather than Clovis (see **BELL SOUND STUDIOS** and **PYTHIAN TEMPLE STUDIO**).

Frustratingly little is known of Holly's activities in New York during late 1958, apart from his involvement in the Lou Giordano session, and the fact that he was also busy composing (see **APARTMENT TAPES**) and setting up home. There were also a few legal meetings following on from his split with Norman Petty, and then there was the forward planning for Prism Records and the Lubbock studio complex too. Sadly, Holly's premature death threw all those cards up in the air and eventually the focus switched back to Clovis and Norman Petty.

TERRY NOLAND

Born in Abilene, Texas in 1938, Terry Noland Church was a contemporary of Buddy Holly who, like Buddy, managed to land a recording deal with Brunswick in February 1957 thanks to the efforts of Norman Petty. But there the similarity ends, for Holly (who joined Brunswick after Terry) quickly hit the big time, whereas Noland laboured away touring and making records without achieving a breakthrough.

Their early careers were also connected in that Noland initially fronted the Four Teens, whose members Larry Welborn and Joe B. Mauldin would both leave to join Holly. The group made their first record – a cover of 'Hound Dog' – in a Dallas studio in 1956, but it remained unissued for years until it was put out by Bear Family on the 1990 *Hypnotized* album.

After Joe B. and Larry had left, Terry cut the excellent 'Ten Little Women' *b/w* 'Hypnotized' at Clovis, but the single failed to lift off despite decent reviews. His follow-up, likewise recorded at Clovis (but with backing by Trini Lopez and the Big Beats) was 'Patty Baby' coupled with 'Don't Do Me This Way'. Although this too failed to chart, it did get him a spot on Alan Freed's Christmas 1957 *Holiday of Stars* show alongside the Crickets, Fats Domino and others.

Certainly, Noland and Holly were acquaintances and exchanged letters in late 1958, when Buddy suggested that Terry record in New

Terry Noland, Brunswick recording artist, 1957.

York, saying that he had a couple of his own songs he thought might suit him. Intriguingly, Buddy also mentioned working with Jesse Stone (composer of 'Shake, Rattle And Roll' and many other hits), although absolutely nothing further is known about this. He then proposed that he and Terry get together in mid-February 1959 when his tour was done, which of course never happened.

Noland had several more releases on Brunswick before the company decided not to renew his contract. Later on, he quit the music business and moved to Oklahoma, where he became a successful property developer. But, like many others, his heart was still in music and he eventually began reappearing at Holly-related events in Lubbock and a few years back put together a complete CD of Holly material on the Silver label entitled *To Terry Noland From Buddy Holly*. He finally got to record the songs that Holly left behind on tape in his apartment, some of which he felt sure Buddy was going to offer to him a lifetime ago.

NORMAN PETTY RECORDING STUDIOS / NOR-VA-JAK

Derived from the names of the Norman Petty Trio (*Nor*man Petty, *V*iolet *A*nn Petty and *Jak*ck Vaughn), 'Nor-Va-Jak' was the name of Norman Petty's main music publishing business (he also owned Dundee Music Publishing) and also his record label, on which he released a string of records by his trio, Myron Lee, Sonny West and others during the '50s and '60s.

It was not, however, the name of Norman Petty's famous studio at 1313 West 7th Street, despite the fact that it had the legend *'Nor Va Jak Music Inc'* emblazoned on its wall in large letters. That was simply the 'Norman Petty Recording Studios'. The administrative centre of the Petty empire was at 1321 West 7th Street, originally the home of Norman's parents.

Shortly after Norman passed away in 1984, Jerry MacNeish reactivated the Nor-Va-Jak label for a new series of record releases. The original studio has since been reopened as a museum, and most current recordings are made at the Lyceum Theater complex which is rented by the Vi Petty estate.

See also **NORMAN & VIOLET PETTY**.

'NOT FADE AWAY'

Recorded May 1957 at Norman Petty Recording Studios, Clovis, New Mexico
Personnel: Buddy Holly (guitar, vocals), Jerry Allison (cardboard box percussion), Joe B. Mauldin (double bass)
Overdubbed May 1957: Buddy Holly, Jerry Allison and Niki Sullivan (backing vocals)

The Crickets were known to be big fans of Bo Diddley, and this is obvious when listening to the rhythms employed by the group on 'Not Fade Away', surely one of the finest tracks ever consigned to the 'B' side of a record in the history of rock'n'roll. It was issued as the flip of 'Oh Boy!', a worldwide hit for the Crickets in 1957, meaning that a great many people got to hear the track. Jerry Allison actually came up with many of the lyrics, although he's not listed as co-composer.

The song's effect was akin to a depth charge, in that it seemed to have minimal impact at the time. However, faint ripples surfaced, and in 1964 the Rolling Stones reworked the number in a heavier style and took it to No.3 in the British charts. It also became their first-ever US hit.

Since those days, more than fifty artists have recorded their own interpretations, although those that have managed to chart with it remain thin on the ground. Interestingly, country star Tanya Tucker had a minor US pop hit with 'Not Fade Away', while the flip, 'Texas (When I Die)', went to No.5 in the Country chart. Luminaries such as Bob Dylan and the Grateful Dead have also been known to perform the song – the latter sometimes closing their act with it. But surely the most unlikely version has to be Dick & Dee Dee's 1964 cover on the Warner Bros. label.

The way the Crickets recorded their version is interesting in that Jerry Allison played a cardboard box to get the exact sound he was looking for, while Niki Sullivan helped Buddy and Jerry with the backing vocals, which were added afterwards, making it one of the rare occasions when neither the Picks nor the Roses were used for overdubs.

An incomplete second half of an alternate take survives and has been spliced with the opening of the released version to create a pseudo-master. This appeared on the 1995 4-CD Vigotone bootleg, *What You Been A-Missin'*. It's relatively easy to spot the splice, as the backing vocals disappear before the instrumental break.

As for Buddy plagiarising Bo Diddley, well Bo got his own back by recording 'Not Fade Away' for his 1976 album, *The 20th Anniversary of Rock'n'Roll*.

NOT FADE AWAY *(film)*

Not Fade Away was the proposed title of a made-for-TV movie about the life of Buddy Holly that was in the works in 1975 – three years before the *Buddy Holly Story* biopic hit the big screen. Based on an original script by Tom Drake and Jerry Allison, it was to have focused on the time the Crickets found themselves on an all-black tour bill and the whole way that played out. 20th Century-Fox reportedly shot two weeks of footage before they got cold feet about the racial overtones and abandoned the project.

Gary Busey, who had been hired to play Jerry Allison, got a second bite of the cherry when he was subsequently offered the lead role in *The Buddy Holly Story*, but the Crickets were glossed over as

they had sold their rights to the makers of *Not Fade Away*.
See also **THE BUDDY HOLLY STORY** *(Film)* and **GARY BUSEY**.

NOT FADE AWAY *(tribute CD and documentary)*

Not Fade Away (Remembering Buddy Holly) was the title for a 1996 MCA-promoted Holly tribute commemorating the 40th anniversary of Buddy recording his first commercial sides in Nashville. The venture brought together a mass of musicians and technicians, and resulted in a major two-part US TV documentary and a commemorative CD which featured artists from across the musical spectrum including Waylon Jennings, the Band and Los Lobos.

The choice of material was equally inspiring, with several of the more obvious Holly numbers being avoided in favour of the likes of 'Wishing', 'Midnight Shift' and the title track, 'Not Fade Away'. The latter brought together the Crickets and the Band and features *three* drummers on the one track! But surely the most innovative of all the recordings had to be the conflation of Buddy Holly and the Hollies on 'Peggy Sue Got Married', a musical marriage that contrasts Holly's original vocals with the layered vocals and instrumentation of the Hollies, specially re-joined by Graham Nash for this one-off project.

'NOW WE'RE ONE'
Recorded June 1958 at Pythian Temple Studio, New York
Personnel: Buddy Holly (vocals), George Barnes (guitar), Al Chernet (guitar), Sanford Bloch (bass), Ernest Hayes (piano), Panama Francis and Philip Kraus (drums), Sam 'The Man' Taylor (alto sax), Helen Way Singers (backing vocals)

This came from the brief session when Buddy was asked by his record company to cut a couple of Bobby Darin songs for rush release (see **'EARLY IN THE MORNING'** for the full story). In effect, Holly ended up covering Darin, but both artists ended up having fair-sized hits with the top deck, 'Early In The Morning'.

It's said that the Holly recordings were produced in stereo, but that is unconfirmed and only mono versions have ever been traced. The master take was included on the 1995 4-CD Vigotone bootleg, *What You Been A-Missin'*, along with a brief false start and count-in.

Jerry Allison reportedly put 'Now We're One' on the turntable minutes after Buddy and Maria Elena had performed their wedding vows. It was on the back of his current hit, so it really was hugely appropriate. However, the song itself has seldom been covered and only rarely crops up on Holly compilations.

O

DES O'CONNOR

Des O'Connor (born Conrad Desmondson in 1932) has had a lengthy international career that remains ongoing at the time of writing. At the time of the Crickets 1958 British tour, he had yet to make his mark in the world of show business, but, thanks to his training as a Butlin's redcoat, Des was the ideal man to compère the show (posters for the tour described him as the *'comedian with the modern style'*). He recalls that he was paid £100 per week – a considerable sum of money back then.

Famously, Buddy asked Des to buy him a guitar. The one he picked out was an acoustic Hofner President, which Holly presented to him when the tour finished. In 1990, it was put up for auction through Phillips of London, but failed to meet its reserve price of £40,000-£60,000.

With a mixture of comedy and song, O'Connor was soon topping bills himself. Then, towards the end of the '60s, he suddenly found his recording career taking off. He went on to have a string of hit records in Britain including an enduring No.1 with 'I Pretend' and has gone on to record almost forty albums.

As the years have gone by, Des has talked more and more of the undoubted pleasure the tour gave him and how friendly Buddy, Jerry and Joe were. He often includes an affectionate medley of Buddy's hits in his cabaret act, albeit with some poetic licence (for example, recalling Buddy singing 'It Doesn't Matter Anymore' to him on the tour bus, despite the fact that the song had not yet been written) – but that's showbiz! A much-loved entertainer, he was awarded a CBE in 2008.

OFF THE RECORD

British TV never quite got to grips with rock'n'roll in the late '50s, and no show exemplified this malaise more than the BBC's *Off The Record*. The weekly show was hosted by Jack Payne, a former big band leader of the '20s who had been leader of the BBC Dance Orchestra for years until he was replaced by the equally elderly Henry Hall. It was painful for teenagers to see this dinosaur of the pre-war era anchoring a programme which somehow tried to incorporate a few of the pop hits of the day.

It was on this show that we saw the Crickets performing 'Maybe Baby' on 26 March 1958. Although *Off The Record* was normally a live show, Holly's segment was actually filmed on 14 March, shortly before his appearance at Woolwich that evening. A few years ago, a reel of audio tape was discovered in the loft of a fan, which confirmed that the group had performed live. An excerpt from this was featured in a radio documentary, but the recording is otherwise unissued at the time of writing.

'OH BOY!'
Recorded June or July 1957 at Norman Petty Recording Studios, Clovis, New Mexico
Personnel: Buddy Holly (guitar, vocals), Jerry Allison (drums), Joe B. Mauldin (double bass)
Overdubbed August 1957: The Picks (backing vocals)

For many fans, this surely constitutes Holly's greatest ever recording: 'That'll Be The Day' may have been the first, and 'Peggy Sue' the most distinctive, but 'Oh Boy!' surely has to be the most iconic.

Released in October 1957, 'Oh Boy!' become a Top 10 hit in most world markets, earning the Crickets a gold record. (For good measure, it even got to No.13 in the *Billboard* R&B chart!)

To realise just how great the recording is, one needs to listen to the original demo by Sonny West (who co-wrote the song with Ben Tilghman) under its original title, 'All My Love'. Recorded at Clovis in February '57 with Glen D. Hardin on piano, West's version lopes along nicely, but pales in comparison with Holly's dynamic hit.

In 1995, a good-quality copy of the Crickets recording, *sans* overdubs, surfaced on the 4-CD Vigotone bootleg, *What You Been A-Missin'*, and is worth seeking out. Live performances of the song from the second *Ed Sullivan Show* (January 1958) and *Sunday Night At The London Palladium* (March 1958) also exist. (And, while we are on the subject of television, it should also not be forgotten that, in 1958, Jack Good purloined the exciting *'Oh Boy!'* name for his equally exciting weekly ITV pop show.)

At least forty cover versions of 'Oh Boy!' exist, although one feels the power and the tension of the original will never be bettered. Nonetheless, in Britain, an acapella version by Mud went all the way to the top of the charts in 1975, almost twenty years after the original hit.

Of course, the latter-day Crickets have never left the stage without performing the song during their set, and have also re-recorded it several times – most recently in 2004 for John Prine's Oh Boy label.

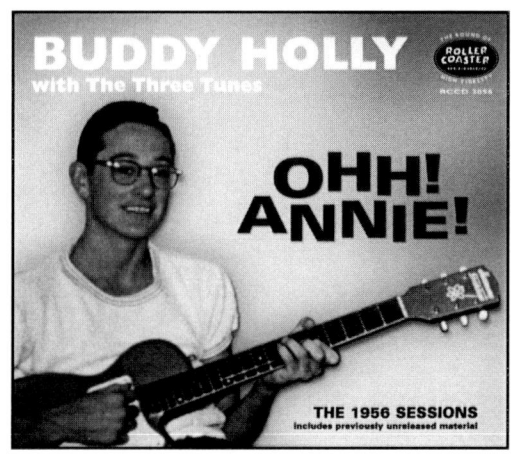

OHH! ANNIE! *(2-CD, UK only)*
❶ *Love Me / Don't Come Back Knockin'* [2 versions] / *Midnight Shift* [2 versions + false start] / *Blue Days, Black Nights / Baby Won't You Come Out Tonight / I Guess I Was Just A Fool / It's Not My Fault / I'm Gonna Set My Foot Down / I'm Changin' All Those Changes* [demo] / *Rock-A-Bye Rock / Because I Love You / Rock Around With Ollie Vee* [guitar version + fragment] / *I'm Changin' All Those Changes / That'll Be The Day / Girl On My Mind / Ting-A-Ling / Rock Around With Ollie Vee* [sax version] / *Modern Don Juan / You Are My One Desire* [+ false start]
❷ *Have You Ever Been Lonely / Bo Diddley / Ain't Got No Home / Buddy's Bop* [aka *Holly Hop*] / *Gone* [3 versions] / *Have You Ever Been Lonely* [2 versions + fragment] / *Brown Eyed Handsome Man / Good Rockin' Tonight / Rip It Up / Blue Monday / Honky Tonk / Blue Suede Shoes / Shake, Rattle And Roll / Bo Diddley / Brown Eyed Handsome Man*

    It's been fifty years since Buddy Holly left us and, musically speaking, there have probably been only a handful of albums over that time which have been truly groundbreaking. Sure, there have been all manner of classic albums along the way, but so many have been repackaging exercises that they haven't necessarily made the heart skip a beat or fallen into that 'must have' category. With the twenty-first century rolling along surely there couldn't be anything new that we hadn't heard for the umpteenth time – could there?

    The surprising answer is that yes there was, and *Ohh! Annie!* is the living proof. Rollercoaster Records, the small British independent, have a thirty-year pedigree where Holly, Crickets and West Texas-related releases are concerned, and this 2007 release is probably their finest hour. Collected together in one package is everything that Holly and his colleagues were busy rehearsing in Lubbock and Clovis during 1956, together with the complete output from the three Nashville sessions for Decca that year, and unfailingly all are in better sound quality than previously heard. Not only that, but we also have a completely different take of 'Midnight Shift' to savour, and it is that that gives rise to the album's title: Holly excitedly shouting *'Ohh! Annie!'* midway through Take 11 (the released take we are all familiar with is Take 4).

Whilst no actual new song titles are in evidence, there are other fragments that have never been heard before, and two incomplete versions of 'Don't Come Back Knockin' ' have been spliced together to create a new performance. In addition to the music itself, we have several previously unseen photos of Holly, Sonny Curtis and Don Guess relaxing in Nashville and the most comprehensive of sleevenotes from Holly guru John Ingman. There's not an overdub in sight and furthermore the whole release is strictly legal. It doesn't come much better than this.

JOHNNY O'KEEFE

John Michael O'Keefe (1935-78) was without a doubt the Elvis Presley of Australia, and it's a curious coincidence that he only outlasted his hero by a little over twelve months before he himself succumbed to a heart attack at the age of just 43. However, it is his connection with the Crickets that is under scrutiny here.

As Australia's top home-grown rock'n'roll singer, O'Keefe had been on the bill for Little Richard's tour in 1957, and was also booked onto the Crickets/Jerry Lee Lewis/Paul Anka package in 1958. It was on this tour that, standing in the wings, Jerry Allison would nightly listen to Johnny singing his show-stopper, 'Wild One', which he decided to record as soon as he set foot back on US soil. Released under the pseudonym 'Ivan', his own version, 'Real Wild Child', became a minor US hit later that year. Interestingly, O'Keefe's recording initially appeared only on EP in Australia, and wasn't issued as a single until much later. Norman Petty also arranged for it to be released in the US, but without much success.

O'Keefe suffered a major setback in 1960 as a result of a car crash and this triggered off all sorts of long-term problems, both physical and emotional. He then relocated to America for a while, but never achieved the breakthrough he deserved.

In 2000, Damian Johnstone published the definitive biography of O'Keefe entitled *The Wild One*.

Roy Orbison *(second from left)* with the Teen Kings.

ROY ORBISON

The careers of Buddy Holly and Roy Kelton Orbison (1936-88) are interlinked, although, according to an interview with the latter, the two never spent much more than twenty-four hours together after meeting by chance when they were on the road: *'I only really got to know Buddy Holly that day... it was from early morning to early morning... we were kindred souls, we became quite close.'* But it seems it was an intense coming-together, and Roy would thereafter often talk about the friendly rivalry between himself and Buddy.

Orbison, who hailed from Vernon, just west of Wichita Falls, Texas, had a head start on Holly. As lead singer with the Wink Westerners (later renamed the Teen Kings), he recorded 'Ooby Dooby' at Norman Petty's studio in 1955, which was released on the Je-Wel label. (This and Orbison's other Clovis material was later issued on a Bear Family box set). Sadly, the single did nothing and, discouraged by his lack of success, Roy moved on to Memphis to try his luck with Sam Phillips.

The man who was responsible for all of Elvis's great Sun label recordings had a long and illustrious career in independent record production and the roll-call of other famous names that passed through his Union Avenue studio is legion: Carl Perkins, Jerry Lee Lewis, Johnny Cash and Charlie Rich must do for starters. Despite this, Orbison only met with limited success at Sun, though a remake of 'Ooby Dooby' did make the *Billboard* 'Top 100' in 1956.

Meanwhile Holly memorably picked out two of his compositions, 'You've Got Love' and 'An Empty Cup', for inclusion on the *Chirping Crickets* album (the songs presumably having been left at Clovis with Norman Petty).

Orbison became an international star in the '60s after signing with Monument and was inducted into the Rock and Roll Hall of Fame in 1987. He died of a heart attack the following year at the age of just 52.

OVERDUBS

References are made throughout the book to various 'overdubs' and may have created some confusion. Hopefully the list below will help to clarify matters:

- The Picks were the first group used by Norman Petty back in 1957 to overdub backing vocals onto selected Buddy Holly recordings, which were then issued as by the Crickets. These overdubs were usually added days or weeks after the tracks were recorded.

- In 1958, the Roses replaced the Picks. The Roses also toured with the Crickets on one occasion.

- The exceptions to both of the above were 'That'll Be The Day', 'I'm Looking For Someone To Love', and 'Not Fade Away'. See the separate entries for those songs for more information.

- In 1959 and 1960, Jack Hansen at Coral Records in New York masterminded a series of vocal and instrumental overdubs of the December 1958 Apartment Tapes. All of these were Holly compositions.

- From 1962 to 1968, Norman Petty used the Fireballs to add (in most cases) instrumental overdubs to Holly's recordings, in order to make the material more suitable for commercial release. This process also allowed stereo masters to be created from mono originals with the notable exclusion of the Buddy & Bob recordings. As with the Picks and Roses, these overdubs were done at Clovis.

- In 1984, the Picks overdubbed some 35 Holly tracks in Houston, Texas. Many of these are now widely available – though they are frequently not identified as such – and should not be confused with the older overdubs mentioned above. The author has no hidden agenda regarding the thorny subject of these overdubs except to say that they are now so prevalent, that those coming to Holly's music for the first time may be unaware that they are not listening to the original classic recordings. That is rather sad, however well-intentioned the motive.

    See also **PICKS** *and* **ROSES**.

P

PALLADIUM THEATRE

During their extensive tour of Britain in March 1958, Holly and the Crickets managed to fit in a few extras, from visiting Austin's Longbridge car works to appearing on several TV shows. But probably the most prestigious extra-curricular activity of the lot took place soon after they set foot on British soil. This was an appearance in the 100th gala edition of *Sunday Night At The London Palladium*, which was being televised live on 2 March.

Compère for the night was the rotund actor, Robert Morley, and with Bob Hope being the night's main headliner, the Crickets were programmed to close the first half of the show, racing through their three biggest hits – 'That'll Be The Day', 'Peggy Sue' and 'Oh Boy!' – in six minutes flat.

Unlike the usual tour dates, where Buddy would get to briefly chat or joke with his audience, the Palladium turned out to be quite different and there was no time for any such niceties. Having already played a show at the State Cinema in Kilburn in the early evening, they had to rush back for the second house, thus forfeiting the thrill of going round on the revolving stage at the end, as was traditional.

Their performance may not have been the greatest of their illustrious career – Buddy later told critic Keith Goodwin that it had been one of their worst ever – but ogling their TV sets that night were a host of wannabe rock'n'roll stars watching every move of the Texan's plectrum. The world was never quite the same again.

Although the show wasn't filmed, a whole gallery of photos exists of the group on stage. Also, an audio recording made by a fan appeared in 1977 on an American bootleg called *Buddy Holly Recorded Live (Volume 1)* on Crickets Records..

Some 32 years after their TV appearance, the Crickets (Jerry, Joe B. and Gordon Payne) returned to the Palladium in 1990. Their show was recorded and later issued by Rollercoaster as a cassette-only release called *Sunday Night At The London Palladium*.

SUE PARRISH

In the '50s, Sue Parrish lived near Lubbock and wrote a couple of songs for Buddy & Bob after hearing them on KDAV. We know from a lengthy interview conducted by Bob Dees that Sue submitted the songs directly to Buddy in Lubbock, as he hadn't yet become involved with Norman Petty. Unusually, she only wrote lyrics but had no partner to write the music, so Buddy was able to set them to a melody of his own choosing. He duly recorded 'Don't Come Back Knockin'' and 'Love Me' at his first Nashville session for Decca in January 1956.

Sue also submitted other sets of lyrics to Buddy after he became famous, but he never recorded anything else she sent him. By the time he was killed, she had moved to California to raise a family. She wasn't a professional songwriter for very long, but had another one of her compositions recorded under her married name of Sue Utela. Sue has very fond memories of her brief involvement with Buddy Holly in the early days of his career.

GORDON PAYNE

In the late '70s, the Crickets as a stage act were temporarily at a crossroads. At the invitation of their old friend, Waylon Jennings, Jerry Allison, Sonny Curtis and Joe B. Mauldin joined his stage show in 1978. After five years, however, relationships soured and they again went their separate ways. Sonny opted to return to Nashville to pursue various solo projects, while Jerry and Joe B. hooked up with Waylors singer/guitarist Gordon Payne to relaunch the Crickets as a three-piece. Originally from Chickashay, Oklahoma, Payne had come to Jennings via Tulsa, where he'd played with various local musicians and served a lengthy apprenticeship with J.J. Cale.

Rejuvenated, the Crickets went out on tour and also cut a brand new album called *Three Piece*, which came out in Britain on the Rollercoaster label in 1988. However, this was quickly deleted and reissued on CBS – with a slightly amended track listing – as *T-Shirt*. With Paul McCartney producing and playing on the title track, and Payne contributing a powerful Fender Stratocaster lead, the group were given a new lease of life.

A real asset, Payne wrote quite a bit of material with and for the Crickets, and was the lead singer/guitarist on two more albums (1990's live *Sunday Night At The London Palladium* and 1993's *Double Exposure*) and the EP, *Back Home In Tennessee*. One of the nicest by-products of his lengthy involvement with the group was that they returned to playing a lot of Holly songs which they hadn't tackled for years.

Payne remained with the Crickets until 1994, and it was a real shock to fans when he decided to hang up his guitar and take up a full-time job outside of music selling vacuum cleaners! However, that must have been a stepping stone, as he has since gone on to write novels, amongst other things.

BOBBY PEEPLES

Born February 1937, Bobby Peeples was a classmate of Holly's at Lubbock High, and constitutes an intriguing footnote in the Buddy Holly story. Late in 1956, Buddy and Jerry Allison recorded a wealth of demo material and it was said that Peeples had engineered the sessions. For years his whereabouts were unknown until longtime British Holly fan Ray Needham tracked him down in the Dallas/Fort Worth area. It turned out that he had been involved in the design of recording studios for many years, but later switched to satellite TV and made his fortune.

In an interview published in *Holly International*, Peeples recalled that Buddy had also recorded some gospel material and that the tapes had been handed over to the Holley family. It had also long been thought that Peeples's Venture Studio in Lubbock was where Buddy had recorded in 1956, but on reflection he didn't think that the studio was operational until 1958 – by which time Buddy was already recording at Clovis. Likewise, it had been rumoured for years that Peeples may have recorded the Crickets playing live on stage at Carlsbad, New Mexico, but this also turned out to be without substance.

See also **VENTURE STUDIO**.

'PEGGY SUE'

Recorded June or July 1957 at Norman Petty Recording Studios, Clovis, New Mexico
Personnel: Buddy Holly (guitar, vocals), Jerry Allison (drums), Joe B. Mauldin (double bass)

Released in late 1957, 'Peggy Sue' *b/w* 'Everyday' has to be one of the strongest couplings in pop history. Holly's first solo hit, 'Peggy Sue', made it to No.3 in the *Billboard* 'Top 100' that year, and his trademark hiccups probably link the singer more closely with this one recording than any other. Equally captivating are Jerry Allison's efforts on the snare drum, which, with producer Norman Petty switching the echo on and off, gives the track a 'rolling' sound. Niki Sullivan quipped that all he got to do on the recording was flick the tremolo switch on Buddy's Fender – something the singer couldn't do himself without missing a beat.

The composer credits are interesting. If you look at the original vinyl album, you'll note with some surprise that the writers are listed as *'Allison-Petty'*. Jerry reputedly wrote the song as 'Cindy Lou', dedicated to Buddy's niece, but it ended up being retitled 'Peggy Sue', after Jerry's girlfriend, Peggy Sue Rackham (see next entry). However, if you look at one of the later reissues, you will find this amended to *'Holly-Allison-Petty'*. Obviously, it cannot have been easy to work out just who contributed what, but certainly it's acknowledged that Buddy was heavily involved.

The hit recording is actually Take 2, but a few years ago an inferior Take 1, which varies little from the original, came out on the 1995 4-CD Vigotone bootleg, *What You Been A-Missin'*. The Picks overdubbed some vocal backings in 1984 (see **OVERDUBS** and **PICKS** for more info), although it's debatable as to whether anything needed to be added to such a momentous recording.

Holly also recorded a short radio jingle for KLLL to the tune of 'Peggy Sue', and there are also three live recordings of him performing the song on TV. Chronologically these are the first *Ed Sullivan Show* (December 1957), *Arthur Murray's Party* (December 1957) and *Sunday Night At The London Palladium* (March 1958).

Twenty-one years after Buddy's original hit, 'Peggy Sue' re-entered the US charts courtesy of the Beach Boys – the most successful of numerous covers that have turned up over the years. The Crickets, of course, play it at every gig, and have also recorded it more than once, including a version with Bobby Vee. Naturally, female covers are thin on the ground, though Connie Francis (with rejigged lyrics, thanks to Sonny Curtis) produced an excellent one. On the other hand, instrumental versions (Sandy Nelson, Hank Marvin, Hank C. Burnette, etc) abound. And, stranger than fiction, Julian Lloyd Webber wove in the 'Peggy Sue' rhythm as part of a cello work based on Paganini's variations!

PEGGY SUE

An acquaintance of Buddy's from Lubbock High School days, Peggy Sue Gerron (born 1940) was the inspiration behind one of his most seminal recordings. And, as if that connection wasn't enough, she also started dating Jerry Allison, whom she eventually married in July 1958, just weeks after her eighteenth birthday. Meanwhile August 1958 saw Buddy marrying Maria Elena, after which the foursome travelled to Acapulco in Mexico for a joint honeymoon.

Honeymoon in Acapulco.
Left to right: Maria Elena, Buddy, Jerry and Peggy Sue.

According to Peggy Sue's account in her 2008 memoir, *Whatever Happened To Peggy Sue?*, her marriage was far from happy and she and Jerry divorced in 1967. She later remarried and raised a family, but divorced from her second husband, Lynn Rackham, in 1993.

'PEGGY SUE GOT MARRIED'
Recorded December 1958 in Apartment 4H, The Brevoort, 11 Fifth Ave, New York
Personnel: Buddy Holly (acoustic guitar, vocals)

It's said that Buddy's father suggested writing a sequel to 'Peggy Sue', but fans wouldn't learn of the follow-up's existence during the singer's lifetime, for he only got as far as taping a demo in his New York apartment. Overdubbed (in mono only) by Coral's Jack Hansen, it became a major posthumous hit in Britain in 1959, but saw no chart action in the US.

Later on, we got to hear Holly's vocals with new overdubs by the Fireballs on the 1965 UK EP, *Buddy Holly Sings* (American fans had to wait until the *Buddy Holly: A Rock And Roll Collection* LP was released in 1972), and also in undubbed form on the 1979 *Complete Buddy Holly* box set on MCA. A fourth version – again with the same lead vocal – appeared in 1996, when the Hollies added their harmonies to the original track in Nashville for the 1996 MCA Holly tribute, *Not Fade Away (Remembering Buddy Holly)*.

For some reason, the whole 'Peggy Sue saga' appears to hold a strange fascination and has gradually insinuated itself into public consciousness. Both 'Peggy Sue' and 'Peggy Sue Got Married' have been covered a surprising amount of times, and surely one of the best examples of the latter is the Crickets' 1960 version with the urgent lead vocals of David Box. Propelled along by furious 'Peggy Sue'-style drumming c/o Jerry Allison, it's a major surprise that it failed to chart – especially in Britain, where the Crickets maintained such a big following.

In 1986, a Francis Ford Coppola film titled *Peggy Sue Got Married* hit the silver screen (although the plot itself had nothing to do with Buddy Holly as such). In 1999, as if to demonstrate how far Holly's influence and the Peggy Sue mystique have permeated throughout the world, Polish rock band Myslovitz went out on a limb with the potentially controversial 'Peggy Sue nie wyszła za mąż' ['Peggy Sue Didn't Get Married']. More recently still, Tim Rice wrote another Peggy Sue anthem, 'Whatever Happened To Peggy Sue?', which Bobby Vee recorded in 2002.

ROGER PETERSON

Pilot of the Iowa air-crash that cost four men their lives, Roger Peterson (1937-59) was as much a victim as the three singers who perished that day. A young married man, he came from a large, supportive family living near Storm Lake, Iowa. His father, Art Peterson, was of Swedish descent. Although only 21 years of age, he'd been with the Dwyer Flying Service for several years and was a relatively experienced pilot, though not used to night flying. He was not qualified to fly with the aid of instruments only, and the Civil Aviation Board investigation subsequently blamed pilot error for the fatal crash. Be that as it may, it is gratifying to see that his name is included on the memorial statue at the Surf Ballroom dedicated to the victims of the crash.

See also **WINTER DANCE PARTY MUSIC SCHOLARSHIP**.

NORMAN & VIOLET PETTY

Norman Petty (1927-84) has been unjustly savaged in the years since his passing, and this reached a crescendo in Philip Norman's 1996 Holly biography, where he was disparagingly referred to throughout as 'Clovis Man' (the critic's slur alluding to the area's famed prehistoric inhabitants). The author's view is that it's wrong, decades later, to take a one-sided view of events when all the parties are not here to speak for themselves.

Certainly, it's common knowledge that Holly had parted company with Petty in a dispute over the latter's habit of appropriating songwriter's royalties as part of his remuneration, and lawyers on both sides were beginning to fire salvos at one another. However, Petty was anxious to ensure that the Crickets, whose management he had taken over, didn't lose out. Had the fatal crash not taken place, one hopes that something would have been worked out fairly swiftly and maybe amicably. Instead, the worst possible scenario arose when Holly's life ended so abruptly, immediately freezing whatever efforts were being made to resolve the issue.

But let's move on from that tragic event and its difficult aftermath, and instead briefly tabulate the ups and downs of Norman Petty's career, as well as those of wife, Violet Ann, Vi or Pansy (1928-92), who survived him by several years.

After a period in the services, Petty had started off as a studio engineer with local radio station KICA, where he doubled as an announcer. Always a gifted musician himself, he'd played in small combos for years and it wasn't be long before he decided to form his own group featuring himself on organ, his wife on vocals/piano and his friend, Jack Vaughn, on guitar. With the Norman Petty Trio becoming well known, they launched the Nor-Va-Jak label to release a cover version of Duke Ellington's 'Mood Indigo', which was rapidly picked up by RCA's X subsidiary and reached No.14 nationally in 1954.

Income from the disc allowed Petty to immediately start building his own studio in Clovis. As word spread, he found that more and more artists were seeking him out, and, as with Sam Phillips in Memphis, he was soon running quite a busy independent recording business. Indeed, Petty's main claim to fame is as a record producer. He is remembered chiefly for his work with Buddy Holly and the Crickets, whom he also managed, but also for Buddy Knox and Roy Orbison, who came before them, and for the String-A-Longs and the Fireballs who came afterwards, both of whom would record

The Big Beats with Norman Petty. *Left to right:* Earl Slocomb, Donny McCord, Jerry Zapata, C.W. Kendall Jr. and Larry Randall. *Seated:* Norman Petty.

million-sellers at Clovis.

In the autumn of 1982, Norman Petty visited the UK to celebrate *Buddy Holly Week* and was interviewed by Stuart Colman for BBC Radio London. Less than two years later, he died of leukaemia aged 57. His long-term secretary, Norma Jean Berry, had died earlier that same year, so Vi Petty was left totally on her own – which is how Jerry McNeish, a professional guitarist from Maryland, and John Ingman ended up sorting out the Clovis tape vaults and record warehouse in 1985. This led to the reopening of the original Norman Petty Recording Studios at 1313 West 7th Street in Clovis to visitors in September 1986, and the launch of an annual *Norman & Vi Petty Music Festival* commemorating Holly and the other artists they worked with.

Sadly, Vi Petty died in 1992 at the age of 63, but the festival continued until organiser Robert Linville (see **ROSES**) passed away in 2001. In 2005, the Clovis Chamber of Commerce revived it as the *Clovis Music Festival*, which takes place each September around the time of Buddy Holly's birthday.

See also **NORMAN PETTY RECORDING STUDIOS / NOR-VA-JAK**.

CHARLIE PHILLIPS

Charlie Phillips was born on his family's farm in Farwell, on the Texas-New Mexico border in 1938, and he was one of many country artists who recorded in Norman Petty's studio. His debut release was 'Sugartime' *b/w* 'One Faded Rose', both of which are co-credited to Odis Echols Sr, the owner of KICA (Farwell), though it's reasonably certain that it was Phillips who actually wrote the songs. Issued on Coral in 1957, 'Sugartime' failed to chart, only for the McGuire Sisters to put their version out on the same label soon after and sell a million. In Britain, sales of 'Sugartime' were split between the McGuire Sisters, Alma Cogan and Jim Dale. In his autobiography, Coral A&R Director Bob Thiele (who was responsible for the McGuire Sisters hit) recalls he first heard the song when Sonny Curtis sang it for him.

Charlie Phillips has an entry here because Buddy Holly played guitar on the single and also sang harmony vocals on the flip. The Roses and the Norman Petty Trio were also involved.

Phillips went on to have a couple of country hits in the '60s on Columbia and appeared on the *Big D Jamboree* and the *Louisiana Hayride*. He was also a disc jockey on the KZIP in Amarillo, which he eventually purchased from KDAV's Pappy Dave Stone. He still performs around Amarillo with his band, the Sugartimers.

PHOTOGRAPHS

While moving film of Buddy Holly and the Crickets is relatively rare, the same cannot be said for photographic images. These have proliferated as the years have gone by, and ever more images have come to light – from family photos of Buddy quite literally as a bouncing baby, to sets of both early and late publicity shoots, to poses of him *sans* glasses; from black & white images to colour pics of the singer lounging in his hotel room. There's a rare candid shot of Holly having make-up applied just prior to going onstage in Britain, and, while the *Sunday Night At The London Palladium* appearance may not have been recorded, over a dozen still images were taken from the TV screen by a dedicated fan. A wonderful discovery were the incredible colour photos taken by Larry Matti of Holly's appearance on 1 February 1959 at the Riverside Ballroom in Green Bay, Wisconsin, and photos also exist from the singer's last appearance at Clear Lake, Iowa. Chris Rees, a friend of the author's, has well over 600(!) different photographs of the singer and is still busily collecting as we go to press.

See also **FILMS**.

PICKS

The Picks were a vocal trio comprising brothers Bill and John Pickering and their friend Bob Lapham, whom they originally met when they were all studying at Texas Tech. Bill and John came from a musical family, and as the Pickering Family Singers had been performing gospel with their parents for years in and around Texas.

Bill Pickering later worked as a deejay at Lubbock radio station KLLL. He first met up with Buddy Holly when the singer turned up with his latest single ('Blue Days, Black Nights') and he played it on air.

Norman Petty knew the Pickering brothers from way back, so it was no real surprise that he called upon their services when he needed some backup vocalists. The Picks overdubbed nine Crickets tracks during 1957 including 'Maybe Baby', 'Tell Me How' and 'Oh Boy!' (recordings issued under Holly's name didn't have any backing vocals). However, John Pickering, who had meanwhile started working as a geologist in Houston, found commuting back and forth to Clovis too much of a strain and the Picks broke up. From that point on, Petty used the Roses instead. Bill Pickering did eventually return to Clovis in the '60s and worked with Homer Tankersley and J.B. Mann.

In the '70s and early '80s, the Picks made a few recordings, but their biggest project came up in June 1984, when they decided to re-form for a one-off project to dub backing vocals onto a range of Buddy Holly's recordings. This included almost every Nashville cut to a handful of the Apartment Tapes and a whole load of others in between – 35 songs in all. Although the author has always had mixed feelings about the outcome, no-one can doubt the group's sincerity in embarking upon such an undertaking. John Pickering later defended their integrity by explaining that the group had been airbrushed out of the Holly legend and that all the credit for the Crickets' recordings had gone to Jerry and Joe B., who at the time never sang a solitary note. This was their way of redressing the historical imbalance.

The author recalls meeting John Pickering in Lubbock, and was struck by his love of the music and the sound they helped create. But it also has to be said – and again is subjective – that the group could not expect to sound the same in 1984 as they had sounded in the studio nearly thirty years earlier. Additionally, such perfectly-honed classics as 'Everyday' and 'Peggy Sue' surely didn't need any extra embellishment – although it is always interesting to hear something new. There seems little reason to completely savage these overdubbed versions, but in recent years they have saturated the market to such an extent that it's difficult to find the original classic recordings, which surely cannot be right.

As to the Picks themselves, Bill Pickering passed away in January 1985, only months after the overdubs were completed.

BRIAN POOLE

Born in 1941 in Barking, Essex, Brian Poole formed the Tremeloes in 1958, and there was little doubt that he was greatly influenced by the music of Buddy Holly and the Crickets. Their debut single, 'Twist Little Sister', sounded like a Crickets recording, while early publicity photos featured Poole sporting heavy horn-rims (although it may sound quaint nowadays, he wasn't the only artist to be influenced in that way – ask Hank Marvin).

When they became a chart act in 1963, Poole sought out Norman Petty, who became involved in several of the group's recordings. The most successful of these was their reworking of the Crickets' 'Someone, Someone', which Petty both engineered and played piano on. A No.2 in Britain, it also became the group's first American hit, albeit at a lowly No.97. Up to that point, all their hits had been frantic workouts ('Twist And Shout', 'Do You Love Me', etc), but this heralded a change in direction. With Petty's active involvement, several softer numbers followed, although only 'Three Bells' made the British Top 20.

Brian Poole left the Tremeloes in 1966 to pursue a solo career. Still active today, he linked up with the group for a special 40th Anniversary tour in 2006.

POSTAGE STAMPS

In 1988, Buddy Holly's image appeared on one of a set of four stamps issued in West Germany commemorating influential singers who were no longer alive (the others being Elvis Presley, Jim Morrison and John Lennon).

More than 56 years after his birth, Holly's face also made it onto a postage stamp in the USA as part of a 1993 series honouring a range of popular rock'n'roll and rhythm & blues singers from Elvis, Bill Haley and Ritchie Valens to Otis Redding, Clyde McPhatter and Dinah Washington.

There may have been others since, but the author is not aware of them.

ELVIS PRESLEY

Elvis (1935-77) needs little additional testimony here as he remains a giant artist despite the fact that more than thirty years have elapsed since his untimely passing. The author has always felt that the lives of Presley and Holly were inextricably linked, and several years ago amplified his thoughts in *Elvis & Buddy – Linked Lives*, which is still in print (see *Selected Bibliography*).

Certainly, it's well documented that Elvis and Buddy (& Bob) played together on the same tour bills when Presley passed through Lubbock on several occasions in 1955, and there is even a grainy snap of him at the Cotton Club with Sonny Curtis, Holly and others visible. It's quite definite that they all met up, although it was well before Buddy's name was known. At the time of the plane crash, Elvis was serving his country in Germany, but sent telegrams of condolence to the bereaved families.

Excluding the Million Dollar Quartet's 'Brown Eyed Handsome Man', Holly covered seven songs recorded by Elvis. However, whilst the King recorded his in the studio, most of Buddy's versions are rough demos that only surfaced as posthumous releases.

Even rougher is the so-called duet of the two singing 'Ready Teddy', which came out several years ago on a bootleg album called *Elvis, You Ain't Nothing But The King*. A total aberration, this basically consists of the two versions (each recorded at a different tempo!) playing simultaneously and being faded in and out. Even completists should give this one a wide berth!

Elvis was, of course, one of the first group of artists to be inducted into the Rock and Roll Hall of Fame in 1986 – only one of the hundreds of awards that have come his way both before 16 August 1977 and since.

JOHNNY PRESTON

Born John Courville in 1939, Johnny Preston hailed from the same part of Texas as the Big Bopper and became the latter's protégé in late 1958 after being discovered at the Twilight Club in Port Neches, near Beaumont. Preston not only signed with the same label as the Bopper (Mercury), but also recorded several of his songs during his career – most notably 'Running Bear', a No.1 around the world in 1960. The record included backing 'grunts' courtesy of the Big Bopper and his friend, George Jones, and because of this, its release was delayed for a time following the former's death.

PRISM RECORDS

In September 1958, Buddy Holly formed Prism Records as a future project with himself as President, Ray Rush as Promotion Manager, George Atwood as PR Manager and Norman Petty as Sales Manager (this was before their acrimonious split in October 1958). Shortly before he married, Buddy had purchased a large tract of land in Lubbock for $55,000 – a substantial sum – in the joint names of himself and his father. Apparently, the idea was to build a facility including accommodation for Holly's parents, a recording studio, rehearsal rooms and even a pressing plant, as well as somewhere for Buddy and his wife to stay (it's likely they would have remained based in New York for quite a while). Certainly, it was a major undertaking and would have been completed in phases. Sadly, all these exciting plans ultimately came to nothing because of the disastrous events of 3 February 1959.

PYTHIAN TEMPLE STUDIO

The Coral Records studio on 70th Street, New York where Buddy recorded a handful of his greatest tracks. At the behest of his record company, he first went there in June 1958 to record covers of Bobby Darin's 'Early In The Morning' and 'Now We're One' for immediate release, then returned in October to cut four titles with a string section – three of them ('It Doesn't Matter Anymore', 'Raining In My Heart' and 'True Love Ways') surely amongst his finest ever.

Milt Gabler, head of Artist Acquisitions and also chief producer for Decca, had long championed the use of this unique studio. It was a large converted ballroom, acoustically superb on account of its high, vaulted ceiling, and had been used to record Bill Haley's 'Rock Around The Clock' in 1954. Certainly, it wouldn't have been physically possible to do the string session back at Clovis: there was neither the physical space needed, nor the range of musicians on tap.

According to arranger Dick Jacobs, Buddy was very comfortable at the Pythian and was not overawed by the facilities, so it's more than likely he would have returned there in the future.

Q

Sonny Curtis, Bob Montgomery, Buddy Holly and Larry Welborn playing at the opening of Rallo Henry's Superette, Lubbock on 1 June 1955.

'QUEEN OF THE BALLROOM' *(Buddy & Bob)*
Recorded August 1955 at KDAV, Lubbock, Texas
Personnel: Buddy Holly (guitar, vocals), Bob Montgomery (guitar, vocals), Sonny Curtis (fiddle), prob. Don Guess (double bass)

A composition by bassist Don Guess, this is one of a handful of demos recorded at the local radio station by Buddy & Bob and would doubtless have remained unissued if new Holly recordings hadn't been so avidly sought in the '60s. This particular one saw the light of day in 1965 on the British version of the *Holly In The Hills* album; it didn't come out in the USA until much later. The only issued version is the one overdubbed by the Fireballs in either 1963 or '64.

Sonny Curtis played fiddle on this number, and around the same time recorded his own demo (likewise a vocal version) at the Nesman Studio in Wichita Falls with Buddy on guitar.

R

PEGGY SUE RACKHAM – *See* **PEGGY SUE**

'RAINING IN MY HEART'

Recorded October 1958 at Pythian Temple Studio, New York
Personnel: Buddy Holly (vocals), Al Caiola (guitar), Sanford Bloch (bass), Ernest Hayes (piano), Doris Johnson (harp), Clifford Leeman (drums), Boomie Richman (tenor sax) plus string section

The last Buddy Holly single to chart in the USA, 'Raining In My Heart' entered the *Billboard* chart as a posthumous hit just a week after the 'A' side, 'It Doesn't Matter Anymore', at the end of March 1959. Composed by Nashville-based songwriters Boudleaux & Felice Bryant, it had been turned down by the Everly Brothers and Elvis before Holly made it his own. Now widely acclaimed as a classic, it's mystifying that it only reached No.88 in the 'Hot 100', and failed to show at all on most other charts. Indeed, it needed Leo Sayer to reinterpret it in 1978 for it to become an international hit.

Like the other three songs from the final session, 'Raining' was recorded in true stereo, but wasn't issued in that format in Britain until many years later, as the stereo master had gone missing. (It later transpired that the stereo cut had been issued in the US on a 1959 compilation album called *Hitsville*, and that the tape was then filed away under that title, rather than being put back with Holly's other material.)

His legendary recording has since been used in various commercials and still regularly makes 'easy listening' playlists.

Additionally, all manner of singers have covered the song over the years, from country songbirds Anne Murray and Skeeter Davis to more regular Holly acolytes such as Bobby Vee, Mike Berry and Tommy Roe. The song is also reputed to be one of Larry Holley's favourites, and he produced a solo version by his daughter Sherry, as well as a duet by Sherry and Tinker Carlen.

'RAVE ON'
Recorded late January 1958 at Bell Sound Studios, New York
Personnel: Buddy Holly (vocals), Al Caiola (guitar), Donald Arnone (guitar), Jerry Allison (drums), Joe B. Mauldin (double bass), Norman Petty (piano), session singers (backing vocals)

This was the first time that Buddy had recorded in New York and the two tracks cut at the session, 'Rave On' and 'That's My Desire' were knocked out *post haste*. The Crickets had only just come off of an Everly Brothers tour a couple of days earlier and were poised to fly off to Australia almost immediately, having also squeezed in a second *Ed Sullivan Show* appearance along the way. Holly's urgency permeates the song and it never fails to thrill, although, at the time, it was described as *'music to steal hubcaps by'*, demonstrating that rock'n'roll had still not been accepted by the Establishment at large.

Another Sonny West composition (see also **'OH BOY!'**), 'Rave On' hit No.5 in Britain and No.1 on the *World's Fair* 'Juke Box Chart' – probably a result of the wash created by the Crickets' tour of a month or two before. In the USA, it made No.37 in the *Billboard* 'Top 100'.

Intriguingly, composer/arranger Milton DeLugg is listed in *Remembering Buddy* as the producer of the session, although Coral boss Bob Thiele insists that he was in charge on the day. Also, in *Buddy: The Biography*, Philip Norman incorrectly names the backing vocalists on the session as the 'Jivetones', whereas they were in fact a collection of New York session singers.

Of course, 'Rave On' has been covered endlessly over the years, but again it's difficult to see how the hit version could be bettered, even with today's technology. Who else could stretch the opening, *'We-he-he-hell'* in such a unique way as Holly and yet make it work so effortlessly? Well, many have tried – some more than once!

Amongst the more unexpected covers are ones by veteran British rockers Status Quo and, introducing a tinge of folk music, both Steeleye Span and the Nitty Gritty Dirt Band. Record producer Joe Meek, who was so fixated by Holly that he sadly committed suicide on the anniversary of his death, got one of his better protégés, Michael

Cox, to record it, albeit without success. Naturally enough, the Crickets have performed the song endlessly over the years and have recorded it a few times too – most recently with the assistance of Phil Everly and his son, Jason.

Interestingly, when the original New York tape box was forwarded to Norman Petty in Clovis after the 1958 session, it listed three versions of 'Rave On' as being included. The other two have never been located, and it's possible the tape may have been reused or even lost. However, John Ingman, who spent some time at Clovis helping Vi Petty several years back, reckons there are all manner of tapes there which have never been catalogued. With an alternate take of 'Midnight Shift' suddenly turning up 52 years on, who knows?

'READY TEDDY'

Recorded early Summer 1957 at Norman Petty Recording Studios, Clovis, New Mexico
Personnel: Buddy Holly (guitar, vocals), Niki Sullivan (guitar), Jerry Allison (drums), Joe B. Mauldin (double bass), Vi Petty (piano)

All the Crickets were huge Little Richard fans, so perhaps it was no surprise that they went into the studio sometime between May and July 1957 and recorded this guitar-based version of 'Ready Teddy' for Holly's first solo album. Although one cannot really fault the flat-out performance, it has to be said that many of rock'n'roll's early compositions were fairly simplistic affairs lyrically speaking, and this is certainly no exception. But then perhaps they weren't meant to be analysed or scrutinised fifty years on, just danced to.

Written by John Marascalco and producer Bumps Blackwell, the song had been a US hit for Little Richard back in 1956 as the flip to 'Rip It Up', and was featured in *The Girl Can't Help It* film.

It's known that the Crickets would often perform 'Ready Teddy' and 'Keep A-Knockin'' on stage in the '50s, and years later they still featured the latter number in their playlist. As Holly's version is itself a cover, it's fatuous to list others, but the author couldn't resist the chance to mention the tremendous reading by Big Wheelie & The Hubcaps on Scepter.

Several years ago, a bootleg album called *Elvis, You Ain't Nothing But The King* included what was purportedly Presley and Holly singing 'Ready Teddy' as a duet. This travesty basically consists of the two versions (each recorded at a different tempo!) playing simultaneously and being faded in and out. Even completists should avoid this one.

'REAL WILD CHILD' *(Ivan)*

This is a number that the Crickets heard Johnny O'Keefe sing nightly on their short 1958 Australian tour under its original title, 'Wild One'. Recorded at Clovis by Jerry Allison ('Ivan') it was released in the USA on the same day as the Crickets' new single, 'It's So Easy'. Amazingly, 'It's So Easy' never charted in the US, while Ivan's record made No.68.

Holly played lead guitar on 'Real Wild Child' and his voice is readily identifiable among the background chants. The flip side of the single has Jerry delivering a cod vocal on the old standard, 'Oh You Beautiful Doll' with Norman Petty playing water-filled wine glasses in the background. Although only one take exists, an undubbed version (without Holly's guitar, backing vocals and handclaps) appeared on the 1995 4-CD Vigotone bootleg, *What You Been A-Missin'*.

This iconic song has been recorded by a raft of artists over the years from Jerry Lee Lewis at Sun to Albert Lee to Iggy Pop, who had a particularly big hit with it in 1986. Allison himself still performs it regularly – although always from the safety of his seat behind the drums!

RECORD COLLECTION

When details came to light many years after his death, it was intriguing to discover what records Buddy Holly had in his own record collection – even if one or two of those listed confusingly post-dated 1959! But the bulk of them seemed genuine enough and included a host of releases by black artists including six singles by Ray Charles from the days before he hit the main charts. Jimmy Reed was also in there, as were Little Walter, Bo Diddley and 'I'll Be Alright' by the Angelic Gospel Singers, said to have been the inspiration for 'True Love Ways'. There were also a few by female singers such as the McGuire Singers, Peggy Lee and Valerie Carr, while others were by people Buddy knew personally, such as Buddy Knox ('Party Doll'), Peanuts Wilson ('Cast Iron Arm') and Ray Campi. However, he seems to have had a surprisingly wide taste in music, and also included were discs by British bandleader Mantovani, cha-cha king Perez Prado and Martin Denny, whose 'Quiet Village' was released in late 1958 but ironically didn't chart until a couple of months after Holly's death.

See *Now Dig This* No.138 for the complete list.

RECORD LABELS

Buddy Holly's US label history is reasonably clear-cut, given that he made his first commercial recordings in 1956 for US Decca, after which he recorded for the Decca subsidiaries Brunswick (as the Crickets) and Coral (as Buddy Holly).

In the UK, Holly's 1956 Decca recordings appeared on Brunswick, and his later recordings, regardless of whether they were by the Crickets or Holly, were all released on Coral.

During the '70s, US Decca morphed into MCA, and subsequently into Universal in the '90s, but effectively they have remained Buddy Holly's parent label through to the present day. However, much of his material seems to be licensed to other labels these days, and it is outfits such as Rollercoaster who have come up with the most innovative releases of late. If you are still wondering why there is no Buddy Holly/Crickets official box set on compact disc, don't ask, but writing to Universal might help. Meanwhile, the long waiting game goes on...

When Holly split with the Crickets in late 1958, the group immediately started recording at Clovis with new lead singer Earl Sinks. After releasing a couple of singles on Brunswick, they were switched to Coral when Brunswick was relaunched as a R&B label. Thereafter, the list of labels playing home to the post-Holly Crickets recordings is a lengthy one: Liberty, Barnaby, MGM, Vertigo, Rollercoaster... the list just goes on and on, and it's a good enough reason to subscribe to the *Crickets File* magazine if you want to know more details of their prolific and ongoing recording career.

See also **CRICKETS** and **JOHN FIRMINGER**.

'REMINISCING'

Recorded September 1958 at Norman Petty Recording Studios, Clovis, New Mexico
Personnel: Buddy Holly (guitar, vocals), Jerry Allison (drums), Joe B. Mauldin (double bass), King Curtis (tenor sax)

This is surely one of Buddy Holly's finest recordings and features the added attraction of ace saxophonist King Curtis. Although Joe B. Maudlin is sometimes listed as bassist on this cut, George Atwood recalls playing on the session. Of course, no written records exist of exactly who played what.

Recorded at a four-song session split 50/50 between Holly and Waylon Jennings, Holly's 'Reminiscing' and 'Come Back Baby' were caught up in the legal mess following his death and didn't see the light of day for three and a half years. However, when 'Reminiscing' did finally come out in 1962, the single reached the UK Top 20, while the eponymous 1963 album (see next entry) charted in both the US and the UK.

Although only the one take has surfaced, the original single and album versions differ slightly in that there is an extra guitar line on the album (added to create a stereo master). A third version was created in 1984 when the Picks overdubbed backing vocals (see **OVERDUBS** and **PICKS** for more info). All versions feature the same lead vocal by Holly.

Covers of the song are thin on the ground, although the Beatles performed it in Hamburg (a live version appeared on *The Beatles Tapes* album in the '70s), while the exotically named Flamin' Groovies also released a decent version on their 1978 *Flamin' Groovies Now* album.

It is rumoured that Buddy wrote the song, but gave the royalties to King Curtis as part-payment for the session, though this remains unsubstantiated.

REMINISCING *(LP)*
Reminiscing / Slippin' and Slidin' / Wait 'Til The Sun Shines, Nellie / Baby, Won't You Come Out Tonight / Brown-Eyed Handsome Man / Because I Love You / It's Not My Fault / I'm Gonna Set My Foot Down / Changin' All Those Changes / Rock-A-Bye-Rock

Although the 'Reminiscing' single had been out for some time, and had charted in the UK, it seemed like an eternity before the *Reminiscing* album was released (February 1963 in the USA, and April in the UK). However, it was worth the wait, as it included a wealth of material that up until then had only been rumoured to exist. The only possible criticism that could be levelled at the content was that it was somewhat uneven, whereby a host of early demos appeared alongside a couple of Apartment Tape songs from January 1959 and one studio recording (the title track).

Holly's cuts had all been overdubbed by the Fireballs (Norman Petty's big group at that time), which led to some further controversy among fans as it appeared to them that the Crickets had been sidelined. In fact, the situation was a lot less clear-cut, and certainly, with hindsight, no-one can doubt the ability of George Tomsco and the other Fireballs to add sympathetic backings to what was decidedly a mixed bag of recordings.

The whole package was a good one – from the exceptional 'porthole' colour photo of Buddy looking out of a plane window *en route* to Hawaii in 1958, to the touching sleevenotes penned by Buddy's mother, Ella. In the States, the album reached No.40 on the *Billboard* 'Top LPs' chart, while in Britain it got to No.2 and was listed for an amazing 31 weeks.

ROBERT REYNOLDS

Bass player with the Mavericks, who had a huge international hit in 1998 with 'Dance The Night Away', Robert Reynolds has always been quick to stress his love of Holly and his musical influences. He got the chance to literally become involved when he played on the Mavericks' version of 'True Love Ways' (with Raul Malo on vocals), one of the highlights of the 1996 MCA tribute album, *Not Fade Away (Remembering Buddy Holly)*.

SIR TIM RICE

Tim Rice is a fine wordsmith probably most well-known for his fine musical collaborations with Andrew Lloyd Webber, but he has never been afraid to proclaim his love of rock'n'roll, as espoused by the likes of Elvis, Buddy Holly, Ricky Nelson and the Everlys. Not too many people remember that he himself cut a powerful vocal version of 'Not Fade Away' for the Chrysalis label in the '70s. Since then, other occasional links with Buddy Holly have floated to the surface: for instance, a few years ago he wrote a heavyweight article for the *Daily Telegraph* entitled *'That'll be the day cricket met Crickets'*, describing in detail the unusual meeting between English cricket legends Dennis Compton and Godfrey Evans and the rock'n'roll trio during their 1958 UK tour. Since then, he's gone on to pen the lyrics of 'Whatever Happened To Peggy Sue?' for Bobby Vee, taking the mythical saga of Peggy Sue even further.

'RIP IT UP'
Recorded late 1956 at Buddy's home in Lubbock, Texas
Personnel: Buddy Holly (guitar, vocals), Jerry Allison (drums)

In the '50s, Buddy and his group appeared on tour bills which featured both Bill Haley and Little Richard, both of whom enjoyed big US hits with this generic classic of the rock'n'roll genre. (Apart from being a pop hit, Richard's original – which was also featured in *Don't Knock The Rock* – went to No.1 on the R&B chart and sold a million in the process.) While Richard's version was pretty frantic, Haley's was a tad more melodic – which is perhaps appropriate, given that composer John Marascalco is said to have originally envisaged it as a country number.

That said, the Holly demo is much more Little Richard or Elvis (who cut it in 1956), than Haley. It was released posthumously on the 1964 *Showcase* album, with overdubs by the Fireballs. Decades later, the raw, undubbed version appeared in Britain on the 1986 *Something Special From Buddy Holly* LP, and in the US on the 1995 4-CD Vigotone bootleg, *What You Been A-Missin'*. Rollercoaster also included it on their 1987 *Good Rockin' Tonight* EP.

MARTY ROBBINS

Martin David Robinson (1925-82) hailed from Arizona and was one of those rare individuals who seemed to excel at whatever they turned their hand to – which in Marty's case was stock car racing, as well as his greatest love, making music. His star burned bright from the '40s, when he first started out in country radio, through to the early '80s, when he died from heart failure at the age of just 57.

We would run out of space were we to list all his achievements, but he was a member of the *Grand Ole Opry* for years and, in addition to his 90 hits on the *Billboard* Country chart during his lifetime – around half of them self-penned – also had several worldwide pop hits for good measure. He is deservedly in the Country Music Hall of Fame, as well as the Nashville Songwriters' Hall of Fame. Perhaps we should also tack on that he won several Grammies and acted in several films.

But why does his name appear here? Well, not everyone realises that Robbins started out as a rockabilly singer, and that Holly and his musical chums hung around his office when they went down to Nashville in 1956. Indeed, it was his manager, Eddie Crandall, who was instrumental in getting Buddy his first shot at fame with Decca. In interviews, Marty would fondly recall those bygone days, although sadly the paths of the two stars rarely crossed again.

Coincidentally, Buddy's pal from Lubbock, Bob Montgomery, was Marty's producer in the months leading up to the singer's death. They had completed his *Come Back To Me* album together and had recorded eight songs towards another when his untimely death occurred.

JIM ROBINSON

A native of Littlefield, Texas, where he was born in 1926, Jim Robinson first met Buddy Holly at Clovis at the time 'That'll Be The Day' was being recorded. Like many others, Robinson went along to Petty's studio to record, and Buddy ended up playing guitar on three of the numbers that he cut there: 'A Whole Lotta Lovin'' *b/w* 'It's A Wonderful Feeling' (released on Epic) and 'A Man From Texas' (released on Brill). Neither release charted.

One of the sessions was split with Jack Huddle and Buddy played on a couple of those recordings too. Readers are urged to track down a copy of the *Remembering Buddy* book (see *Selected Bibliography*), where the 'Session File' section sets out all known details from such sessions (for instance, the fact that the rhythm on 'A Whole Lotta Lovin'' was supplied by Jerry Allison on his trusty cardboard box!).

Jim Robinson was a first cousin of Johnny Horton, and in an interview once remarked that the West Texas sound of the '50s became the British sound of the '60s! An intriguing observation. Robinson also penned several numbers with Peanuts Wilson. Although he went on to have a career outside music, he has returned to recording on an occasional basis over the years.

RED ROBINSON

A charismatic Canadian disc jockey, Red Robinson got to play host to virtually every visiting rock'n'roll singer throughout the '50s and beyond. Such was his influence that it's said – and is undoubtedly true – that he helped to break 'That'll Be The Day' when it came out in Canada. Of all the various interviews with Buddy Holly that have surfaced, one of the finest has to be the one with Robinson backstage at the Georgia Auditorium in Vancouver, from when the Crickets were appearing there on the *Biggest Show of Stars for 1957*.

Although little-known outside of North America, Robinson has been given several broadcasting awards, while RCA presented him with a double platinum album for his *Canadian Tribute To Elvis*, one of six records he produced and narrated from his thirty-year collection of interviews. He has remained active in the entertainment business over the years and also founded one of Canada's biggest advertising agencies. In 1983, he published his musical memoirs, *Rockbound*, where he reminisced about meeting up with Holly, Buddy Knox and a host of other big names from those days who played Canada.

'ROCK-A-BYE ROCK'
Recorded early 1956 at Norman Petty Recording Studios, Clovis, New Mexico
Personnel: Buddy Holly (guitar, vocals), Sonny Curtis (guitar), Jerry Allison (drums), Don Guess (double bass)

Like many other recordings from those days, this was one of a series of demos that Buddy cut at Norman Petty's studio in the run-up to his big hit, probably sometime between his first two Nashville sessions (January and July 1956). Self-penned (although the melody is redolent of Hank Ballard's 'Sexy Ways', which Buddy loved) and undoubtedly rockabilly, Holly manages to endow the lyrics with a plaintive quality that makes the song quite a favourite, although it's seldom heard or covered.

Like other demos from the same session, it made its first appearance on the 1963 *Reminiscing* album, with overdubs by the Fireballs. In 1984, the Picks overdubbed backing vocals onto this recording (see **OVERDUBS** and **PICKS** for more info). It was released in undubbed form on the 1983 *For The First Time Anywhere* album.

ROCK AND ROLL HALL OF FAME
It's sometimes surprising to remember that, although the Rock and Roll Hall of Fame had been in gestation for some time, it was to be fully thirty years before it opened its doors in Cleveland, Ohio. Justice was seen to be done when Holly was included among the ten initial inductees in 1986. Many other deserving names have been added over the years, though the connection with '50s rock'n'roll has long been lost. A list of some of the inductees would appal the average reader.

'ROCK AROUND WITH OLLIE VEE'

(1) Recorded July 1956 at Bradley's Barn Studio, Nashville, Tennessee
Personnel: Buddy Holly (guitar, vocals), Sonny Curtis (guitar), Jerry Allison (drums), Don Guess (double bass)
(2) Recorded November 1956 at Bradley's Barn Studio, Nashville, Tennessee
Personnel: Buddy Holly (vocals), Harold Bradley (guitar), Grady Martin (guitar), Don Guess (double bass), Floyd Cramer (piano), Farris Coursey (drums), Dutch McMillin (alto sax)

    This classic number is from the pen of Sonny Curtis, and it's fitting that Sonny played lead guitar on the original July 1956 recording. However, we can only assume that Buddy was unhappy with his first attempt, as he had a second go at the song when he returned to Nashville in November 1956, this time with saxophone accompaniment. The latter version was released in September 1957 on his third Decca single, but remained unknown outside the US for many years.

    Curtis has often told the story of how he came to write the song and where the unusual name of Ollie Vee came from. It turns out that it was actually the name of a cleaning lady who worked on his father's farm in Meadow, Texas, but it just seemed to fit the lyrics. A personal favourite of Sonny's (he confesses the number was influenced by Bill Haley), he's recorded it himself during his solo career and also, on more than one occasion, as vocalist with the Crickets. Several singers have also recorded rhythmic versions of the number including Shakin' Stevens and the Country Rockers. But Bobby Vee, perhaps spooked by the name, has not covered it to date.

    The sax version wasn't officially released in Britain until its inclusion on the 1975 *Nashville Sessions* album. These days, both of Holly's versions can be tracked down relatively easily. The earlier one was also overdubbed with backing vocals by the Picks in 1984 (see **OVERDUBS** and **PICKS** for more info), making it three versions in all. For completists, a short fragment of an alternate take of 'Rock Around With Ollie Vee' (again from the first session) came out in 2007 on the *Ohh! Annie!* Rollercoaster CD.

A great song which sounds even greater live, it was included both in the *Buddy Holly Story* biopic and the *Buddy* musical.

'ROCK ME MY BABY'
Recorded September 1957 at Tinker US Air Force Base, Oklahoma
Personnel: Buddy Holly (guitar, vocals), Niki Sullivan (guitar), Jerry Allison (drums), Joe B. Mauldin (double bass)
Overdubbed October 1957: The Picks (backing vocals)

A superlative number which first appeared on the *Chirping Crickets* album and illustrates that nothing Holly ever recorded after his first hit came out could ever be termed a filler. This was one of the four numbers that the quartet recorded in Oklahoma after rendezvousing with Norman Petty when they were out on tour.

Written by Shorty Long and Susan Heather, it's surprising that it's seldom been covered, though Holly acolyte Mike Berry recorded it when he recently teamed up with the Crickets in Nashville (unusually, it wasn't included on his 2005 *About Time Too!* album, but on a 2006 Rollercoaster CD EP entitled *Before I Grow Too Old*). But the most fascinating version surely has to be the one by the Roses, who backed Buddy so often and whose version was also cut at Clovis in 1957, making it one of the first-ever covers of a Crickets/Holly number. Unissued at the time, it can be heard on the 2008 Rollercoaster CD, *Clovis Rocks: Stars of the Clovis Music Festival*.

Incidentally, none of the four songs from this session has ever appeared without the backing vocal overdubs, and it's uncertain whether the tapes still exist in this format.

TOMMY ROE

Born in Atlanta, Georgia in 1942, Tommy Roe racked up over 22 'Hot 100' hits between 1962 and 1973, including two Number Ones and four million-sellers – a far greater total than the combined hits of Buddy and the Crickets in the same chart. He was inspired by Holly's vocal style and also the drumming patterns of Jerry Allison, and recorded several Holly songs during the course of his career including 'That'll Be The Day', 'Heartbeat' and 'Raining In My Heart'. Although none of these charted, 'Sheila' (a virtual rewrite of 'Peggy Sue') and both sides of the follow-up, 'Susie Darlin" *b/w* 'Piddle De Pat', owed a debt to the group from Lubbock. Definitely one of the better Holly copyists.

'ROLL 'EM UP, HONEY'

A few lines of lyrics allegedly scribbled down by Buddy Holly that were auctioned off a few years ago. In fact, of several such fragments, quite a few are possibly from the pen of Buddy's mother, Ella Holley.

CHAN ROMERO

Chan Romero is one of the unsung heroes of Chicano rock'n'roll. He wrote and recorded the wonderful 'Hippy Hippy Shake', inspiring many a musician – not least the Swinging Blue Jeans, a British outfit who succeeded where he failed by having a worldwide hit with the number. Romero is mentioned here primarily on account of his little-known link with the post-Holly Crickets, in that he played bass and sang with them on tour for a couple of weeks in 1965, having been introduced to the group via his friend Jerry Naylor. However, it was at a time when the Crickets weren't in the studio very much, and consequently Romero didn't appear on any of their recordings.

FRED & WESLEY ROSE

Fred Rose (1897-1954) was one of the founding fathers of country music. Having started off as both a songwriter and a small-time performer himself, he went on to form the influential Acuff-Rose music publishing empire in Nashville with singer Roy Acuff, later headed by his son, Wesley. Two of the main songwriters with Acuff-Rose, Boudleaux & Felice Bryant, penned 'Raining In My Heart'. Having been turned down by the likes of the Everly Brothers, the song thankfully ended up being offered to Norman Petty in Clovis and recorded by Buddy Holly.

ROSES

The Roses were a male trio consisting of Robert Linville, Ray Rush and David Bigham, and were one of the groups that Norman Petty liked to use at Clovis for backing vocals when the material warranted it. As regards the Crickets' recordings, the Roses took over from the Picks around the end of 1957.

In addition to backing others, the Roses also had three singles out under their own name on Dot. It is known that they also covered

'Rock Me My Baby' during 1957, while one of their later releases was as 'Don & The Roses' – the lead vocals being handled by Donnie Lanier, the guitarist who was associated so closely with Buddy Knox during his most successful years.

Unusually, the Roses actually got to sing on stage with the Crickets during their October 1958 tour – the one and only time Holly's group went out with backing vocalists.

They eventually split up and David Bigham went on to a career in banking before retiring to live in Clovis in Norman Petty's former house on Hull Street. Robert Linville deejayed for a time on KTQM, a local Petty-owned FM radio station, and later organised the *Norman & Vi Petty Music Festival* from 1987 until his death in 2001 at the age of 65.

See also **RAY RUSH**.

ROYAL TEENS

A New Jersey group famous for having Bob Gaudio in its line-up prior to his involvement with the Four Seasons. As a group their success was modest indeed and mainly revolved around the novelty, 'Short Shorts', which reached No.3 in the US charts. Another member of the Royal Teens was Joey Villa, who signed up with them in late 1958 although by that time their star was already on the wane. A friend of the Everly Brothers (they met while touring together), Joey joined up with Holly and Phil Everly to help out with the 1958 single they produced for Lou Giordano, 'Don't Cha Know' *b/w* 'Stay Close To Me'. Sadly, it fell stillborn from the presses.

RAY RUFF

Ray Ruff and Ray Rush were contemporaries of Buddy Holly, but had no connection with one another. However, because of the occasional confusion with their names, a few words about both men have been included. Ruff hailed from Amarillo in Texas and claims to have met Buddy Holly by pure chance, though not through music. Apparently he was a pro baseball player until an injury intervened and he decided to go into music.

Said to sound rather Holly-ish, and wearing heavy horn-rims to get into the part, he went on to cut singles for various labels including 'Love', released in 1961 on Norman, and 'The KIXZ Twist' *b/w* 'The KIXZ Waltz' on the KIXZ label, sponsored by the Amarillo radio station of the same name. That one at least would have been assured of airplay! Years later, one of his most Holly-like records, 'I Took A

Liking To You' (originally released on Lin in 1964) was included on a compilation entitled *The Buddy Holly Sound*. Thereafter, Ruff gravitated to production and went on to have a lengthy career in the industry both as a producer and record company executive.

RUMOURS

Over the years, many rumours about Holly's material have come and gone, but frankly most aren't worthy of repetition at this late stage. But remember while reading this today that the world wasn't as connected-up in the 1950s and '60s, and the paucity of information that existed regarding rock'n'roll singers was truly staggering. In Britain, there were hardly any fan clubs in existence, and when the Crickets arrived here in 1958, they were part of a new phenomenon and we had few yardsticks against which to measure things. Reviews and analysis that we take for granted these days were virtually non-existent, although Bill Haley's 1957 UK tour was an exception and attracted a blaze of tabloid publicity. For some thirty years, it couldn't even be categorically confirmed that the Crickets had performed live on the *Off The Record* BBC-TV show, with some fans claiming that the performance was mimed. An audio tape of the broadcast which came to light in 1996 put that particular rumour to bed, but it typifies the struggle Holly fans and researchers faced.

Most rumours have concerned precisely what is or isn't still in the tape vaults and might one day get issued. But what about the possibility that some live recordings existed? Had a tape been made of the Crickets' show in Stockton during their British tour? Had one of their earliest gigs in Carlsbad, New Mexico been captured on tape? The answer is that we simply don't know.

And then there was the speculation arising from Holly's sudden and unexpected death. Tapes surfaced all over the place, but the singer had died intestate, leaving a widow in New York, a close-knit family back in Lubbock and an estranged ex-manager in Clovis. An extremely messy situation to say the least. Rumours abounded for years as to who owned what, and what was going to be released.

In the early twenty-first century, conspiracy theorists began to speculate about the fatal plane crash, suggesting that Holly himself may have taken over the controls of the doomed aircraft, or that firearms may have somehow been involved. Thankfully, all such outlandish theories have now been disproved. Hopefully we can now concentrate on what matters: the music.

RAY RUSH

A member of the Roses vocal trio, Ray Rush first became friendly with Buddy Holly when they recorded together at Clovis. He was lined up to be Promotion Manager for Holly's proposed Prism label, but had to withdraw after Buddy fell out with Norman Petty, who was also to have been involved in Prism. Rush later briefly managed David Box, helping him to get an RCA contract just before the singer's untimely death.

See also **PRISM RECORDS** *and* **ROSES**.

S

MARIA ELENA SANTIAGO – *See* MARIA ELENA

Frankie Sardo enjoys some backstage refreshment at the Riverside Ballroom, Green Bay, Wisconsin on 1 February 1959.

FRANKIE SARDO

Singer Frankie Sardo was born in Italy in 1939, but grew up in the New York City of the 1950s. In 1958, he formed a duo with his brother called Frankie & Johnny and cut several singles before going solo in 1959. When his debut single, 'Fake Out', started to break out in the Midwest and became a *Billboard* 'Spotlight Winner of the Week', he was added to the *Winter Dance Party* tour bill.

Not too much is known about Sardo, although from photos of the time he has the look of a teenage heart-throb *à la* Fabian – but even that failed to help make his record a hit and it didn't even bubble under the 'Hot 100'. Between 1959 and 1962, he made further solo singles for ABC-Paramount, Lido, MGM, Newtown, 20th-Fox, SG, Studio and Rayna, all of which were uniformly unsuccessful. Eventually, he called it a day, got married and found success in films as an actor, writer, producer, and as a nightclub proprietor.

SAXOPHONE

Some say that Holly's original group formation of lead singer/guitar/bass/drums was the template for the classic rock'n'roll combo, but in reality Buddy and his friends were doing no more than copying others and, like the search to find who made the first rock'n'roll record, the result will always feel somewhat contrived.

What we do know is that, although the saxophone didn't routinely feature in the original Crickets' hit-making line-up, Holly and his group were receptive to all sorts of musical sounds from the start – from the celeste on 'Everyday' to Jerry getting the percussion sound he wanted via a cardboard box or slapping his Levis. They were certainly an innovative bunch of musicians and were prepared to do whatever was necessary to come up with the hits they wanted. (It's also said that Buddy made some tapes at school with his friend, Bob Harris, who played the saxophone – but they have never surfaced.)

The author read somewhere that if drumming was the heartbeat of rock'n'roll, then the sax was its muscle. Certainly, from the '40s onwards it was increasingly employed in the instrumental breaks on records, and it wasn't long before full-length sax-led instrumentals like 'Honky Tonk' and 'Raunchy' were getting into the charts. With Jerry Allison's help, Buddy put together a fine guitar-based demo version of the former in late 1956, while a month later Dutch McMillin contributed some Nashville sax on 'Modern Don Juan' and the re-cut of 'Rock Around With Ollie Vee'.

Thereafter, Holly's career was too fleeting for him to ever do anything but flirt with the instrument, and the occasions it was used were minimal. In fact, it wasn't until mid-1958, when he was rushed into a New York studio to cover Bobby Darin's 'Early In The Morning' that it cropped up again, this time with the great Sam 'The Man' Taylor taking care of business. Whether the experience whetted Buddy's appetite isn't known, but three months later he imported King Curtis to Clovis to play on 'Come Back Baby' and 'Reminiscing', plus a couple of Waylon Jennings cuts.

That's not quite it, as, of course, a superlative sax solo puts in an appearance on 'True Love Ways', laid down at his final studio session in October 1958, and one can't help but think there would have been more to come had Holly lived.

The saxophone's ability to add rich texture or extra punch to recordings is undisputed, and the post-Holly Crickets have relished the chance to occasionally use the instrument to augment their sound – for example, Joe Sublett on 'That'll Be The Day' and Bobby Keyes on 'Think It Over' on their 2004 *Crickets And Their Buddies* CD.

SCHOOLS

It's of academic interest only (no pun intended) as to what schools Buddy Holly went to in Lubbock, but brief details are supplied here, particularly for those that may be Lubbock-bound at some point.

Buddy's family moved around the Lubbock area quite a bit when he was a child. He evidently didn't go to a kindergarten, but entered the school system in 1943 at Roscoe Wilson Elementary before moving on to Roosevelt Elementary in 1947. Thereafter, Buddy attended J.T. Hutchinson Junior High (where he later met the younger Jerry Allison) from 1949 through to 1952, and finally Lubbock High from 1952 through to graduation in 1955.

Looking at the sessions listed in the *Remembering Buddy* book (see *Selected Bibliography*) that start to proliferate from 1954 onwards, one feels that Holly's studies started fading away almost from the day he left the Hutchinson Junior High. For those requiring more detailed information, Bill Griggs's series of booklets, *Buddy Holly Day-by-Day*, highlights as far as possible the minutiae of the singer's daily life.

SEARCHERS

This heading can serve the dual purpose of giving a name-check to the British group who still go by the name, and also the title of the classic John Wayne western which inspired 'That'll Be The Day' to be written.

The Searchers had been around since 1960, but didn't rise to fame until the Mersey Beat boom of 1963. Thereafter, they were ever-present in the singles charts for the next few years with a sound that leant towards that of the Crickets, whom group member Mike Pender would often cite as an early inspiration. Indeed, they recorded versions of 'Listen To Me' and 'Learning The Game' (for some reason mistitled 'Led In The Game'), while their British No.1, 'Needles And Pins' – written by Sonny Bono and Jack Nitzsche – was Crickets-like both in sound and instrumentation.

As for the John Ford-directed movie, *The Searchers* (one of the all-time great westerns), we know that Buddy, Jerry and Sonny went to see it one day in early 1956 and, laughing about Wayne's repeated use of the phrase *'That'll be the day'*, Buddy and Jerry decided to try and turn it into a song lyric. Holly subsequently recorded an inferior version of it at his second Nashville session in July 1956. Re-recorded at Clovis in early 1957, 'That'll Be The Day' became the worldwide hit we all know and love.

'SEND ME SOME LOVIN''
Recorded July 1957 at Norman Petty Recording Studios, Clovis, New Mexico
Personnel: Buddy Holly (vocals), Niki Sullivan (guitar), Jerry Allison (drums), Joe B. Mauldin (double bass)
Overdubbed October 1957: The Picks (backing vocals)

Little Richard's 'Send Me Some Lovin'' was the flip side of 'Lucille', and both sides were US pop hits in the spring of 1957. Since the Crickets were big fans of the Georgia Peach, it's not surprising that they elected to record their own version of the John Marascalco-Lloyd Price composition for the *Chirping Crickets* album. Once again, it is one of those masterly tracks which demonstrated that this was not any old group we were listening to, but really something very special.

The Crickets version most fans are familiar with came with backing vocals added by the Picks some three months after it was first recorded. An undubbed version has since appeared on the 1995 4-CD Vigotone bootleg, *What You Been A-Missin'*, but in a very rough state. There is some debate as to whether the undubbed version is an alternate take in view of the bass sound: readers will have to decide for themselves.

'SHAKE, RATTLE AND ROLL'
Recorded late 1956 at Buddy's home in Lubbock, Texas
Personnel: Buddy Holly (guitar, vocals), Jerry Allison (drums)

We can name the writer of this rock'n'roll classic as either Charles Calhoun or Jesse Stone, but of course they were one and the same – the former simply being a songwriting pseudonym for the latter.

Holly would have been very familiar with the raunchy song, as it was a No.1 R&B hit for Joe Turner in 1954 and – with tamer lyrics – a Top 10 pop hit for Bill Haley & His Comets. Elvis also included it in his act, so he would have seen him perform it on stage in Lubbock.

Sadly, Buddy only got as far as cutting a demo of it, which first appeared – with heavy overdubs by the Fireballs – on the 1964 *Showcase* album. Much later, the raw, undubbed track came out on the 1986 Rollercoaster LP, *Something Special From Buddy Holly*, allowing us to see what had been added.

TONY SHERIDAN

A name forever associated with the Beatles and Hamburg, Anthony Sheridan Esmond McGinnity and the author grew up together in Norwich, Norfolk and even briefly played in the same school orchestra. Thereafter the shared musicality ended and, while Tony went on to fame and fortune and a million-seller with 'My Bonnie', the author got his musical fix by studying the pages of the *New Musical Express* and playing his Dansette record player.

Tony was a massive Buddy Holly/Crickets fan from the outset and even got to sing 'Oh Boy!' on the weekly rock'n'roll show of the same name on British TV. It's said that he was the very first British artist to play the electric guitar live on TV when he became a regular on the same show. A professional musician all his life, he often uses 'Not Fade Away' as the finale for his shows.

These days he lives permanently in Hamburg with his wife, Anna. The author is currently working on his authorised biography.

SHOWCASE *(LP)*
Shake, Rattle and Roll / Rock Around With Ollie Vee / Honky Tonk / I Was Just A Fool / Ummm, Oh Yeah (Dearest) / You're The One / Blue Suede Shoes / Come Back Baby / Rip It Up / Love's Made A Fool Of You / Gone / Girl On My Mind

A hotch-potch of overdubbed early and late demo material, plus some Nashville tracks and a few others thrown in, it's extraordinary in retrospect to recall that this album reached the No.3 spot in the British LP charts during 1964 and was listed for 16 weeks in total. It clearly demonstrated the continuing love affair that British fans had with Buddy Holly. In stark contrast, the same album failed to chart at all in the USA, despite their listings being far deeper.

But, coming a year after the *Reminiscing* album and five years after Holly's death, this surely meant that the well was dry and nothing more would ever trickle out... didn't it? Well, as we know, first of all the previously unknown Buddy & Bob material materialised in 1965 on *Holly In The Hills*, while a full decade after the singer's passing the 1969 *Giant* album revealed even more unheard material. Although the bulk of Holly's recordings have long since been issued, life is never dull if you're a keen fan, for sundry releases over the years have contained all manner of snippets from radio station IDs, interviews and rehearsal material (eg 'Mona') to – in 2007 – a wholly new alternate take of 'Midnight Shift'.

EARL SINKS

Henry Earl Sinks was born in Whitharrel, Texas on 1 January 1940, close to the musically fertile area of Littlefield (birthplace of Waylon Jennings and Jim Robinson). His family background was rooted in Western swing, but like so many contemporaries from that era, he was pulled towards rock'n'roll and gravitated to Clovis. It's very likely that he made his recording debut there backed by the Big Beats. Certainly, as a youthful eighteen year old, he was part of Tommy Allsup's Western Swing Band, who appeared on the 1958 *Summer Dance Party* tour along with the Crickets.

When Holly and the Crickets split up shortly thereafter, he was recruited as replacement lead vocalist for the group and was featured on all their remaining Coral material from November 1958. However, the relationship ended in 1960, when Earl left and briefly joined a group called the Omegas.

Throughout much of the '60s, he recorded for the Hickory label and worked as a session guitarist. In 1966, he changed his professional name to 'Earl Richards', and it was under this identity that he finally made the *Billboard* Country chart with 'The House Of Blue Lights', which old rockers will remember from the Merrill Moore recording. Several other hits followed during the first half of the '70s.

He also collaborated with Bob Montgomery during this period, evidently becoming one of the most-recorded country music harmony vocalists in history. And all of that doesn't include the many films he featured in over the years, or the fact that he ran a couple of record labels! A most versatile ex-Cricket, he also diversified his interests and even owned – wait for it! – an abattoir.

'SLIPPIN' AND SLIDIN' '

Recorded January 1959 in Apartment 4H, The Brevoort, 11 Fifth Ave, New York
Personnel: Buddy Holly (acoustic guitar, vocals)

When it was first released in America, 'Slippin' And 'Slidin' ', the flip of Little Richard's No.6 hit, 'Long Tall Sally', was one of the defining records of the era. Based on Eddie Bo's 'I'm Wise', its full title was 'Slippin' And Slidin' (Peepin' And Hidin')' and it reached No.33 in the *Billboard* 'Top 100' in the spring of 1956.

Holly was known to be a huge fan of the singer, so it's not surprising that he cut the number himself. The shock, perhaps, is that it was on the January 1959 Apartment Tapes, rather than on an earlier demo.

As with so many recordings listed in these pages, the record-buying public didn't catch up with Buddy's version – a strangely slow, ponderous reading – till it popped up as the 'B' side of a British 45 rpm release in 1963 complete with overdubs by the Fireballs (see **CHIPMUNKS** for a theory behind this unusual recording). An undubbed version duly surfaced in 1979 on the *Complete Buddy Holly* box set.

For some time, this was thought to be the only recording of the song, but in 1969, a much faster, 'normal speed' version, again overdubbed by the Fireballs, came to light on the 1969 *Giant* album.

In 1995, an alternative 'slow' version, on which the singer's phraseology is noticeably different, appeared on the 4-CD Vigotone bootleg, *What You Been A-Missin'*, but so far has not been officially released.

The post-Holly Crickets also cut the song (for Liberty in 1964), with Jerry Naylor on lead vocals.

RONNIE SMITH

A name that has been sadly absent from nearly every musical reference book of the past fifty years, Ronnie Smith came from Odessa in West Texas, and was known to the Crickets from having recorded at Clovis during the late '50s. In fact, it's said that Holly was present at one of his sessions, although he didn't play on it.

At that time, Ronnie's group, the Poor Boys, included guitarist Tommy Allsup and drummer Carl Bunch, who later formed the nucleus of Buddy's road band during his final tour. Smith, who was left back in Texas, later found himself in the unenviable position of having to fly up North and join the fated tour in the absence of three of its main stars.

Although bassist Waylon Jennings was in a state of shock following Holly's death, he was more familiar with the Crickets' material and handled most of the vocals, though Smith did a strong Elvis-like act that also went down well. Afterwards, he briefly contemplated remaining with the stricken group, but ultimately opted to return to Texas as the aftershocks from the tragedy continued to reverberate.

It was expected that Smith's career would soon take off, and he did have a few releases on national labels (eg 'Lookie, Lookie, Lookie' on Brunswick in 1959), but his career dipped and he became seriously hooked on pills. Thereafter, he switched to glue-sniffing and, according to Larry Lehmer's *The Day The Music Died*, took his own life in a state hospital in Rusk, Texas in 1962 while undergoing treatment for drug dependency. He was still only in his twenties.

'SMOKEY JOE'S CAFÉ'
Recorded January 1959 in Apartment 4H, The Brevoort, 11 Fifth Ave, New York
Personnel: Buddy Holly (electric guitar, vocals)

This was one of two Leiber & Stoller songs that Holly cut during his lifetime, although unlike 'Baby I Don't Care', it wasn't a studio recording but one of the final Apartment Tapes.

It was first released in 1969 on the *Giant* album, with the customary instrumental overdub by the Fireballs plus, unusually, a vocal group overdub courtesy of Homer Tankersley and others. Much later, the undubbed version appeared on the 1995 4-CD Vigotone bootleg, *What You Been A-Missin'*. It is believed that only one take of the song exists.

The composition is a classic 'story-in-song' that Jerry Leiber and Mike Stoller had honed to an art form, and it's surprising to discover that the Robins' original 1955 version only reached No.79 in the US pop chart. Buddy was familiar with it from those days, and it was one of several titles that he had jotted down in notebooks to learn at the start of his stage career. Although the song never had the success it deserved, it was adopted as the title for a West End musical a few years ago, which also featured many other Leiber & Stoller numbers.

'SOFT PLACE IN MY HEART' *(Buddy & Bob)*
Recorded 1955 at Nesman Recording Studio, Wichita Falls, Texas
Personnel: Buddy Holly (guitar, vocals), Bob Montgomery (guitar, vocals), Sonny Curtis (fiddle), Don Guess (double bass)

The only known version of this early Buddy & Bob recording came out on the 1965 *Holly In The Hills* album – in an overdubbed format like so many others. Songs like this Bob Montgomery composition were typical of the material that the duo used to perform weekly on the *Sunday Party* at KDAV. It's possible that another version of this song by Buddy & Bob exists.

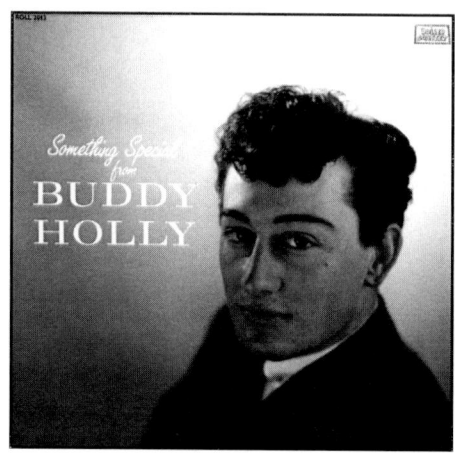

SOMETHING SPECIAL FROM BUDDY HOLLY *(LP, UK only)*
Gone [2 versions] / *Have You Ever Been Lonely* [3 versions] / *Brown-Eyed Handsome Man* / *Good Rockin' Tonight* / *Rip It Up* / *Blue Monday* / *Honky Tonk* / *Blue Suede Shoes* / *Shake, Rattle and Roll* / *Bo Diddley* / *Ain't Got No Home* / *Holly Hop*

    This long-deleted Rollercoaster album from 1986 was only issued in the UK, and at the time gave fans their first-ever chance to hear a whole slew of early Holly demos in their original, undubbed state: twelve different numbers to be precise, with a couple of them ('Gone' and 'Have You Ever Been Lonely') attempted more than once.

    The joy in hearing such recordings at that time was that they were raw, uncluttered, and sounded like duets between Holly's vocals/guitar and Jerry Allison's powerhouse drumming. What's more, the demos also included some engaging bits of studio chatter. Formerly, we'd only heard the good, if more sanitised versions that had been overdubbed and came out in the '60s.

    This was one of two landmark albums released during the '80s (the other being 1983's *For The First Time Anywhere*), which featured material that we'd previously only heard heavily overdubbed. In the last two years, the entire contents of the *Something Special* LP augmented by other 1956 recordings have been released on the Rollercoaster CD *Ohh! Annie!* in far superior sound and with an alternate take of 'Midnight Shift'.

SOUNDALIKES

In a Holly documentary a few years back, Keith Richards laconically remarked that there wasn't a piece of music being created today that didn't owe something to the man from Texas. Expansive though those words undoubtedly were, there is indisputably a long and ongoing list of singers, songwriters and musicians who have been influenced by Buddy Holly in some way – from his vocal mannerisms, to his writing style, to his image.

Buddy's own influences, of course, came in equal measure from his country roots and the rhythm & blues he'd absorbed, but what he handed down to others has branched out into a far greater number of tributaries. What follows can be little more than a roll-call of the more deserving names, chosen mainly to illustrate the diversity of Holly's influence on different musical styles.

The Crickets (Jerry Allison, Joe B. Mauldin and Sonny Curtis) as a group must head any list here. Their erstwhile leader may have gone, but he wasn't forgotten back in 1959, and neither is he today.

Leading the list of soundalikes are Bobby Vee and Mike Berry, though we'll never know what David Box's full potential might have been, or, come to that, Bobby Fuller's (as one of his group later commented, *'If Buddy Holly wore a red sock, then Bobby would have to wear a red sock too!'*). But there have also been dozens of others who tried to follow in Holly's footsteps including Tommy Roe, Bob Osborn, the Hollyhawks, Ray Ruff, Gene Evans, Rick Tucker and the Turks to name just a few. Casting the net even wider, artists as diverse as Weezer, Alvin Stardust, Joe Ely, the Flatlanders and even the Dixie Chicks all owe a debt to Charles Hardin Holley. So, come to think of it, perhaps Keith Richards was right after all.

ALVIN STARDUST

Born in 1942, Bernard Jewry first materialised as 'Shane Fenton' in the early '60s, having been inspired by the rock'n'roll singers he had seen at first hand when growing up in the '50s. In 1958, he not only saw Buddy Holly perform live with the Crickets on stage, but also managed to infiltrate the singer's dressing room, and he has often told the tale of how Buddy showed him how to pick out 'Peggy Sue' on the guitar, leaving his 16-year-old fan star-struck for life.

Having drifted out of the public eye in the later '60s, he successfully reinvented himself as 'Alvin Stardust' during the glam rock era of the '70s. In 1984, he recorded Mike Batt's 'I Feel Like Buddy Holly' and took it to No.7 in the British charts.

'STAY CLOSE TO ME' *(Lou Giordano)*

As stated in the entry for Lou Giordano, this is one of a few original Holly compositions that Buddy never got to record himself. At least, if he ever did commit his own version to tape, it has never been traced. It is possible that he intended to cut it at his last recording session in October 1958, but dropped it in favour of 'It Doesn't Matter Anymore'.

Although lyrically simple (as was so much of the pop music of the '50s), it is set to a uniquely beautiful melody. Giordano's version, produced by Holly and Phil Everly, was released on Brunswick in 1959, but didn't sell. It would appear that only the released take (Take 4) has survived in the vaults. It appeared on the 1995 4-CD Vigotone bootleg, *What You Been A-Missin'*, complete with a count-in by Holly.

Frankly, Giordano didn't do the song justice, but years later Mike Berry reprised it and finally gave it the beautiful rendition it deserved, though again with little commercial success.

STEREO RECORDINGS

As most of the Holly/Crickets material was recorded at the time when stereo recording was still in its infancy, a few words of explanation might be helpful. During the late '50s, the majority of singles were issued in mono, even though many recordings were actually made in stereo.

Although Holly was contracted to a major label in 1957-58 (Coral and Brunswick being subsidiaries of Decca), the majority of Holly/Crickets recordings were made at Norman Petty's independent studio in Clovis, New Mexico. While Petty was a fine engineer and his Ampex equipment was state of the art from the outset, in Buddy's day he only had the capability of recording in mono.

The only true stereo recordings made by Holly were the four songs he recorded at the Pythian Temple studio in New York in October 1958: 'It Doesn't Matter Anymore', 'Moondreams', 'Raining In My Heart' and 'True Love Ways'. (It's also worth remembering that the stereo master of 'Raining In My Heart' was mislaid and the song was only available in mono format for many years.)

Additionally, there are numerous other stereo recordings scattered throughout Holly's catalogue, but most of these were created in the '60s when the Fireballs overdubbed Holly's original mono masters (Petty began using stereo equipment in 1960).

In the 1960s, there was an industry move to recycle mono recordings in 'electronically reprocessed stereo' – a recent RCA invention whereby a quasi-stereo effect was created by separating frequencies into two channels. Whilst most Holly compilations that came out doctored in this way sounded quite reasonable, others (for example, Elvis's Sun sessions) were frankly terrible. Although that era is now thankfully a distant memory, electronic stereo recordings still crop up on new reissues with inexcusable regularity.

In 1986, MCA listed *The Stereo Album* as a forthcoming release. However, despite being allocated a catalogue number (MCL-1827), the record never appeared.

JESSE STONE

A legendary name from the world of R&B, Jesse Stone (1901-99) was a multi-talented individual and his CV is far too long to detail here. As well as being a recording artist in his own right, he also wrote songs under the pseudonym of Charles Calhoun and was responsible for rock'n'roll hits like 'Money Honey', 'Razzle Dazzle' and 'Shake, Rattle And Roll', which Holly recorded a demo of in late 1956.

In a letter to Terry Noland written shortly before his death, Buddy mentions the possibility of using Jesse Stone to write some arrangements. In hindsight, this sounds more than feasible, given that King Curtis and Bobby Darin both had connections to Stone and Holly. However, this is something we can only guess at.

PAPPY DAVE STONE

Country music radio pioneer Pappy Dave Stone was born David Pinkston in Post, Texas in 1913 and started his career in the early '30s as a bookkeeper at KSEL in Lubbock. He later became a deejay, but his big career leap was in opening KDAV in Lubbock, an all-country station, in 1953. Over the next four years, he also opened KZIP in Amarillo, KPEP in San Angelo and KPIK in Colorado Springs.

It was, of course, at KDAV where Buddy & Jack and then Buddy & Bob had a regular spot. Stone's right-hand man at the station, William 'Hi-Pockets' Duncan, also played a crucial role in the Buddy Holly story, becoming his manager shortly before his recording career took off in earnest.

In addition to operating radio stations, Stone also promoted live shows in Lubbock. Buddy & Bob were frequently included on the bill, giving Holly an opportunity to hone his craft and the exposure he needed to land his first recording contract.

Retiring to Colorado Springs in the early '70s, Stone passed away in 2004 at the age of 90.

STRING-A-LONGS

Although most '50s fans run the names of Petty and Holly together, Norman Petty was always proud of the handful of other acts he put on the road to stardom, even if none had the staying power of Buddy Holly. Buddy Knox, Jimmy Bowen and the Fireballs have already been mentioned in these pages, and the String-A-Longs, with their 1961 million-seller, 'Wheels', were another group that became a huge earner for Petty.

Sadly, the group never had any more monster hits, although a couple of smaller ones made it into the US Top 50 before they broke up in 1965. They are mainly mentioned here because Keith McCormack, who handled the occasional vocals and played rhythm guitar, sat in with the Fireballs for the many overdubbing sessions on Holly's posthumous recordings which Petty oversaw at Clovis. McCormack is said to have been a bit of a Holly clone himself, and one of his recordings ('So Shy' by the Leen Teens on Imperial) is included on the *Buddy Holly Days* soundalikes compilation.

ED SULLIVAN

Holly and the Crickets played the prime-time *Ed Sullivan Show* just twice, with decidedly mixed results. Their first appearance (as a quartet) was on 1 December 1957 on the back of their second Top 10 hit that year, 'Oh Boy!' and Buddy's solo No.3, 'Peggy Sue'. Sullivan famously interviewed Holly – some say rather condescendingly – repeatedly stressing that the group were from Texas. The boys performed 'That'll Be The Day' and 'Peggy Sue' live, and overall the show was felt to be a great success. But it marked the final appearance of rhythm guitarist Niki Sullivan (see next entry), who reputedly played without his guitar being plugged in!

Invited back on 26 January 1958, the group – now a trio – again expected to perform a couple of numbers. However, according to John Goldrosen's Holly biography, they managed to annoy the show's host and ended up only doing 'Oh Boy!' – a number Sullivan evidently didn't approve of. Although the film clips from both shows are good, they were certainly badly lit on that second show – perhaps deliberately so – and Sullivan's introduction seems offhand.

Ed Sullivan continued to host prime-time American variety shows for many years and passed away in 1974 at the age of 73. Despite the negative comments *vis-à-vis* the Crickets, he had a long and distinguished career in many fields and was also a syndicated columnist for the *New York Daily News* for years. He has a star on the Hollywood Walk of Fame.

NIKI SULLIVAN

Unlike the other original Crickets, Niki Martin Sullivan (1937-2004) was not born in Texas, but in California, though his family moved to Lubbock soon after. Intriguingly, he was a distant cousin of Buddy Holly by marriage. Even more intriguingly, he was also very similar in appearance: take a look at the cover of the *Chirping Crickets* album and you will see the group had two skinny, bespectacled members, and it's not immediately obvious which one was its leader, as Holly hadn't yet started wearing his trademark specs. (Incidentally, Sullivan later also switched to heavy frames when he embarked on his brief solo career.)

Whether there was ever room for both of them in the Crickets is, of course, academic, but Holly's lead guitar-playing was highly rhythmic, which left little for Sullivan to do as rhythm guitarist. Perhaps the seeds were already sown, as his contribution to the group

The Crickets tear it up at the Brooklyn Paramount, September 1957.
Left to right: Niki Sullivan, Jerry Allison, Buddy Holly and Joe B. Mauldin.

appears to have been somewhat peripheral from the outset, his greatest moments being reserved for performing on stage. For example, he only sang backing vocals on 'That'll Be The Day', only had a non-playing role on 'Peggy Sue', and according to the 'Session File' in the *Remembering Buddy* book, didn't play at all on 'Words of Love', 'Listen To Me' and quite a few others. The situation must have caused him a modicum of anguish, but there appears to have been no single factor that caused Sullivan to leave the group on 5 December 1957, shortly after their debut appearance on the *Ed Sullivan Show*.

After a brief hiatus, he embarked on a solo career and had a record out on Dot in 1958, 'It's All Over' *b/w* 'Three Steps To Heaven', both self-composed songs which he recorded at the small Hester studio in Lubbock.

In 1960, he recorded at Clovis with guitarist Gene Evans and the Fireballs as 'The Hollyhawks', but their Jubilee release, 'When Came The Fall' *b/w* 'I Cry All The Time' again met with little success. The Hollyhawks were managed for a time by Buddy's father, L.O. Holley.

By now with a young family to support, Sullivan decided to call it a day and embarked upon a long and successful career with a major electronics company, only dusting down his guitar for occasional Holly-related events. He died in April 2004 from a sudden and unexpected heart attack at the age of 66.

SURF BALLROOM

This was the venue of the very last performance by Buddy Holly, Ritchie Valens and the Big Bopper, and as such the name resonates in the mind of most rock'n'roll fans who go back to the '50s, and maybe several that don't. We know from extant memorabilia that the admission price for the show was $1.25 and that it was advertised as being *'for ages 12 to 21'*. A few years ago, photos from that last concert were discovered, although the finder has not seen fit to publish them – a situation that seems rather strange to the author.

Annual tribute shows have been held at the Surf Ballroom and at nearby venues every February for a great many years, although it's sobering to note that such events didn't actually start until 1979, when a local radio deejay called the Mad Hatter helped set them up and persuaded Wolfman Jack to attend the inaugural show. Since then, a veritable galaxy of stars have played the venue including Carl Perkins, Bobby Vee, Tommy Roe, Freddie Cannon, the Diamonds, the Drifters, the Crickets, the Shirelles, Johnny Tillotson, Wanda Jackson, Jimmy Clanton and the late, great Del Shannon. A favourite at Holly tributes over the years, he was there at the Surf in 1979. Sadly, he committed suicide in February 1990, just days after appearing in nearby Fargo, North Dakota with the Crickets and Bobby Vee.

Fans who visit the ballroom in Clear Lake, Iowa invariably travel out to the crash site, although – as is to be expected – it isn't very accessible, and involves a long trek across open fields. Close by the Surf, a statue has been erected commemorating the four men who died in that plane crash some fifty years ago.

See also **WINTER DANCE PARTY**.

T

'TAKE THESE SHACKLES FROM MY HEART' (Buddy & Bob)
Recorded 1952 at Buddy's home in Lubbock, Texas
Personnel: Buddy Holly (mandolin, vocals), Bob Montgomery (guitar, vocals)

It's possible that this number and 'I'll Just Pretend' predate 1952, as both Buddy and his pal Bob sound like adolescents whose voices hadn't yet reached maturity. The song is from the pens of early *Opry* stalwarts Pee Wee King and Redd Stewart (they also wrote 'Tennessee Waltz') and is a typical country number with a tinge of gospel that would have been staple fare on the C&W radio stations. Buddy & Bob would both have been familiar with it, particularly as the Maddox Brothers & Rose recorded it for Columbia in 1952.

Had Holly not met an untimely death, this is another recording that would probably have remained unissued. For years, collectors only had this Buddy & Bob song on a cassette tape, if at all. It eventually appeared on the 1995 4-CD Vigotone bootleg, *What You Been A-Missin'*, and has since also been issued elsewhere.

'TAKE YOUR TIME'
Recorded February 1958 at Norman Petty Recording Studios, Clovis, New Mexico
Personnel: Buddy Holly (guitar, vocals), Jerry Allison (cardboard box), Joe B. Mauldin (double bass), Norman Petty (organ)

Written by Buddy Holly (though Norman Petty copped for half of the royalties), this understated number was recorded just after the group had returned from their successful Australian tour and subsequently came out as the flip of 'Rave On'. It's not often that Norman Petty got to play an organ solo on a Holly number, but here it works well, while Jerry Allison's innovative cardboard box drumming is as effective as ever. In 1984, the Picks overdubbed backing vocals onto this recording (see **OVERDUBS** and **PICKS** for more info).

The number of the released take isn't known, but a few years ago four surviving versions appeared – some incomplete, but with enlightening studio chatter – giving us an insight into how the recording was put together. For diehard fans it was all something of a revelation.

A version of 'Take Your Time' by folk singer Carolyn Hester was one of four songs from a June 1958 session uncovered in the Clovis tape vault by Jerry MacNeish and John Ingman in 1985, though all remain unissued at the present time. Photos from this session confirm Holly's participation. Other covers are thin on the ground, although Denny Laine and Albert Lee have both produced their own interpretations. One of the best was by Ted Roddy *aka* Ted & The Tall Tops, who cut a version in Texas for the 1989 tribute album, *Everyday Is A Holly Day*.

When the author was visiting America a year or two ago, the Holly recording of 'Take Your Time' was being used as part of a pizza TV commercial: both the pizza and the song sounded good.

See also **CHRISTMAS RECORDS**.

HOMER TANKERSLEY

An obscure name from the past, Homer Tankersley played a small walk-on part that is worthy of a brief mention. A local singer, he recorded 'If I Had Known' (under the pseudonym 'Ken James') at Clovis in mid-1958. According to the 'Session File' in *Remembering Buddy*, Holly played acoustic guitar on this cut, which was released on Norman Petty's Nor-Va-Jak label. During the '60s, Petty also enlisted his help for the vocal overdubs on a couple of the Apartment Tape songs ('Smokey Joe's Café' and 'Wait Till The Sun Shines Nellie').

Tankersley operated a clothing shop in Clovis for many years, was the musical arranger at Norman Petty's church in Clovis and recorded many albums of gospel material. He also recorded as 'Ken Pepper'.

'TELL ME HOW'

Recorded mid-1957 at Norman Petty Recording Studios, Clovis, New Mexico
Personnel: Buddy Holly (guitar, vocals), Niki Sullivan (guitar), Jerry Allison (drums), Joe B. Mauldin (double bass)
Overdubbed October 1957: The Picks (backing vocals)

'Tell Me How' was surely one of the Crickets' greatest recordings, despite being relegated to the 'B' side of 'Maybe Baby'. As the single came out in February 1958, it meant that 'Tell Me How' actually sat in the Clovis vaults for an incredible six to nine months before it was released. That may not sound long in everyday terms, but in the fast-moving world of rock'n'roll around 1957-58, it was an eternity. Likewise the Picks' backing vocals, usually applied within days, weren't added for several months (incidentally, the undubbed master has never been issued).

Of course, there was nothing sinister in such a delay, as it was an extremely creative period for Buddy and the boys, and things had to be fitted around their endless touring, TV appearances and the madcap life that a hit group led.

Unusually, the music publishing rights for this Crickets number were assigned to Sherwin Music, a company owned by Jack Hooke – who just happened to be Alan Freed's business manager! No doubt this will have ensured extra plays in a world where payola was shortly to cause a furore.

Written by Holly and Jerry Allison (with Norman Petty listed as co-writer, as per usual), 'Tell Me How' has long been a favourite with fans, many of whom prefer it to the million-selling 'A' side. Certainly, the unusual guitar break, which sees Holly using the lower strings for the solo, was not only innovative but also extremely effective.

The song seems to have been a favourite with other musicians too, and, considering its flip-side status, it has been covered by relatively many artists over the years including Nanci Griffith, Matchbox, Peter & Gordon, Bobby Vee, Mike Berry, the Hollies and the (post-Holly) Crickets.

TEX-MEX MUSIC

In the years immediately following Buddy's demise, Holly/Crickets music was labelled as 'Tex-Mex', although anybody from around the Texas area would have known that this was really a misnomer. Certainly, the *Buddy Holly Story* album liner notes from 1959 enthused about the singer's *'Tex-Mex sound'*, but this was surely just a figure of speech that meant nothing. In Britain, this anomaly was fuelled by the release of an EP titled *That Tex-Mex Sound*, although the four tracks on it were all overdubbed demos and no different from other Holly/Crickets EP releases.

Later, as fans gradually became more knowledgeable about all types of World Music, we'd discover recordings that were far more deserving of the 'Tex-Mex' label. And, as we heard other musicians from the Lubbock area, we realised that, if we must use a label, then 'West Texas' would be considerably more accurate.

'THAT MAKES IT TOUGH'

Recorded December 1958 in Apartment 4H, The Brevoort, 11 Fifth Ave, New York
Personnel: Buddy Holly (acoustic guitar, vocals)

This was one of Buddy's final compositions and was discovered among the now-famous Apartment Tapes. Released posthumously, it appeared with vocal and instrumental overdubs courtesy of Jack Hansen on the *Buddy Holly Story (Volume II)* in 1960. As the 'B' side of 'Learning The Game', it also made the Top 40 in Britain that October.

The 'Session File' in *Remembering Buddy* lists the song as being the only one recorded on 8 December 1958, and Tommy Allsup recalls visiting Buddy's apartment and playing guitar on this particular track: it seems Holly was having a problem playing one particular chord on his guitar. But is this the version we have? It's thought that the tape Buddy made in December was passed to Dick Jacobs to work out arrangements, while Allsup and Waylon Jennings probably didn't meet up with him until just before the *Winter Dance Party* kicked off in January. So, who really knows?

As with all the recordings Holly left behind that December, there are three different versions to chose from: the Jack Hansen overdub discussed above, the later instrumental overdub by Norman Petty (first released on the 1965 UK EP, *Buddy Holly Sings*), and the undubbed original (issued on the 1979 *Complete Buddy Holly* box set). Of course, all feature the same lead vocal by Holly. Surprisingly, the song doesn't appear to have inspired any cover versions.

'THAT'LL BE THE DAY'
(1) Recorded July 1956 at Bradley's Barn Studio, Nashville, Tennessee
Personnel: Buddy Holly (guitar, vocals), Sonny Curtis (guitar), Jerry Allison (drums), Don Guess (double bass)
(2) Recorded February 1957 at Norman Petty Recording Studios, Clovis, New Mexico
Personnel: Buddy Holly (guitar, vocals), Jerry Allison (drums), Larry Welborn (double bass), Niki Sullivan, Gary Tollett and Ramona Tollett (backing vocals)

No-one wishes to deny Norman Petty credit for the significant part he played in the creation of Buddy Holly's music, but his appropriation of songwriting credits will always trigger some debate. If this song were a test case, it could be confirmed that the composers of the original 1956 Nashville recording were Buddy Holly and Jerry Allison – the song, of course, having been inspired by John Wayne's catchphrase in *The Searchers* which had so amused them. But, when the hit version – undeniably the identical song – came out the following year, it bore Norman Petty's name on it as co-writer. Such, it seems, was the price that had to be paid in the music industry back then to get hits.

There's not too much to be said about this classic apart from mentioning that, although Joe B. Mauldin was about to be enlisted as the Crickets' permanent bass player, he'd not yet joined the group. The bassist on the hit was Larry Welborn, who in turn had replaced Don Guess. The other notable difference between this and later Crickets recordings was that Niki Sullivan and Gary and Ramona Tollett sang the backing vocals.

The story of how this demo became the actual master recording and took the music world by storm is well known. 'That'll Be The Day' topped most charts around the world in 1957, and even reached No.2 in the *Billboard* R&B listing, but for some reason wasn't certified gold until 1969.

By contrast, the earlier version recorded in Nashville with Jerry Allison, Sonny Curtis and Don Guess sounds laboured and never really lifts off. It's announced as Take 19 (you can hear the studio engineer on the 2007 *Ohh! Annie!* CD from Rollercoaster) – which may have been part of the problem – although Buddy also seems to be straining to sing higher than usual (something he also does on 'Girl On My Mind' from the same session).

Interestingly, although much of the product from the three Nashville sessions wasn't released at the time, 'That'll Be The Day' was released in the US as a single in September 1957. Decca had evidently decided to start competing against its own Brunswick and Coral subsidiaries! A confusing state of affairs for American fans, and one wonders whether the record company was simply diluting sales, or actually gaining any. In Britain, we had to wait until the 1961 Ace of Hearts album, *That'll Be The Day*, to finally hear what was often referred to as the 'country & western' version of the song.

Additionally, the Crickets' live performance of the song on the *Ed Sullivan Show* has been released, as well as one from their *High Time* appearance in Portland, Oregon. Both of these date from 1957 and are both audio and visual. A sound-only live performance from the *Sunday Night At The London Palladium* UK TV show in March 1958 also survives. Plus there is, of course, the trio of jingles that the group recorded as a 'thank you' to the same tune (see **JINGLES**).

Log onto the Internet and search for covers, and you'll quickly find a list of fifty or more. It's virtually mandatory for every Holly tribute album to include a version of the song, and inevitably it has also been covered by Waylon Jennings, Tommy Allsup, Sonny Curtis and the Crickets. It's also interesting to note that the Beatles chose to perform it for their first-ever recording (an acetate by the Quarrymen). A significant number of country singers have also committed it to wax over the years, and Linda Ronstadt had a big US hit with it in the '70s. More recently, country singer-songwriter Rodney Crowell joined forces with the Crickets on their 2004 *Crickets And Their Buddies* CD to pay homage to the number. It seems 'That'll Be The Day' is going to be around for a while longer.

US version

UK version

THAT'LL BE THE DAY *(LP)*
You Are My One Desire / Blue Days, Black Nights / Modern Don Juan / Rock Around With Ollie Vee / Ting-A-Ling / Girl On My Mind / That'll Be The Day / Love Me / I'm Changin' All Those Changes / Don't Come Back Knockin' / Midnight Shift

Released in the USA in April 1958, this was Buddy Holly's third album and the last to appear during his lifetime. Why the UK version didn't come out until October 1961 isn't known, but it was one of the very best posthumous Holly albums as far as British fans were concerned – and all the better as it came out on the newly created budget label, Ace of Hearts, making it almost affordable.

But it wasn't the money so much as the fact that we finally got to hear all – well, *nearly* all – of those 1956 Nashville recordings, some of which had appeared a couple of years earlier on a couple of Brunswick EPs. The artwork may have been somewhat other-worldly, but it was iconic as far as the impressionable youth were concerned. But we had to wait until 1975 for the *Nashville Sessions* album to come out before we could finally acquaint ourselves with the 'saxophone' version of 'Rock Around With Ollie Vee'.

'THAT'S MY DESIRE'
Recorded late January 1958 at Bell Sound Studios, New York
Personnel: Buddy Holly (vocals), Al Caiola (guitar), Donald Arnone (guitar), Jerry Allison (drums), Joe B. Mauldin (double bass), Norman Petty (piano), session singers (backing vocals)

A few days before the Crickets' Australian tour, the group went into a New York studio with the intention of recording a couple of songs for possible release as a single, 'Rave On' and 'That's My Desire'. Life being what it is, things didn't work out that way, and 'Rave On' came out coupled with 'Take Your Time', leaving 'That's My Desire' to moulder in the vaults until its eventual release (with a rather fussy instrumental overdub by the Fireballs) on the 'B' side of the 1966 UK single, 'Maybe Baby'.

The undubbed recording was issued in 1983 on *For The First Time Anywhere*, making us wonder why it had ever been overdubbed at all, although presumably Norman Petty must have considered it to be sub-standard. Eventually, two earlier takes surfaced on the 1995 4-CD Vigotone bootleg, *What You Been A-Missin'*, allowing us to eavesdrop on the backing singers tuning in, which makes for very interesting listening. In *Buddy: The Biography*, author Philip Norman incorrectly names them as the 'Jivetones', whereas they were actually a collection of New York session singers.

It's something of a mystery as to why Holly attempted such an unlikely standard. Was it a song he had always wanted to record, or was it simply a favourite of his mother's? It dated from pre-war days, the melody having been composed by Helmy Kresa (Irving Berlin's arranger), with lyrics by Carroll Loveday. It was widely recorded over the years by everyone from Louis Armstrong to Frankie Laine to rock'n'roll alumni Chuck Berry, Clyde McPhatter, Dion & The Belmonts, and even Buddy's friend, Eddie Cochran. It's difficult to pinpoint the attraction – perhaps it was the mildly lascivious lyrics that made it so irresistible?

'THAT'S WHAT THEY SAY'
Recorded early December 1958 in Apt. 4H, The Brevoort, 11 Fifth Ave, New York
Personnel: Buddy Holly (acoustic guitar, vocals)

This is one of half a dozen self-compositions that Buddy fortuitously left on tape just prior to his final tour, and it has been heard in a variety of guises over the years – naturally all posthumous releases. It was first released with overdubs by Jack Hansen on *Volume II* of the 1960 *Buddy Holly Story* album, and a decade later with the Petty/Fireballs overdub. That version was itself overdubbed with vocal backings by the Picks in 1984 (see **OVERDUBS** and **PICKS** for more info).

The original undubbed version still awaits a legal release, although, like other material, it was unofficially released on the 1995 4-CD Vigotone bootleg, *What You Been A-Missin'*. So, there are four different versions in all, all with the same lead vocal by Holly. Completists might like to note that there is also a short snippet of an alternate take, some thirty seconds long, in circulation.

Although the song is seldom covered, a group called Runaway Express did an album of Holly covers in 2000 called *Yeah Buddy!* and included it in a medley.

BOB THIELE

Bob Thiele (1922-96) was the man at the helm of Coral/Brunswick in New York, and definitely had a lot to do with releasing 'That'll Be The Day' back in 1957, when Norman Petty was desperately looking every which way for a label. Buddy and the boys later recorded a jingle to the same tune as the song by way of a 'thank you' to Thiele, who, according to his 1995 memoir, *What A Wonderful World*, had fond memories of later producing the group in New York.

Whether he was hands-on in the studio is debatable, but what isn't in doubt is his musical pedigree (and it is also a matter of considerable envy that he was married to the delectable Teresa Brewer!). His CV lists him as being a jazz musician, dance band leader, publisher, record producer, multiple record label owner, deejay, A&R man and songwriter. Notably, he (co-)wrote 'Mailman, Bring Me No More Blues' under the pseudonym 'Stanley Clayton', to avoid his management knowing that he was moonlighting as a composer.

And that's not all. His book also lists a roster of singers that he discovered (although perhaps it might be more accurate to say that he gave several stars their big breaks and first hits). Thiele also relates in

Norman Petty *(left)* and Buddy Holly receive gold disc from Coral/Brunswick's Bob Thiele for sales of 'Peggy Sue'.

his memoirs how he and Murray Deutch flew from New York to Clovis to present Buddy Holly with a gold record. Curiously though, Dick Jacobs, Thiele's chief arranger, isn't mentioned once in the course of his autobiography.

'THINK IT OVER'
Recorded mid-Feb. 1958 at Norman Petty Recording Studios, Clovis, New Mexico
Personnel: Buddy Holly (guitar, vocals), Jerry Allison (drums), Joe B. Mauldin (double bass)
Overdubbed February 1958: Vi Petty (piano), The Roses (backing vocals)

    A classic Crickets track that was far more successful in Britain (where it reached No.11) than elsewhere, although this no doubt was on the back of the Crickets' tour of the UK that year. Written by Holly and Jerry Allison, the song was good to start with, but the idea of using a piano solo midway, rather than the *de rigueur* guitar break, was a touch of genius and transforms the cut. In fact, the piano part was overdubbed by Vi Petty at the same time as the Roses' backing vocals. Legend has it that Vi was very busy cooking a meal and was somewhat irritated when Norman called her through to play the piano. The result? She pounded the keys particularly fiercely that day and probably helped to make the record the hit it was. What a thought!

    In recent years, some of the Clovis rehearsals have come to light, and it's actually possible to hear Buddy and the boys working up the song in the studio. Jerry Allison recalls that they tried to replicate the feel they'd had on 'That'll Be The Day'.

Unusually, 'Think It Over' was published by Cedarwood, which was part of the January 1958 agreement to resolve the publishing ownership of 'That'll Be The Day'. (Complications had arisen with Decca when Holly re-recorded 'That'll Be the Day' with the Crickets and it became a colossal hit on Brunswick. As a result, the group ended up passing over 50% of 'Think It Over' to Cedarwood as a *quid pro quo* arrangement.)

HANK THOMPSON

Henry William 'Hank' Thompson (1925-2007) had a very long and successful career in country music fronting the Brazos Valley Boys, and is one of a handful of artists who simply has to be included in any discussion on Western swing. He's mentioned here as Buddy and the boys (Sonny Curtis, Jerry Allison and Don Guess at that point) appeared as a support act on a couple of tours that Hank headlined. He certainly remembered Buddy from those early days, and that he'd thought he had what it took to make the grade.

Thompson hailed from Waco, Texas and it was fate that found him making his last-ever performance in his home town just a few months before he succumbed to cancer at the age of 82.

THREE TUNES

Released in 1957, Holly's third Decca single, 'Rock Around With Ollie Vee' *b/w* 'That'll Be The Day', came out credited to 'Buddy Holly & The Three Tunes'. Strictly speaking, it should have been 'Two-Tones', a name invented by the boys which derived from their stage outfits. 'Three Tunes' was a misnomer and they never used this name on the bandstand.

'TING-A-LING'
Recorded July 1956 at Bradley's Barn Studio, Nashville, Tennessee
Personnel: Buddy Holly (guitar, vocals), Sonny Curtis (guitar), Jerry Allison (drums), Don Guess (double bass)

It's probably no coincidence that, when Buddy Knox and Buddy Holly were looking for material to record, both found themselves choosing hits by the Clovers. After all, the group had had thirteen consecutive Top 10 R&B hits during the early '50s. In the event, Knox picked 'Lovey Dovey' while Holly opted for 'Ting-A-Ling', which had topped the R&B chart in 1952. Both, incidentally, came from the pen of Atlantic executive Ahmet Ertegun *alias* 'A. Nugetre'.

Holly's cut dates from the second Nashville session with Sonny Curtis, Jerry Allison and Don Guess, and the song is transformed from an R&B number into a slab of rockabilly that ranks as one of his best pre-hit parade performances. Decca belatedly thought so too, issuing it as a US single in 1958 when both the Crickets and Holly were on a particularly hot streak. In Britain, it was first heard on a Brunswick EP issued in 1959 shortly after the singer's death. In 1984, the Picks overdubbed backing vocals onto this recording (see **OVERDUBS** and **PICKS** for more info). On the 2007 *Ohh! Annie!* CD, the session engineer is heard announcing Holly's recording as 'Take 7'.

Not many artists have recorded 'Ting-A-Ling', but the post-Holly Crickets, with Earl Sinks on vocals, cut a great version in New York in June 1959. It was produced by Jack Hansen, who shortly after would overdub vocal and instrumental backings onto a bunch of Holly's Apartment Tapes.

TINKER US AIR FORCE BASE

It's interesting to note that the Crickets with Holly at the helm recorded all their material at Norman Petty's studio in Clovis with the exception of the four songs they cut at Tinker. Unusually, these were recorded when they were on the road with the *Biggest Show of Stars for 1957* and passing through Oklahoma City on 29 September 1957.

In fact, the Crickets still had two months of a gruelling three-month tour to run when the above rendezvous at the Officers' Club took place. Fate had decreed that the Norman Petty Trio would be fulfilling an outstanding engagement at the base, and with his usual meticulous attention to detail, Petty spotted an ideal chance to get the group to complete some recordings for their upcoming first album. Not only that, but the premises themselves were ideal at dead of night for him to set up his recording equipment and to record undisturbed. And a momentous session it was too.

After the addition of backing vocals by the Picks, all four numbers – 'An Empty Cup (And A Broken Date)', 'Rock Me My Baby', 'You've Got Love' and 'Maybe Baby' – made their appearance in November 1957 on the *Chirping Crickets* album. (Incidentally, this was the second occasion that the group attempted 'Maybe Baby', the first time being shortly after they'd made 'That'll Be The Day', some six months before. On that occasion, it just hadn't worked out, but here it was reworked with a different rhythm and subsequently became a huge hit.)

On the morning after the session, the Crickets and Petty's trio visited Norman's cousin, Olinda Brown, whose husband Tom recorded a few minutes of ciné-film that has occasionally cropped up in documentaries. It's said that Mr Brown also shot some film around Petty's studio in 1960, but this presumably remains with the family.

GARY & RAMONA TOLLETT

Gary Dale Tollett was born in Amherst near Lubbock, Texas in 1932 and met his future wife, Ramona (born 1936) while stationed with the USAF in her hometown of Merced, California. After settling down together in Lubbock, music soon brought them into contact with Buddy Holly.

From the 'Session File' in the *Remembering Buddy* book, it appears that Buddy, Jerry Allison and Niki Sullivan backed Gary Tollett on a couple of demos, 'Go Boy Go!' and 'Gone', which he cut at KDAV in February 1957. (In 2000, Rollercoaster released a limited edition 78 rpm disc of these two demos as a collectors' item. The originals now only exist as acetates in Tollett's possession.) A few days later, the Tolletts repaid the compliment by helping out on some backing vocals – which is how the couple came to be on the Crickets' legendary hit, 'That'll Be The Day'! This was typical of the incestuous music scene around Lubbock during the mid-'50s, when alliances were forged and broken – mostly amicably – almost on a daily basis. Sadly, none of the recordings that Buddy and his pals helped out on were released at the time, although they have surfaced in later years, most memorably on the 1998 Rollercoaster EP, *Go Boy Go!* and on the 1995 4-CD Vigotone bootleg, *What You Been A-Missin'*.

As 'Gary Dale', Tollett also cut a single in New York for George Goldner's Gone label in 1957 ('Love Is Dynamite' *b/w* 'Pretty Baby'), but this made no impact. He continued making music with Ramona, although it was on an occasional basis and not as a career. Now retired to Arizona, the Tolletts have attended many Holly tributes over the years in both Lubbock and Clovis. It's also interesting to note that Gary Tollett is a cousin of June Clark and Donnie Lanier.

GEORGE TOMSCO

George Tomsco was born in Raton, New Mexico in 1940 and began playing the guitar at an early age, forming his first group while still at high school. A warm-hearted individual, he has gone on to have a long and enduring career in the music business. His main Holly connection is via the Fireballs, as he played lead guitar on all of the material that the group overdubbed. He also played on Tommy Allsup's *Buddy Holly Songbook* album in the '60s, and did a lot of session work at Clovis with other artists over a long period of time. In the mid-'60s, he played several gigs with Jerry Allison performing mainly Crickets material, and has occasionally appeared at Holly tribute shows over the years.

TOURS

Buddy Holly began touring before he ever came to fame, and well before the Crickets came into being. As Buddy Holly & The Two-Tones (named after the stage clothing they wore), the singer and his ensemble were added to C&W packages headlined by Sonny James and Hank Thompson. Of course, Holly and his friends also played in Lubbock itself, either at the Cotton Club or the Fair Park Coliseum, both on their own doorstep (to read more about some of those early gigs check out my earlier book, *Elvis and Buddy – Linked Lives*). Most of these early appearances would have been at smaller venues.

Once fame struck, life for the Crickets became a ceaseless round of domestic touring, ranging in length from a few days (eg 1958's *Big Gold Record Stars In Person*) to several months, plus major overseas tours of Australia and Britain.

The last tour they undertook as the Crickets was the *Biggest Show of Stars for 1958* in October that year, just at the very point that they were breaking up. By the time Holly embarked on the fateful *Winter Dance Party* tour in January 1959, his temporarily estranged buddies, Jerry and Joe B. had already recorded their first post-Holly Crickets single, 'Someone, Someone' *b/w* 'Love's Made A Fool Of You', with Earl Sinks on lead vocals.

See also **AUSTRALIAN TOUR, UK TOUR, WINTER DANCE PARTY**.

TRIBUTE RECORDS – *See* DEATH DISCS

LARRY TRIDER

Born close to Lubbock in Texas, Larry Trider both sang and played bass, and was another fine West Texas musician who worked with Rick Tucker, Don Guess and a posse of others, even broadcasting on KDAV for a while. In the '60s, James Allison introduced his brother Jerry to Larry, and it wasn't long before the two musicians joined forces and circa 1965-66 revived the somewhat moribund

Crickets name for gigs, occasionally augmenting the group with other friends when the venues warranted it.

Trider's name doesn't get too many mentions in Crickets literature as, unfortunately, he never made it into the recording studio with the group. However, he did have several singles issued under his own name (notably 'Don't Stop' (a rewrite of 'When Sin Stops') b/w 'The Ha Ha Song' on Roulette), some of them recorded at Clovis. He also recorded an album called *Country Soul Man*.

Trider is a dynamic stage performer and played Las Vegas for a while in the '70s before returning to Lubbock and holding down a long-running residency at the Red Raider Club. In 1987, he performed at the *Norman & Vi Petty Music Festival* in Clovis.

'TRUE LOVE WAYS'

Recorded October 1958 at Pythian Temple Studio, New York
Personnel: Buddy Holly (vocals), Al Caiola (guitar), Sanford Bloch (bass), Ernest Hayes (piano), Doris Johnson (harp), Clifford Leeman (drums), Boomie Richman (tenor sax) plus string section

The lyrics for this beautiful song were composed by Holly whilst the melody was said to be based on a gospel tune by the Angelic Gospel Singers called 'I'll Be All Right', a particular favourite of the singer – so much so, that it was played at his funeral.

One of four tracks recorded during Buddy's final studio session, the cut is notable for the beautiful arrangement by Dick Jacobs and for the sax player's sublime solo, said to have been ad-libbed rather than scored. If so, it was certainly inspired. It was Holly's only session with a string section, and, being recorded at Coral's main studio, was of course captured in stereo. Norman Petty, Jerry Allison and Joe B. Mauldin were all present – but as non-participants, the boys and Buddy being on the point of going their separate ways.

The song itself has become an evergreen and, although all manner of other artists have recorded fine versions of it, the beautiful simplicity of the original has seldom been surpassed. Suffice it to say that, as you are reading these words, it is featuring on some radio station playlist somewhere in the world.

Ironically, in the UK, where Holly's reputation reigns supreme, his own version was a minor posthumous hit in 1960, though it didn't even dent the Top 20. In 1965, however, Peter & Gordon took it almost to the top of the British charts, while much later Cliff Richard scored a Top 10 hit with it in 1983.

Although it never attained the same level of success in

America's pop charts, Jerry Lee Lewis's cousin, Mickey Gilley, made it a Country No.1 in 1980 – the first of a string of hit ballads for him. Gilley later recalled that his version was in the same key and basically the same tempo as Holly's, and a Dallas deejay spookily put together a tape of the two men singing a 'duet'.

Over the years 'True Love Ways' has been recorded by a string of other country-flavoured artists including the Mavericks, Martina McBride, Mary Duff, Sonny Curtis, Skeeter Davis and Aaron Watson. Vi Petty also cut her own vocal version on the Nor-Va-Jak label in 1960. It would seem the song has plenty of life in it yet, and was recently used for an advertising campaign.

In 1985, Holly's original was released complete with a snippet of studio chatter from the session on the MCA CD, *From The Original Master Tapes*.

RICK TUCKER

Born in Amarillo, Texas in 1938, Rick Tucker recorded a couple of numbers ('Patty Baby' and 'Don't Do Me This Way') at Clovis in 1957 and it has been claimed that Buddy Holly played on these. However, Buddy's touring schedule proves beyond doubt that he wasn't present.

SCOTTY TURNER

Scotty Turner was born Graham Morrison Turnbull in Nova Scotia, Canada in 1931. An international long-jumper, he won a post-grad Athletics scholarship at Texas Tech in Lubbock in 1955. He was also a good guitarist and soon teamed up with fellow students Hal Goodson (guitar, vocals), Gerry Dryer (guitar, vocals) and James Baird (double bass) to form Hal Goodson & The Plainsmen. They performed mainly around Lubbock, on some occasions with Buddy Holly.

Early in 1957, the band cut a few demos at KFYO and were immediately signed by Solo Records in Hollywood, who renamed them 'The Raiders', and arranged a recording session at Norman Petty's studio in Clovis. As they had no drummer in their line-up, Jerry Allison volunteered his services. The session yielded four songs, two of which, 'Later Baby' *b/w* 'Who's Gonna Be The Next One, Honey', were released on 20 May 1957 – one week before 'That'll Be The Day' was issued by Brunswick. The Solo release therefore qualifies as Jerry Allison's disc debut. All four recordings were later issued (under Hal Goodson's name) on the 1990 Rollercoaster EP, 'Texas Rockabilly'.

Following the release of the Solo single, the group (with the exception of Gerry Dryer, who was replaced by Eddie Edwards) then headed for Hollywood, where Solo had good contacts with local clubs, and teamed up with virtuoso drummer Hal Blaine. However, Goodson returned to Lubbock soon after, while the Raiders were signed up as Tommy Sands's backing band and became the Sharks.

Earlier in this book, Colin Cook's entry describes how he came to record a couple of songs that Buddy Holly and Scotty Turner had collaborated on shortly before Holly's death, 'Am I Ever Gonna Find It' and 'September Hearts'. Incredibly, prior to their appearance on *Colin Cook Sings The Lost Songs Of Buddy Holly* in the '90s, very few people had been aware that these existed.

According to the investigations of Holly/Crickets researcher Brian Shepherd, Turner visited Buddy in New York while on tour there in December 1958. They wrote and recorded a couple of numbers together in his apartment ('I'm Gonna Love You' and 'There You Go'), though the tapes for these have never surfaced, and also roughed-out lyrics for another six numbers ('Am I Ever Gonna Find It', 'Lonely Little Lover Lost', 'Not Too Late To Run', 'Our House On The Hill', 'September Hearts' and 'The Memory Of You'), which Turner finished off after Buddy's passing.

Scotty Turner later became head of Liberty/Imperial's country divisions and took up a similar post for United Artists, where he produced both Buddy Knox and Earl Richards. He went on to become one of Nashville's top composers and producers.

U

UK TOUR

The United Kingdom incorporates the historic kingdoms of Scotland and England, the principality of Wales and the province of Northern Ireland – meaning, rather pedantically, that the Crickets didn't get to visit many parts of the UK at all! Looking at the itinerary, every stop during March 1958 was at an English venue, the exception being the penultimate gig at the Capitol Cinema in Cardiff, Wales. However the group did appear on a couple of nationally networked TV shows during their stay, so most of the population got the chance to see them, if only as flickering images on their screens.

Shows were scheduled from 1 to 25 March inclusive with *no* rest days, and it must have been a punishing experience for the Texans! But the trio still managed to fit in several interviews, meeting up with musical journalists such as Keith Goodwin from the *NME*, visit the Austin car plant in Longbridge, stroll around the university grounds in Cambridge, and otherwise fill every waking hour taking in the new sights and sounds. It was certainly a far cry from West Texas and, at that point, only their second overseas visit (they had just returned from Australia the month before).

The complete troupe that toiled around Britain included many more acts in addition to the headliners. Des O'Connor, then on his way to the top of the show business tree, was the comic and compère: the man who really held the show together and befriended the group. The remainder comprised the Tanner Sisters, a well-known vocal duo, but not a chart act, and Gary Miller, who'd had a string of British hits, the latest of which, 'The Story of My Life', was still in the charts when the tour kicked off. Underpinning the bill were Ronnie Keene & His Orchestra, who got to do their own spot during the first half. And we mustn't forget Norman and Vi Petty, who accompanied the Crickets and took care of the logistics, so that the boys could concentrate on the performing.

On stage, the Crickets included many songs they hadn't recorded, such as 'Tutti Frutti' and Be-Bop-A-Lula', and also threw in the occasional ballad.

The above is the sketchiest of outlines. However, Jim Carr of *Holly International* has published the definitive account of the whole tour (see *Selected Bibliography*).

Please quote the following number in any further correspondence A.R.1/O.S.1943/58	MINISTRY OF LABOUR AND NATIONAL SERVICE, Foreign Labour Division, Ebury Bridge House, Ebury Bridge Road, London, S.W.1.	
PERMIT under Article 4(1)(b) of **THE ALIENS ORDER, 1953**		

No. of Permit	Date of Issue	
382633	**5 FEB 1958**	Period covered by Permit FIVE WEEKS months from the date of landing in the United Kingdom.

Employer's Name and Address	Alien's Name, etc.
LEW & LESLIE GRADE LTD., 235, REGENT STREET, LONDON, W.1. (Tel. No. Regent 5821)	Surname HOLLY Other Names CHARLES HARDIN Date of Birth 7th September, 1936 Sex MALE Nationality U.S.C. Employment VARIETY ARTISTE W.2(a).

This permit is issued to the above-named employer subject to the conditions shown below :—

CONDITIONS GOVERNING THE ISSUE OF THIS PERMIT

Voir Dessous. Siehe Rückseite.)

1. This permit does not relieve the employer of his obligations under the Disabled persons (Employment) Act, 1944, as regards engagement of staff.
2. This permit does not constitute any obligation upon the Immigration Officer to give the above-named alien leave to land in the United Kingdom. The alien will be required to satisfy the Immigration Officer on arrival that he (or she) can comply with the provisions of the Aliens Order, 1953, which may include a medical inspection.
3. This permit must be produced to the Immigration Officer at the port of arrival in the United Kingdom. **Thereafter it should be carefully preserved by the alien for production at any time to the competent authorities.**
4. This permit may be used only by the alien named thereon. If an unauthorised person amends the particulars upon the permit it will thereby be rendered invalid.
5. This permit is valid only for the particular employment for which it is issued and not for employment of another kind or with another employer.
6. The alien during the period of stay in the United Kingdom is subject to the restrictions, and must conform to the requirements, of the Aliens Order, 1953. If the permit is for a period of more than three months, the alien will be required to register with the Police and to produce two photographs for this purpose. He/she is, therefore, advised to obtain two extra copies of any photograph taken for passport purposes.
7. This permit ceases to be valid if not produced to the Immigration Officer at the port of arrival in the United Kingdom within **two months** after the date of issue.
8. If it is desired to employ the alien beyond the terminal date of the period for which the alien has been granted leave to land by the Immigration Officer application should be made **by the employer** about one month before such date to the Under-Secretary of State, Home Office, Aliens Department, 271-7 High Holborn, London, W.C.1, marking the envelope in the bottom left-hand corner "M.L. Permit." The alien's passport should be forwarded with the application.

Signed on behalf of the Minister of Labour and National Service,

Joan Fenwick

After its number and date of issue have been noted this permit of **four pages** should be sent intact to the alien, who will be required to produce it together with a valid passport, to the Immigration Officer at the port of arrival.

A.R.2A

Buddy Holly's 1958 UK work permit. This is the only page in this book where you will find him described as an 'alien', or as a 'variety artiste'!

V

RITCHIE VALENS

Buddy Holly's music has endured a long while now, but the fact that Ritchie Valens achieved what he did by the age of seventeen has to be a matter of continued wonderment. There can be no doubt that there was a lot of music still to come, and the world really did lose three fine recording artists in the early hours of 3 February 1959. In several newsflashes, Valens was named as the headliner, as he was still high in the US charts with his double-sided blockbuster, 'Donna' b/w 'La Bamba'. By contrast, Holly's name had been absent from the US Top 20 for nigh on a year.

Ritchie Valens was the first Chicano or Latin artist to break down the racial barriers with his music, personality and demeanour, and it was fitting that a biopic of his life, *La Bamba*, was released in 1987. Born Richard Steven Valenzuela in Los Angeles in May 1941, Valens was from Mexican-Indian stock and grew up in the San Fernando Valley area, where he attended Pacoima Junior High School and later San Fernando High.

A dynamic performer described as 'the Little Richard of the San Fernando Valley', he was signed by Bob Keane to his Hollywood-based label, Del-Fi. Having broken through in the US with 'Come On, Let's Go' in the autumn of 1958, Valens quickly found himself on Dick Clark's *American Bandstand* followed by bookings on package shows like Ted Randal's *Cavalcade of Stars* and Alan Freed's *Christmas Jubilee*.

Shortly before joining the *Winter Dance Party* tour in January 1959, Valens also recorded a cameo appearance for the *Go, Johnny, Go!* movie, where he lip-synched to 'Ooh My Head'. He thus became the only one of the *Winter Dance Party* victims to appear on the big screen (sadly, posters would state *'Starring the Late Ritchie Valens'*). Life was hectic for the singer in the run-up to that final tour, and only days before it started, he appeared on the inaugural *Music Box* show with Buddy Bregman on NBC-TV.

However, as with Holly, the story didn't end that February, and a *Ritchie Valens Music Festival* celebrating his life is held in Pacoima each year around the time of his birthday. He was a precocious talent who was taken from us too soon.

A pensive Ritchie Valens backstage at the Riverside Ballroom, Green Bay, Wisconsin on 1 February 1959.

In addition to his unique vocal style, Valens was also a fine guitarist, and various recordings showcasing his artistry were released after his death. These included instrumental versions of 'Fast Freight' b/w 'Big Baby Blues' issued under the pseudonym of 'Arvee Allens' (a play on the name of 'R. Valens') and a recording of a live concert he'd played at his old school, Pacoima Junior High, in 1958.

In 1990, Ritchie Valens was awarded a star on Hollywood's Walk of Fame; in 1993, he became the first Latino artist to have his likeness appear on a United States postage stamp; and in 2001, he was belatedly elected to the Rock and Roll Hall of Fame. Like Buddy Holly and the Big Bopper, he has not been forgotten.

'VALLEY OF TEARS'
Recorded May, June or July 1957 at Norman Petty Recording Studios, Clovis, NM
Personnel: Buddy Holly (guitar, vocals), Niki Sullivan (guitar), Jerry Allison (drums), Joe B. Mauldin (double bass), Norman Petty (organ), Vi Petty (piano)

The Crickets were big fans of Fats Domino and Little Richard, so it wasn't a great surprise that, when casting around for material for Buddy's solo album, Fats's 'Valley Of Tears' and Richard's 'Ready Teddy' would be selected.

Evidently, his brother Larry loved 'Valley Of Tears', and Buddy's recording is indeed a memorable one, though it wasn't initially intended for single release. Norman Petty persuaded him that the song needed an organ on it, and it really does add an extra dimension. In a surprise move, UK Coral released it as a single in 1961 with 'Baby I Don't Care' on the flip. The record became a double-sided hit, reaching No.12 in the UK Top 20.

It is interesting to note that the Picks didn't add backing vocals to this cut in 1984 (see **OVERDUBS** and **PICKS** for more info), but the instrumentation is probably too full for it to have been effective.

See also **'BLUE MONDAY'**.

JACK VAUGHN

The original guitarist with the Norman Petty Trio, Jack Vaughn was the 'Jak' part of Nor-Va-Jak. He passed away in 1984 at the relatively young age of 55.

In a radio interview, Jack's son claimed his father had played rhythm guitar on a Holly session. If true, this can only be the late '56 Clovis cuts of 'Bo Diddley' and 'Brown-Eyed Handsome Man', for which the second guitarist has never been confirmed.

BOBBY VEE

Perhaps in some alternative universe somewhere Buddy Holly and the Crickets deputised for Bobby Vee & The Shadows after the latter met a premature death in a small plane crash? Fanciful of course, but the underlying point has to be made that the singer's career is so inextricably linked with Holly's, that one's mind can be forgiven for taking flight and imagining that destiny must have somehow been involved. Almost everyone reading these lines knows that Robert Velline (born 1943 in Fargo, North Dakota) ended up being added to the *Winter Dance Party* tour bill of 3 February 1959 when he responded to a radio appeal seeking local replacements for its three deceased main headliners.

But, although he did briefly deputise on the show and this undoubtedly inspired his ambition to succeed in music, he wasn't exactly an overnight sensation. Even so, before the year was out he had a couple of minor hits behind his belt that paved the way for his big breakthrough in August 1960 with 'Devil Or Angel'. (Interestingly, Vee had travelled down to Clovis that June to record under Snuff Garrett's direction, but the session was abandoned after a disagreement between Garrett and Norman Petty.)

There is no doubt that the way in which he made his debut drew Vee towards Holly's music, and it wasn't long before he was recording with the Crickets in Los Angeles – and the rest, as they tritely say, is history. He has gone on to enjoy a long and illustrious career, and his love of the West Texan's music has never wavered.

Indeed, Vee and the Crickets have often joined up over the years, and he was actually responsible for the group's last-ever US 'Hot 100' single, when 'Someday' (with himself on vocals) briefly charted in 1962. The track was taken from the *Bobby Vee Meets The Crickets* album, a hit in the UK, while the 1963 tribute album, *I Remember Buddy Holly*, was equally well received though it didn't chart.

In 1999, Vee completed another project that was dear to his heart: *Down The Line*, an album concentrating mostly on Holly's lesser-known numbers. Mention is also made under the **SIR TIM RICE** entry of the singer's recording of 'Whatever Happened To Peggy Sue', the opening track on his 2002 album, *I Wouldn't Change A Thing*, which he made with the help of his son, Jeff Vee.

And it's not over yet, as Bobby is still touring and working on more projects as these words are being written. His backing band, the Vees, includes his two older sons, Jeff and Tommy. His youngest son, Robby Vee, is also a performing and recording artist in his own right.

VENTURE STUDIO

In Buddy Holly literature it's often mentioned that Holly and Jerry Allison recorded some of their 1956 demos ('Rip It Up', etc) in this small studio at 1926 19th Street, Lubbock, which had been jointly set up by Bobby Peeples, Larry Welborn and Johnny Rackler, close by the high school that they'd all attended.

In the latest interview with Peeples, he states that the studio didn't actually become operational until 1958 and recalls that the demos were in fact cut in the garage of Buddy's home, although Buddy did sometimes use the Venture premises to rehearse in. The studio itself was only open for a few years, although country artist Tommy Overstreet is known to have recorded there.

GENE VINCENT

The name of Eugene Vincent Craddock (1935-71) makes the heart of an old rock'n'roller skip a beat even after this remove in time. A tortured soul, he was also a truly great singer, responsible for some of the most inspired musical output of the era. Anyone who thinks of Gene Vincent merely in terms of 'Be-Bop-Lula-La' or 'Who Slapped John' would do well to search out either the ballads from his early

Capitol albums, or even the quasi-country material he cut for other labels in the last few years of his life.

As contemporaries on the music scene, Vincent and Holly knew one another, and Gene would talk about them meeting when they were both recording in Nashville in 1956 (session listings for the two men show that the dates didn't actually coincide, but disc jockey conventions were frequently held in Nashville and it is possible that they met on one of those occasions).

Incredibly, Vincent's star began to wane soon after in the US, which is how he came to be touring Britain with Eddie Cochran some three years later. Cochran, of course, had an enduring friendship with Holly, and would obsess about his death until his own tragedy overwhelmed him.

In Vincent's 'Story Of The Rockers' (written by deejay Jim Pewter), Buddy is given a name-check and so, of course, is Eddie. Not too much of Vincent's material resembles Holly's, although 'My Heart' certainly sounds more like a Crickets record than a Gene Vincent one.

Vincent was belatedly inducted into the Rock and Roll Hall of Fame in 1998 and is forever immortalised in celluloid through his appearances in *The Girl Can't Help It* (1956) and *Hot Rod Gang* (1958).

VIOLIN

Early publicity material about Buddy Holly describes him as playing the violin at the age of eight, although 'fiddle' is probably a better description. But, from information that has come out since, it's quite clear that Buddy's dalliance with anything other than the guitar, banjo or mandolin was doomed to be very short-lived (his brother Larry recalls a local competition where they had to grease young Buddy's violin bow to render his instrument inaudible!). He also started to learn the piano, but in no time at all switched to an acoustic guitar, and his love of the instrument stayed with him to the end. It seems that he was fascinated by every aspect of making music (see **SAXOPHONE**) and he even volunteered to play drums on the *Winter Dance Party* tour when Carl Bunch was hospitalised with frostbite. But the violin, it seems, remains little more than a figment of a publicist's imagination.

W

'WAIT 'TIL THE SUN SHINES, NELLIE'
Recorded January 1959 in Apartment 4H, The Brevoort, 11 Fifth Ave, New York
Personnel: Buddy Holly (electric guitar, vocals)

This tune dates back to the start of the twentieth century, and as such is one of the oldest songs that Buddy ever recorded (as well as one of the last he ever tackled). It was composed by the American songwriting partnership of Harry von Tilzer (1872-1946) and lyricist Andrew B. Warren (1874-1955), who are probably best remembered for their 'A Bird In A Gilded Cage'.

Quite what prompted Holly to do so is a mystery. It has been suggested that it may have been a favourite of his mother's, or he may have recalled Bing Crosby & Mary Martin's version from the 1941 film, *Birth Of The Blues*, or possibly the 1940s recording by the Sons Of The Pioneers. Whatever the reason, the song is certainly the 'odd one out' of the '59 material he left behind, the others basically being R&B-slanted material which he appears to have been accumulating for a project he had in mind.

First released (with instrumental and vocal overdubs by the Fireballs) on the 'B' side of 'Reminiscing' (a Top 20 hit in the UK), it charted in its own right in Australia. It was also released worldwide on the 1963 *Reminiscing* album, and it was interesting to discover that the LP version contained an additional guitar overdub, which also converted the mono cut into stereo.

In 1995, the undubbed take eventually emerged on the 4-CD Vigotone bootleg, *What You Been A-Missin'*. This lasts only a little over a minute compared to the overdubbed version, which was stretched to approximately two minutes by some judicious editing and repetition of the lyrics.

BILLY WALKER

William Marvin Walker (1929-2006) was a big star in his time and his name was hardly absent from the US Country chart over a twenty year period. Tragically, he recently lost his life in a car crash while on his way home to Nashville.

Born near Lubbock in Ralls, Texas, he got his first big break during the '40s and ended up with his own show on KICA in nearby Clovis. By the '50s, he was a Columbia artist and consequently used

Norman Petty's studio to record (Petty also recorded for Columbia and sometimes steered other artists towards them).

It has also been positively confirmed that, during the mid-'50s, Buddy and his cohorts played on some tour dates headlined by Walker, several of which were in Lubbock itself. There is also a suggestion that Holly, Jerry Allison and Joe B. Mauldin may have played on Walker's March 1957 Clovis session which produced 'On My Mind Again' and 'Viva La Matador!'. Holly researcher John Ingman feels the odds are that they did, but Walker himself gave contradictory answers when questioned over the years.

DON WEBB

Born in Lubbock in 1935, Don Webb was a contemporary of Buddy Holly. After he played him his demo of 'Little Ditty Baby' in December 1958, Buddy agreed to produce him when he returned from the *Winter Dance Party* tour. Sadly, it was not to be.

After Buddy's death, Webb travelled to Clovis and cut four tracks with Norman Petty's help instead, two of which were released as a single on Brunswick. Of these, 'Little Ditty Baby' definitely has Hollyish overtones and has appeared on many soundalike compilations over the years.

There are stories that Webb played piano on some early gospel-style recordings by Buddy, although no such material has ever come to light. He later became active in writing and producing music, and also worked as a painter and decorator around the Dallas area.

LARRY WELBORN

Born in Pleasant Hill, Oklahoma in 1939, Larry Welborn moved to Lubbock as a teenager and played stand-up bass with Buddy & Bob. Heavily involved with Holly for a time, he was part of the group that played the weekly *Sunday Party* on KDAV.

Around 1956, when musical alliances were particularly fluid, he joined Terry Noland & The Four Teens as lead guitarist. Joe B. Mauldin was the group's bassist at that point. They made their first recordings in Dallas that year (the personnel on these is unconfirmed), but the tracks remained unreleased for years until Bear Family put out a Noland anthology, *Hypnotized*, in 2000.

Welborn earned his place in history by playing bass with the Crickets on their million-selling hit 'That'll Be The Day', although by the time the record came out he'd already moved on to pastures new.

At Paul McCartney's instigation, he finally received a belated gold record in 1986 in recognition of his contribution. He also played bass on Holly's demos of 'Bo Diddley' and 'Brown-Eyed Handsome Man' recorded towards the close of 1956. With overdubs by the Fireballs, both became huge posthumous hits in the UK.

In 1959, Welborn did a little session work at Clovis and then linked up with Ben Hall in Big Spring, Texas, where he recorded for his Gaylo label as a session musician and in his own right. In the '60s, he played guitar with the Crickets for a while, but never got the chance to record with them. Later on, he returned to Oklahoma, where he opened his own studio.

In 1972, he played lead guitar on Kenny Vernon's recording of 'That'll Be The Day', which became a minor country hit. He thus had the distinction of playing different instruments when charting with the same title fifteen years apart. How about *that* making the *Guinness Book of Records*?

'WELL... ALL RIGHT'
Recorded February 1958 at Norman Petty Recording Studios, Clovis, New Mexico
Personnel: Buddy Holly (guitar, vocals), Jerry Allison (cymbals), Joe B. Mauldin (double bass)

The surviving Crickets always pay homage to Little Richard, who was indirectly responsible for this song being written. Although totally unlike his style, it was, of course, inspired by his famous catchphrase, which he was wont to shout endlessly both on- and offstage. Jerry and Joe B. have also remarked that it was probably the most collaborative of all their joint songwriting efforts, and indeed their three names – and that of Norman Petty – appear on the sheet music. One of Holly's finest recordings, it was relegated to the flip side of 'Heartbeat', although in Australia it climbed to No.24 in its own right, while 'Heartbeat' itself didn't chart. In 1984, the Picks overdubbed backing vocals onto this recording (see **OVERDUBS** and **PICKS** for more info).

One of the most intriguing points from the session listings is that Jerry Allison is uniquely listed as playing the cymbals rather than the drums, and Buddy plays acoustic rather than electric guitar.

This is a classic track that can be interpreted as a touching love song or as a rocker, as Bobby Vee did in a later version. Needless to say, anybody and everybody has recorded the number, from the British supergroup Blind Faith to the latter-day Crickets, who teamed up with

Nanci Griffith and later Waylon Jennings in what was probably one of his last recordings. It's also worth mentioning that Latin-rock group Santana charted with it in Britain and the US in the late '70s.

SONNY WEST

Joe 'Sonny' West was born near Lubbock in 1937, but moved to New Mexico shortly after, which is where he got his start in music. Those coming late to Holly's music can be excused for not knowing Sonny West's name, but he co-wrote two of the singer's greatest hits, 'Oh Boy!' and 'Rave On', thus playing a small but significant part in his career. ('Oh Boy!' was originally titled 'All My Love (Oh Boy)'. West belatedly recorded his own version in 1990, albeit without the exclamation mark.)

Interestingly, West and Holly both recorded 'Rave On' in 1958 within weeks of one another. West's record (on which he was backed by the Big Beats) came out first, but despite favourable reviews in *Billboard* failed to sell. Had his version been a hit, Holly's recording might have been left as an album track instead of becoming a classic single that has been on radio playlists ever since.

Sonny West is also remembered for two other rockabilly classics which he wrote and recorded in 1956, namely 'Sweet Rockin' Baby' and 'Rock-Ola Baby'. Both were cut at the Lyceum Theatre in Clovis and engineered by Norman Petty. (He later also recorded at Petty's more famous studio on nearby West Seventh Street.) The single was issued on the Nor-Va-Jak label – ordinarily home to much more sedate recordings – as by 'Sonee West'.

In many ways, West missed out on hitting the big time, but it certainly was not for want of trying. He was one of many hopefuls to trek to Memphis in a vain attempt to get an audition with Sam Phillips back in those early days. But he has since seen his music anthologised on the Rollercoaster label, and, although now semi-retired, he's also appeared at several Holly/Clovis tribute shows to great acclaim. He may not have got all of his dues, but he's still alive and well in Abilene, and still making music.

A few years ago, he told his story to *Holly International* magazine and reminisced about meeting Buddy in Lubbock on several occasions, mostly before he hit the big time. Ironically, West also recalled that, having been unable to carve out a full-time musical career, he was reduced to selling jukeboxes.

'WHAT TO DO'
Recorded December 1958 in Apartment 4H, The Brevoort, 11 Fifth Ave, New York
Personnel: Buddy Holly (acoustic guitar, vocals)

This was one of a handful of new songs that Holly left behind on tape and, although simple in construction, it is still a great composition. It first appeared on *The Buddy Holly Story (Volume II)*, released in the United States in 1960 less than twelve months after the best-selling *Buddy Holly Story* LP.

Overdubbed in New York under the supervision of Jack Hansen, the backing for 'What To Do' was provided by session musicians and, as with some of the other recordings, the Ray Charles Singers. Released as a single in the UK, it became a minor hit in 1961. Another version, overdubbed by the Fireballs, did marginally better in 1963. In 1984, the Picks overdubbed backing vocals onto the latter version (see **OVERDUBS** and **PICKS** for more info), while the 1995 4-CD Vigotone bootleg, *What You Been A-Missin'*, finally served up the cut in its original, undubbed state. So, the song exists in four different versions built around the same lead vocal.

'What To Do' has rarely been covered, although those by the Hollies and the Crickets (with Bobby Vee on vocals) are most worthwhile.

HANK WILLIAMS

The direct links between Hiram King Williams (1923-53) from Alabama and Charles Hardin Holley from Texas are perhaps somewhat tenuous, although having been brought up in Lubbock, we know Buddy and his family would have listened along with millions of other to Hank and the Drifting Cowboys on the radio. He may even have seen the singer on one of his endless Southern tours, which occasionally took in Lubbock Fair Park Coliseum as they criss-crossed the South.

What is more surprising, perhaps, is that amongst the 100 or so songs that Holly recorded, not a single one was by Hank! Considering that most of his contemporaries (Jerry Lee, Johnny Cash, Carl Perkins and Roy Orbison) pillaged the Williams songbook, it's quite extraordinary that Buddy seems to have avoided it, though whether this was deliberate isn't known. We certainly know that he often performed Hank's songs on KDAV back in his Buddy & Jack days, and most likely would have recorded something of his at some point, but that's something we can't second-guess.

The quirkiest connections between Buddy Holly and Hank

Williams are the fact that both were elected posthumously to the Rock and Roll Hall of Fame just one year apart, and that, among all the titles they recorded, the last ones were the most bizarre: 'It Doesn't Matter Anymore' in Holly's case, and 'I'll Never Get Out Of This World Alive' in Williams's. Of course, both men died tragic early deaths (Hank a wasted, haggard-looking 29) and would have the dubious honour of having Hollywood biopics (*The Buddy Holly Story* and *Your Cheating Heart*) made about them. Although the Holly movie has its critics, it was surely better than casting heart-throb George Hamilton as Williams. Additionally, recordings by both singers have been posthumously overdubbed, and, of course, both Holly and Williams are legends in their own right.

LARRY WILLIAMS

It briefly seemed as if rock'n'roll had discovered another Little Richard when Larry Williams (1935-80) first burst on the scene in 1957 with a couple of self-penned, double-sided smash hits, but sadly the promise was short-lived and the full history of the singer makes for rather sad reading. Buddy and the Crickets appeared together with him on one of Alan Freed's huge tour bills in 1958 and a glorious photo of Holly, Freed and Williams together exists and has been widely circulated. Williams later died in suspicious circumstances in Los Angeles, aged 44, with his hit parade days well behind him.

CHUCK WILLIS

Buddy Holly and his fellow plane passengers are usually thought of as the first great casualties of rock'n'roll, although, in those unenlightened days, one suspects that perhaps their being white might have added to the legend. Certainly, R&B singers Johnny Ace (1929-54) and Harold 'Chuck' Willis (1928-58) had tragically lost their lives some time earlier without attracting national headlines.

Willis in particular is one of the unsung heroes of rock'n'roll, and was a particular favourite of the Crickets at the time they were starting out. They only got to record one of his compositions, the haunting 'It's Too Late' (a R&B hit on Atlantic in 1956 for Willis, with the Cookies on backing vocals).

Within weeks of his death in April 1958 (from the unglamorous peritonitis), his ironically-titled latest release, 'What Am I Living For' *b/w* 'Hang Up My Rock And Roll Shoes', with King Curtis on both sides, cracked the US Top 10.

BOB WILLS

If the previous two entries highlight Holly's mid-'50s R&B influences, this one gives a nod in the opposite direction to the world of country music – in particular the genre known as Western swing, of which Bob Wills (1905-75) was the undisputed king.

In his early days, Buddy played in several loose-knit ensembles, one of which was the Rhythm Playboys, who not only featured Wills's material in their repertoire, but even derived their name from Wills's band, the Texas Playboys. Buddy would certainly have absorbed much of his music when he was growing up, as did latter-day Crickets Tommy Allsup and Waylon Jennings. Allsup eventually produced what turned out to be Wills's last studio album, and within months of that, Jennings wrote and recorded 'Bob Wills Is Still The King', a live tribute that went straight to the top of the US Country chart. To this day Tommy Allsup still plays with the Texas Playboys.

PEANUTS WILSON

The name of Johnny 'Peanuts' Wilson (1935-80) may only be remembered by a few, but he is one of a cherished minority who got to record at both Clovis and at Sam Phillips's Sun studio in Memphis. On both occasions it was as a member of Roy Orbison's group, the Teen Kings. At Clovis, they cut 'Ooby Dooby' in 1955, which was released on the Je-Wel label, but failed to sell. Later that year, they gravitated to Sun, where they cut several singles, although only their 1956 remake of 'Ooby Dooby' made the *Billboard* Top 100.

Wilson also wrote several songs with Orbison, notably 'You've Got Love' (which appeared on the flip of his rockabilly classic, 'Cast Iron Arm'). Holly's own version was issued on the 1957 *Chirping Crickets* album, and also on a 1964 UK single, which provided him with a posthumous Top 40 hit.

WINTER DANCE PARTY

Because so much has been written about the *Winter Dance Party* elsewhere in these pages (**BEECHCRAFT BONANZA, CRASH, TOURS**, etc) what follows below is a simple overview. For the full story see Larry Lehmer's book, *The Day The Music Died*.

By the time 1959 arrived, the huge multi-artist tours that had exemplified the American rock'n'roll era had almost come to an end. Certainly the *Winter Dance Party* that Buddy, the Big Bopper, Ritchie Valens and Dion & The Belmonts spearheaded was a slimmed-down affair criss-crossing the Midwest by bus. Furthermore, the itinerary

had been put together without much forethought, the artists often doubling back and virtually duplicating their journeys.

In summary, it started on 23 January 1959 in Milwaukee, Wisconsin and was scheduled to end in Springfield, Illinois on 15 February 1959. The tour party had already travelled to eleven different venues spread throughout three States (Wisconsin, Minnesota and Iowa) and was due to travel through another three States (and Wisconsin and Iowa again) before it ground to a halt. Incredibly, despite the tragedy of 3 February 1959, they still fulfilled their engagement at the Armory in Moorhead, Minnesota that evening. Unbelievable.

WINTER DANCE PARTY MUSICAL SCHOLARSHIP

Paul and Dot King from the UK and Dennis and Patti Farland from America are long-standing fans of Buddy Holly and, with the help of others, they decided to put something back into the music that had given them so much. And so in 1998 they agreed to commemorate the 40th anniversary of 'the day the music died' the following year by raising sufficient monies to establish musical scholarships and awards in memory of the four young men who were lost on 3 February 1959.

As an initial fundraiser, a touring tribute show played all eleven cities in the same order and on the same dates as the *Winter Dance Party* tour. A non-profit corporation was established in the State of Iowa in 1999 to administer the scholarships and awards. Since then, fundraising has continued with a further tour and other events, and many musical scholarships and awards have been presented in the hometowns of the three rock'n'roll singers and their pilot. Further musical scholarships are awarded annually in Wisconsin, Minnesota and Iowa, these being the three states visited by the 1959 *Winter Dance Party* tour. By 2009, nearly fifty high school students had graduated to universities and colleges to major or minor in music with the assistance of a Winter Dance Party Musical Scholarship.

'WISHING'
Recorded June 1958 in Norman Petty Studio, Clovis, New Mexico
Personnel: Buddy Holly (guitar, double-tracked vocals), Tommy Allsup (guitar), Bo Clarke (drums), George Atwood (double bass)

'Wishing' is one of a pair of songs Buddy and Bob Montgomery wrote together specifically with Don and Phil Everly in mind. By the time June 1958 arrived, the Everly Brothers had five US Top 30 hits and two Number Ones behind their belts, and Buddy, who had struck a warm friendship with the duo on an earlier tour, felt certain that 'Wishing' and 'Love's Made A Fool Of You' might produce their next hits. Unfortunately, it's likely that Don and Phil didn't even hear the demos, as the material they recorded was supplied by the Acuff-Rose publishing house at that point, and was therefore largely a closed shop as far as outsiders were concerned.

What *is* certain, however, is that 'Wishing' is a superlative Holly recording. Cut at Clovis with the help of in-house musicians Tommy Allsup, George Atwood and Bo Clarke, it was first released as a UK single in 1963 (as a follow-up to 'Bo Diddley') and became his third Top 10 hit that year. The cut certainly didn't need any 'doctoring', but when it appeared on the 1965 *Holly In The Hills* album it came with an additional guitar line overdubbed by Norman Petty, probably played by George Tomsco of the Fireballs.

The composition has inspired surprisingly few covers, although Bobby Vee has tackled it on two separate occasions and it has been recorded several times as an instrumental – most notably by Hank Marvin. Popular country star Mary Chapin Carpenter chose it as her contribution to the 1996 MCA tribute, *Not Fade Away (Remembering*

Buddy Holly). Kevin Montgomery, whose father was the co-writer, helped out on harmony vocals and guitar.

In discussing Buddy's musical legacy a few years back, Jerry Allison was moved to say that 'Wishing' was *'mighty good for a demo'*, and few would disagree.

WOLFMAN JACK

Robert Weston Smith (1938-97) was a legendary deejay who was once described in dramatised form as *'the howling, prowling Wolfman Jack'*. He was a true friend of rock'n'roll and someone who, like Alan Freed, often flew the flag for R&B, although he himself was white and was born to middle-class parents in Manhattan, New York. He became famous for his raucous patter between tracks, and for broadcasting (illegally at first) throughout much of the United States on powerful 250,000-watt stations. He later played himself in the '70s *American Graffiti* movie, a film set in small-town America which featured a rock'n'roll soundtrack.

The Wolfman was also a big fan of Holly/Crickets music and mentioned the singer at several points in his autobiography, *Have Mercy!* (see *Selected Bibliography*), which was published shortly before his death in 1997. He also anchored the first-ever *Anniversary Tribute Concert* at Clear Lake, Iowa in 1979. A true one-off.

'WORDS OF LOVE'
Recorded April 1957 at Norman Petty Recording Studio, Clovis, New Mexico
Personnel: Buddy Holly (double-tracked guitar, vocals), Jerry Allison (drums), Joe B. Mauldin (double bass)

'Words Of Love' is arguably one of Buddy Holly's greatest-ever compositions and it achieved a unique double for the singer, although not too many people knew about it at the time. Firstly, it was his first US hit – thanks to the Diamonds, who took it into the US Top 20 two months before the Crickets charted with 'That'll Be The Day'. Secondly, it was his first solo release on Coral, but never got anywhere near the charts and sank without trace.

Buddy's cut certainly owes a lot to Mickey & Sylvia's influence, both in the guitar sound and the multi-tracked vocals, pioneering a studio practice that was almost unheard of at the time. It was also very different from the Diamonds' version, which was set to a catchy 'Little Darlin' '-type Latin rhythm. In 1984, the Picks overdubbed backing vocals onto Holly's recording (see **OVERDUBS** and **PICKS** for more info).

In Britain, it was only released as an album track on his first solo album, *Buddy Holly*. But the Beatles for one certainly knew a quality song when they heard it, and they faithfully copied his arrangement on their 1964 *Beatles For Sale* album.

The song has since been recognised as a sublime piece of work and, despite its non-hit status, has been included in virtually every 'greatest hits' compilation. In fact, a 1992 compilation of Holly/Crickets hits entitled *Words Of Love* topped the UK album charts, selling over 400,000 units. A poor-quality copy of the undubbed recording by Holly appeared on the 1995 4-CD Vigotone bootleg, *What You Been A-Missin'*.

It was also this song that inspired pioneering Holly biographer John Goldrosen to research his life and help reactivate interest in the singer when it was beginning to wane. In 1989, his British counterpart, Philip Norman, wrote a short story under the title *Words of Love*, then went on to pen a dramatised life-story of Holly for TV under the same title. (He later also wrote a large-scale biography of the singer which was serialised in the British tabloid press, albeit with some lurid headlines.)

Y

'YOU AND I ARE THROUGH' *(Buddy & Bob)*
(1) Recorded June 1955 at Nesman Recording Studio, Wichita Falls, Texas
Personnel: Buddy Holly (guitar, vocals), Bob Montgomery (guitar, vocals), Jerry Allison (drums), unknown (double bass)
(2) Recorded August 1955 at KDAV, Lubbock, Texas
Personnel: Buddy Holly (guitar, vocals), Bob Montgomery (guitar, vocals), Sonny Curtis (guitar), prob. Don Guess (double bass)

It wasn't always easy to recall just who wrote what with those early Buddy & Bob songs and, although this one is attributed to Bob Montgomery, it's one that Jack Neal insists he penned. Although not particularly memorable, it's a pleasant enough country-styled effort with plenty of fiddle in evidence, courtesy of a youthful Sonny Curtis. The fiddle-playing is especially noticeable on the undubbed versions (there are two different ones in existence, and both appear on the 2006 Rev-Ola CD, *Gotta Roll! The Early Recordings 1949-1955*). Long-standing Holly fans will be more familiar with the KDAV cut, which was overdubbed by the Fireballs and released on the 1965 *Holly In The Hills* album and also the 1979 *Complete Buddy Holly* box set.

'YOU ARE MY ONE DESIRE'
Recorded November 1956 at Bradley's Barn Studio, Nashville, Tennessee
Personnel: Buddy Holly (vocals), Harold Bradley (guitar), Grady Martin (guitar), Don Guess (double bass), Floyd Cramer (piano), Farris Coursey (drums)

Written by bass player Don Guess, this slow ballad was one of only three numbers cut at Holly's third Nashville session, and there is speculation that the visit to Decca wasn't pre-planned and that Buddy had simply travelled there in the hope of recording more material. Although a sax was used on the other two tracks recorded at the session, it's not in evidence on this particular number. However, Floyd Cramer, who also worked with Elvis and Johnny Cash, contributed a memorable 'cling-cling' piano line throughout. It was released on the flip of 'Modern Don Juan' on Christmas Eve 1956, but, despite attracting some reasonable reviews, the single met with little success.

In 1984, the Picks overdubbed backing vocals (see **OVERDUBS** and **PICKS** for more info), which in this instance worked particularly well, giving the track a much fuller, textured sound.

Completists might also like to note that the 2007 Rollercoaster CD, *Ohh! Annie!* also includes Take 2 (a false start), though it only lasts for a few seconds.

Despite its merits, 'You Are My One Desire' is frequently overlooked when Holly's songbook is discussed and has seldom been covered.

'YOU'RE THE ONE'
Recorded late December 1957 at KLLL, Lubbock, Texas
Personnel: Buddy Holly (guitar, vocals), Waylon Jennings and Slim Corbin (hand-clapping)

This has to be one of the most unlikely recordings ever released and, once again, one that surely wouldn't have seen the light of day if fate hadn't cruelly intervened. In his autobiography, Waylon Jennings describes how he and Buddy, with the assistance of Slim Corbin, decided to compose an 'instant' song when Holly called in at the radio station over Christmas.

It remained unissued for years, but, reversing the trend, when it surfaced on the 1964 *Showcase* album, it was in its original, undubbed form with Buddy singing and playing guitar, and the others clapping along. Jennings also recorded two of his own compositions ('More and More' and 'When You Are Lonely') at the same session with Buddy on guitar, which have circulated among fans for years.

Later on, Norman Petty got the Fireballs to overdub the cut, and this version appeared on the 1969 *Giant* album and on the flip of the 1969 'Love Is Strange' single. In 1984, the Picks overdubbed backing vocals onto the Fireballs version (see **OVERDUBS** and **PICKS** for more info).

In Britain, rockabilly revivalists Matchbox included their version of this little-covered song (plus the better-known 'Love's Made A Fool Of You') on their 1981 *Flying Colours* album.

'YOU'VE GOT LOVE'
Recorded September 1957 at Tinker US Air Force Base, Oklahoma
Personnel: Buddy Holly (guitar, vocals), Niki Sullivan (guitar), Jerry Allison (drums), Joe B. Mauldin (double bass)
Overdubbed October 1957: The Picks (backing vocals)

Surely one of the Crickets' greatest recordings, 'You've Got Love' was laid down when they were on the road and needed several songs to complete the *Chirping Crickets* album. This one was penned by Roy Orbison and Teen Kings member Johnny 'Peanuts' Wilson. Wilson had already recorded the song at Clovis for the flip side of his rockabilly classic, 'Cast Iron Arm'.

Without warning, the Crickets' cut was suddenly plucked out in 1964 for single release in Britain (*b/w* 'An Empty Cup') and, incredibly, went on to make the Top 40 – yet another posthumous hit for Holly.

None of the four songs from this session have appeared undubbed, and it's uncertain whether the tapes still exist in that format.

Z

ZAGER & EVANS

American folk-rock duo Denny Zager and Rick Evans are surely the ultimate one-hit wonders, responsible for most unlikely of chart singles, 'In The Year 2525', a sermon on the grand sweep of history from the beginning to the end of time... and all delivered in less than three minutes! Initially released on the Truth label in 1968, it was picked up by RCA the following year and shot to the No.1 spot. Amazingly, it turns out that this futuristic song was produced by Buddy Holly's former lead guitarist, Tommy Allsup, at his AOK recording studio in Odessa, Texas.

JERRY ZAPATA

It's a personal indulgence, but perhaps it's fitting to end this book with a short entry on Jerry Zapata, the drummer with the Big Beats, a Dallas group who were taken under Norman Petty's wing and spent some time in Clovis in 1957 hoping to hit the big time. Somehow, it was never meant to happen, even if they did get to tour nationally and cut some singles for Columbia. What I would like to end with is a personal story of how the author and Jerry unexpectedly met up in 1996 in circumstances that owed everything to chance, coincidence, or perhaps pure fate. It shouldn't have happened, but it did, and the brief tale that follows is worth telling.

By the time 1996 came around, Jerry's musical days were far behind him and he was driving a Las Vegas taxi for a living. My wife and I had just finished the Vegas leg of our vacation and, as I picked up the phone in the motel lobby at 5:00 a.m. that morning to order a cab to the airport, a fussy desk clerk intervened, insisting he'd make the call personally and lay on the transport.

So, Jerry and his cab duly arrived, and as we chatted together during the brief ride I let slip that we were then heading for Lubbock.

'Oh', said Jerry 'I used to play in Clovis with Buddy Holly. Have you heard of him, and did you know that he was from Lubbock?'

Not only did I happen to know that, but I just happened to have a copy of an earlier edition of *A to Z of Buddy Holly* in my suitcase which included an entry on the Big Beats, which I scrambled to present to him before the plane left.

A comedy of errors was to follow. He gave me his address,

which I promptly lost, and my efforts to trace him upon returning to England drew a blank. But Jerry somehow found me and a fast friendship developed. Maybe it was meeting me that resulted in the Big Beats coming back together for a Reunion Concert in Dallas a few years later – I'd like to think so. Since then, we've corresponded and visited as often as was humanly possible but Jerry now finds himself battling a life-threatening illness. We send him and his wife Kathy our love and support, and value his friendship, which has been of the highest.

Other fans and musicians have doubtless found their lives touched by the power of Buddy Holly and his music in all sorts of unexpected ways. Maybe with far greater stories than mine. But I'm really proud to let Jerry have the final word in this book, which has been a labour of love throughout.

Selected Bibliography

Someone once paid credit to every album sleeve they'd ever read and every music magazine they'd ever opened in putting together a work of reference such as this, and the author feels a bit this way too. Thus, the few books listed below are restricted to ones spanning the last few decades and ones in my own possession that I referred to more than once. But the list is indeed ridiculously selective:

Armburn, Ellis - *Buddy Holly: The Real Story*
    (St Martin's Press, New York) 1995
Bowen, Jimmy, & Jim Jerome - *Rough Mix*
    (Simon & Schuster, New York) 1997
Carr, Jim - *Buddy Holly: The UK Tour*
    (Holly International Publishing, Doncaster) 2005
Clark, Dick, & Michael Shore - *The History of American Bandstand*
    (Ballantine Books, New York) 1985
Collis, John - *Gene Vincent & Eddie Cochran: Rock'n'Roll Revolutionaries*
    (Virgin Books, London) 2004
Dawson, Jim, & Spencer Leigh - *Memories of Buddy Holly*
    (Big Nickel Publications, Milford, New Hampshire) 1996
Dellar, Fred - *NME Guide To Rock Cinema*
    (Hamlyn, Feltham, Middlesex) 1981
Gerron, Peggy Sue, & Glenda Cameron - *Whatever Happened To Peggy Sue?*
    (Togi Entertainment, Tyler, Texas) 2008
Goldrosen, John, & John Beecher - *Remembering Buddy*
    (Omnibus Press, London) 1996
Ingman, John - *Crickets Factfile*
    (Ingman Music Research, Chesterfield) 1998
Jackson, John A. - *Big Beat Heat*
    (Schirmer, New York) 1991
Jennings, Waylon, & Lenny Kaye - *Waylon*
    (Warner Books, New York) 1996
Johnstone, Damian - *The Wild One*
    (Allen & Unwin, Sydney, Australia) 2001
Lehmer, Larry - *The Day The Music Died*
    (Schirmer, New York) 1997
Mann, Alan - *The A-Z of Buddy Holly*
    (Sound of Tex-Mex, Little Melton, Norwich) 1994 • *First edition*
Mann, Alan - *The A-Z of Buddy Holly*
    (Aurum Press, London) 1996 • *Second edition*

Mann, Alan - *Elvis & Buddy – Linked Lives*
    (Music Mentor Books, York) 2002
Norman, Philip - *Buddy: The Biography*
    (Macmillan, London) 1996
Repsch, Joe - *The Legendary Joe Meek: The Telstar Man*
    (Woodford House, London) 1989
Skinner, Quinton - *Casualties of Rock*
    (Simon & Schuster, New York) 2001
Talevski, Nick - *Tombstone Blues: Encyclopaedia of Rock Obituaries*
    (Omnibus Press, London) 1999
Thiele, Bob - *What A Wonderful World*
    (Oxford University Press, New York) 1995
Wallis, Ian - *American Rock'n'Roll: The UK Tours 1956-72*
    (Music Mentor Books, York) 2003
Warner, Alan - *Who Sang What In Rock & Roll?*
    (Blandford Press, London) 1990
White, George R. - *Bo Diddley: Living Legend*
    (Castle Books, Chessington, UK) 1995
White, George R. - *(35 Years of) British Hit EPs*
    (Music Mentor Books, York) 2001
Wolfman Jack - *Have Mercy! Confessions of the Original Rock'n'Roll Animal*
    (Warner Books, New York) 1995
Wolff, Daniel - *You Send Me*
    (Virgin Books, London) 1996

In random order, the following have also all been invaluable:

Buddy Holly Day By Day, a series of five booklets by Bill Griggs.
Crickets File, quarterly magazine.
Holly International, quarterly magazine.
Now Dig This, monthly rock'n'roll magazine.
Alan Clark's series of booklets on Holly, Cochran, Valens, etc.
Pete Frame's series of *Rock Family Tree* books.

Also innumerable sleevenotes and booklets from sundry Rollercoaster and Bear Family LP and CD releases. There are undoubtedly others in addition to the above which I've forgotten to mention. My heartfelt thanks to all.

Useful addresses

Again, this list is selective, but all deal in Holly/Crickets material to a greater or lesser degree:

Crickets File
John Firminger
5 Springwell Gardens
DONCASTER
DN4 9AH
UK

Down The Line
Trevor Lailey
16 Seymour Avenue
Eaglescliffe
STOCKTON-ON-TEES
TS16 0LD
UK

Holly International
Jim Carr
PO Box 1436
DONCASTER
DN11 9YQ
UK

Ingman Music Research
John Ingman
17 Damon Drive
Brimington
CHESTERFIELD
S43 1JD
UK

Now Dig This
Trevor Cajiao
19 South Hill Road
Bensham
GATESHEAD
NE8 2XZ
UK

Simon Pritchard Rock'n'Roll Artwork
10 Longe Road
Old Catton
NORWICH
NR6 7JD
UK

Rockin' 50s
Bill Griggs
PO Box 6123
LUBBOCK, TX 79493
USA

Rollercoaster Records
John Beecher
Rock House
London Road
St. Mary's
STROUD
GL6 8PU
UK

Alan Mann can be reached c/o the publishers.
Writs will be returned *'Gone away: author deceased'*.

PHOTO CREDITS

Front cover photo: Courtesy Lou Barile.
Back cover photo: Courtesy of Jeebasmoka.
Label shots: pages 37, 110, 166, 191, 218, 242, 252, 268 and 277 courtesy Ian Higham collection.
Sleeve shots: pages 62, 63, 64, 75, 124, 131, 154, 163, 223, 247, 262, 266 and 279 courtesy Ian Higham collection.
Photos/illustrations: page 33 courtesy George Atwood/Author's collection; page 47 © Mike Berry/courtesy Rollercoaster Records; pages 48, 235 and 312 courtesy Jerry Zapata/Author's collection; pages 50, 258 and 293 photo by and © Larry L. Matti/Author's collection; pages 55, 217 and 225 courtesy Johnny Vallis collection; page 57 courtesy Rita Box-Peek/David Gibsone; pages 60, 68, 93, 125, 152, 209, 232, 273 and 304 courtesy Author's collection; page 88 photo by Elwin Musser/courtesy Mason City *Globe-Gazette*; page 90 courtesy David Gibsone collection; pages 91 and 177 photo by Lorne 'Flash' Eckford/© Johnny Vallis Archive page 105 photo by John Chown/© John Beecher/Rollercoaster Records; pages 119, 121, 128 and 291 courtesy Ian Higham collection; page 130 courtesy Snuff Garrett/Johnny Vallis collection; pages 140 and 212 © Thelma King/courtesy Rollercoaster Records; page 171 photo by and © Steve Lassiter/Author's collection; page 207 courtesy Larry Holley/ C.J. Rees collection; page 182 and 241 courtesy Bill Griggs/BHMS; page 272 © Arsene Photography/courtesy C.J. Rees collection; page 282 courtesy C.J. Rees collection.

A very special thank you to Ian Higham for supplying all the label shots and sleeve illustrations in this book. Many more examples from Ian's amazing collection may be found on Hans Werner Finking's **http://www.buddyhollylives.info** website.

OTHER TITLES FROM MUSIC MENTOR BOOKS

American Rock'n'Roll: The UK Tours 1956-72
Ian Wallis
ISBN-13: 978-0-9519888-6-2 *(pbk, 424 pages)*

The first-ever detailed overview of every visit to these shores by American (and Canadian!) rock'n'rollers. It's all here: over 400 pages of tour itineraries, support acts, show reports, TV appearances and other items of interest. Illustrated with dozens of original tour programmes, ads, ticket stubs and great live shots, many rare or previously unpublished.

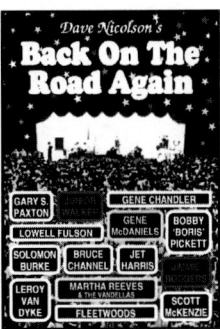

Back On The Road Again
Dave Nicolson
ISBN-13: 978-0-9547068-2-1 *(pbk, 216 pages)*

A third book of interviews by Dave Nicolson in the popular *On The Road* series, this time with more of a Sixties flavour: Solomon Burke, Gene Chandler, Bruce Channel, Lowell Fulson, Jet Harris, Gene McDaniels, Scott McKenzie, Gary S. Paxton, Bobby 'Boris' Pickett, Martha Reeves & The Vandellas, Jimmie Rodgers, Gary Troxel (Fleetwoods), Leroy Van Dyke and Junior Walker.

The Chuck Berry International Directory (Volume 1)
Morten Reff
ISBN-13: 978-0-9547068-6-9 *(pbk, 486 pages)*

For the heavyweight Berry fan. Everything you ever wanted to know about Chuck Berry, in four enormous volumes compiled by the world-renowned Norwegian Berry collector and authority, Morten Reff. This volume contains discographies for over 40 countries, plus over 700 rare label and sleeve illustrations.

The Chuck Berry International Directory (Volume 2)
Morten Reff
ISBN-13: 978-0-9547068-7-6 *(pbk, 532 pages)*

The second of four volumes in this extensive reference work dedicated to rock'n'roll's most influential guitarist and composer, Chuck Berry. Contains details of bootlegs; radio albums; movies; TV shows; video and DVD releases; international tour itineraries; hits, achievements and awards; Berry's songs, roots, and influence on other artists; tributes; Chuck Berry in print; fan clubs and websites; plus annotated discographies of pianist Johnnie Johnson (post-Berry) and the ultimate Berry copyist, Eddy Clearwater.

Daynce of the Peckerwoods: The Badlands of Texas Music
Michael H. Price
ISBN-13: 978-0-9547068-5-2 *(pbk, 350 pages)*

From a childhood spent among such key roots-music figures as Bob Wills and Big Joe Turner, and an extended dual career as a musician and journalist, Michael H. Price has forged this frenzied chronicle of life among the denizens of the vanishing borderlands of Texas' indigenous music scene over the past half-century. Contains essays on Billy Briggs, Ornette Coleman, the Light Crust Doughboys, Big Bill Lister, Rudy Ray Moore, Eck Robertson, Ray Sharpe, Robert Shaw, Major Bill Smith, Stevie Ray Vaughan and many more.

Elvis & Buddy – Linked Lives
Alan Mann
ISBN-13: 978-0-9519888-5-5 *(pbk, 160 pages)*

The achievements of Elvis Presley and Buddy Holly have been extensively documented, but until now little if anything has been known about the many ways in which their lives were interconnected. The author examines each artist's early years, comparing their backgrounds and influences, chronicling all their meetings and examining the many amazing parallels in their lives, careers and tragic deaths. Over 50 photographs, including many rare/previously unpublished.

Last Swill and Testament
– The hilarious, unexpurgated memoirs of
Paul 'Sailor' Vernon
ISBN-13: 978-0-9547068-4-5 *(pbk, 228 pages)*

Born in London shortly after the end of World War II, Paul 'Sailor' Vernon came into his own during the 1960s when spotty teenage herberts with bad haircuts began discovering The Blues. For the Sailor it became a lifelong obsession that led him into a whirlwind of activity as a rare record dealer, magazine proprietor/editor, video bootlegger and record company director. It's all here in this one-of-a-kind life history that will leave you reaching for an enamel bucket and a fresh bottle of disinfectant!

Let The Good Times Rock!
– A Fan's Notes On Post-War American Roots Music
Bill Millar
ISBN-13: 978-0-9519888-8-6 *(pbk, 362 pages)*

For almost four decades, the name 'Bill Millar' has been synonymous with the very best in British music writing. This fabulous new book collects together 49 of his best pieces — some previously unpublished — in a thematic compilation covering hillbilly, rockabilly, R&B, rock'n'roll, doo-wop, swamp pop and soul. Includes essays on acappella, doo-wop and blue-eyed soul, as well as detailed profiles of some of the most fascinating and influential personalities of each era.

On The Road
Dave Nicolson
ISBN-13: 978-0-9519888-4-8 *(pbk, 256 pages)*

Gary 'US' Bonds, Pat Boone, Freddy Cannon, Crickets Jerry Allison, Sonny Curtis and Joe B. Mauldin, Bo Diddley, Dion, Fats Domino, Duane Eddy, Frankie Ford, Charlie Gracie, Brian Hyland, Marv Johnson, Ben E. King, Brenda Lee, Little Eva, Chris Montez, Johnny Moore (Drifters), Gene Pitney, Johnny Preston, Tommy Roe, Del Shannon, Edwin Starr, Johnny Tillotson and Bobby Vee tell their own fascinating stories. Over 150 illustrations including vintage ads, record sleeves, label shots, sheet music covers, etc.

On The Road Again
Dave Nicolson
ISBN-13: 978-0-9519888-9-3 *(pbk, 206 pages)*

In this second book of interviews with the stars of pop and rock'n'roll, Dave Nicolson delves deeper into the dazzling and often treacherous world of the music industry, with more revealing and highly personal first-hand accounts from 15 pioneering performers who were at the forefront of the Fifties' music revolution: Freddie Bell, Martin Denny, Johnny Farina (Santo & Johnny), the Kalin Twins, Robin Luke, Chas McDevitt, Phil Phillips, Marvin Rainwater, Herb Reed (Platters), Tommy Sands, Joe Terranova (Danny & The Juniors), Mitchell Torok, Marty Wilde and the 'Cool Ghoul' himself, John Zacherle.

Railroadin' Some: Railroads In The Early Blues
Max Haymes
ISBN-13: 978-0-9547068-3-8 *(pbk, 390 pages)*

This groundbreaking book, written by one of the foremost blues historians in the UK, is based on over 30 years research, exploration and absolute passion for early blues music. It is the first ever comprehensive study of the enormous impact of the railroads on 19th and early 20th Century African American society and the many and varied references to this new phenomenon in early blues lyrics. Includes ballin' the jack, smokestack lightning, hot shots, the bottoms, chain gangs, barrelhouses, hobo jungles and more.

Music Mentor books are available from all good bookshops or by mail order from:

**Music Mentor Books
69 Station Road
Upper Poppleton
YORK YO26 6PZ
England**

Telephone: +44 (0)1904 330308
Email: music.mentor@ntlworld.com
Website: http://musicmentor0.tripod.com